Mrs. Dorothy Richards
126 Lakeside Dr.
Council Grove, KS 66846-1413

WHY THE END ?

TWO MILLENIA OF PROPHECY

AND IT'S FRUITLESS ATTEMPT

TO AWAKEN HUMANITY

By J. T. Revelator

WHY THE END ?

TABLE OF CONTENTS

FOREWORD

Whether or not you believe in the Great Spirit (God), Earth Changes or the validity of prophecy, look around yourself, and this country. Although we may not yet experience a personal accounting of our past (mis)deeds and thoughts, they are collectively accumulating around the planet. One only has to hear the news of earth quakes, volcanic eruptions, radioactive testing and accidents; atmospheric puncturing by microwaves, chemicals, satellites and rockets; climactic changes, animal mutations, and destructive human behaviors - to hear the message - the Earth is cleansing and reacting to release man's negativity heaped upon it. Many of the forces and events foreseen by intuitive wise men and women have already transpired. This book is written to decipher the myths, shed light on confusion, to make clear the clues, and explain the obvious evolutionary flow of consciousness and the projected results. Just because the majority of Americans have followed the projected "script" of the minority manipulators through lies and deceit, which causes us all to experience dramatic degenerative changes in events and the times since we became conscious, seeing much of the old world odor's greed, deceit, concentration of power and viciousness grow with underhanded erosion of common personal liberties and property rights; all this criminal trickery won't deter, or cause us to abandon, our personal gifts of greater brain and spirit awareness, overcoming and transforming negativity with love. Our religion is a personal identification and resonance with divinity, and we are moving with the planet Earth and the Great Spirit God to remove manipulated deceit and monopolies of corrupt agents, self-empowering the golden "Now Age" of brotherly love and consciousness. Awaken in joy and expectation! Vast changes are upon us and are happening, the Earth will be cleansed, the severity of events proportional to the amount of conscious love versus the toxic negativity emanating from We The Sovereign People and government employees at that time. It is true, we shall reap what we sow - we have failed as caretakers of the earth and our dignity; and events are transpiring not simply to purify mother Earth and our lives, but more essentially to bring human consciousness closer to universal values for those who can comprehend the grand cosmic plan. Like Americans who went before us, do your patriotic part pioneering progressive values into a frontier of expanded opportunities for those who dare to see the vision. Victorious adventure awaits those who can adapt with an evolving cosmos. On the other hand, frustration from not knowing, hardship from traumatic changes, imbalance and destruction befall those unaware and unprepared. Open your eyes, perceive the environmental, intellectual, and spiritual deprivations and degradations already wrought, and extrapolate into the future. Consider the plans that corrupt powers dangle, and with foresight prepare for intended slavery under the bankster's communist and vicious U.N. troops, or survival as a patriotic American child and freeman of God, because there is no middle ground. As Sovereign individual freeholders under the Constitution, the majority of Americans have allowed middlemen (politicians) to change our laws and give up our rights to foreign powers (Federal Reserve Bank, I.M.F., U.N.). So like a camel, nosing into the sovereign's tent, soon the animal pushes the master freeholder out of the tent, and the master becomes a foreigner in his own house. Now with the Year 2000 (Y2K) computer breakdown impending, the first in a series of planned catastrophes to weaken the population into accepting "help" from the foreign powers (I.M.F., U.N.) if we just give up our rights and succumb under martial law (by subterfuge of the Hegelian principle - change peaceful security by creating both a problem, and the deceitful solution that overthrows the lawful order). To be part of the lawful order and godlike solution, and not part of the arrogant communist gestapo problem, knowledge is your best insurance. Precision perception of future events is what this manuscript gives to you. Use this information to protect and defend yourself, your friends and family. Even though you may not change the final outcome alone, to the extent that you raise your awareness and mental stamina to that of diligent honest freemen, the surviving remnant, you will expand your creative gifts to experience and create the now-evolving script of sovereign dignified self-empowerment in the golden age. The choice is yours. *[The Editor]*

" ... In all ages there have been persons possessed of the spirit of prophecy, not for the purpose of announcing new doctrines, but to direct human action." *(St. Thomas Aquinas in 'Summa' circa 1273)*

WHY THE END ?

" ... Your sons and daughters shall prophesy; your old men shall dream dreams, and your young men shall see visions." *(Joel 2:28, Bible)*

" ... And I will show wonders in heaven." *(Joel 2:30, Bible)*

"If you know how to interpret the look of the sky, can you not read the signs of the times?" *(Matthew 16:3, Bible)*

"Do not despise prophecies. Test everything; retain what is good."
(Thessalonians 5:19, Bible)

"Many men have prophecied that a cataclysm is coming. Over the last one thousand years many seers and prophets have spoken of this event. Before you dismiss these prophecies as the warnings of cranks, seek to establish why they were warning you ... the only motivation they had ... was to foretell what was to come ... so as to warn a race of men which would be far removed from them both in its way of life and evolution. You may disregard the voice of God at your peril." *(Ramala Prophecy in 'The True Meaning and Significance of Cataclysm' circa 20th Century)*

6   Information Pioneers Publisher

THE WORD PROMISED
BEFORE THE END OF THIS AGE

"And this Gospel of the Kingdom shall be preached in the whole world, for a witness to all nations, and then will come the end." *(Matthew 24:14)*

"This is his Promise: He would send THE WORD of truth unto you and you will do with that which you will ... " *(Excerpt from 'Murder By Atomic Suicide', a Phoenix Journal, 1991)*

"The final promise for this civilization prior to the final fulfillment of the 'prophecies' was that Man would be given THE WORD and it would flow to the corners of the globe so each could make choices of his divine journey and so it is ... " *(Excerpt from 'Science of the Cosmos', a Phoenix Journal, 1991)*

"The words of truth were disallowed from the tampering for it would be that God's WORD would go forth in truth before the final closing - and it is done and so be it." *(Aton in 'Firestorm In Babylon', a Phoenix Journal, 1990)*

"The time has come when these things shall be again laid before you so that man can look within and choose - for THAT is the promise of God - to send forth THE WORD unto the lands that man may come into choosing of his divine path." *(Excerpt from 'I And My Father Are One', a Phoenix Journal, 1991)*

"We are giving THE WORD and thrusting it out to the world ... with the hope and deep prayer that it will give you ability to save the Earth from becoming a barren thing." *(Excerpt from 'Murder By Atomic Suicide', a Phoenix Journal, 1991)*

" ... The just shall be delivered by knowledge." *(Proverbs 11:9, Bible)*

"My people are destroyed for lack of knowledge." *(Hosea 4:6, Bible)*

WHY THE END ?

"And you shall know the truth: and the truth shall make you free." *(John 8:32, Bible)*

"The greatest homage to truth is to use it." *(Emerson)*

"He that is of God heareth the words of God ... " *(John 8:47, Bible)*

"He that despiseth me and receiveth not my words hath one that judgeth him. THE WORD that I have spoken, the same shall judge him in the last day." *(John 12:48, Bible)*

"Take the helmet of salvation and the sword of the spirit, the WORD of God." *(Ephesians 6:17, Bible)*

"For the WORD of God is living and effectual and more piercing than any two edged sword ... " *(Hebrews 4:12, Bible)*

"And out of his mouth proceedeth a sharp two-edged sword, that with it he may strike the nations." *(Revelation 19:15, Bible)*

"And the people shall cease to understand one another. They shall forget the meaning of the word teacher. But just then shall the Teachers appear and in all corners of the world shall be heard the true teaching. To this WORD OF TRUTH shall the people be drawn, but those who are filled with darkness and ignorance shall set obstacles." *(Tibetan Prophecy)*

"But woe unto them that falsify my WORD and commandment, and draw away them that hearken to the commandment of life; for together with them they shall come into everlasting judgement." *(The Epistle of the Apostles)*

"For our wrestling is not against flesh and blood; but against principalities and powers, against the rulers of the world of this darkness, against the spirit of wickedness in the high places." *(Ephesians 6:12, Bible)*

"The eyes of those who will see will not be blinded and the ears of those who hear will listen and the mind of the hasty will discern truth." *(Isaiah 32:3-4, Bible)*

" ... God ... wants all men to be saved and come to know the truth." *(1 Timothy 2:4, Bible)*

"He that knoweth God, heareth us: He that is not of God, heareth us not: by this we know the spirit of truth and the spirit of error." *(1 John 4:6, Bible)*

" ... Man has slipped more and more deeply into the mire of chaos and evil intent that he must again be in the final reminding of that which is coming. For that was the greatest promise: that THE WORD shall go forth unto the four corners of the world that all men who will see and hear shall have opportunity of knowing that which is God and Godly! I come to fulfill the prophecy - not 'save' a bunch of criminals and lawbreakers - only the individual can 'save' self ... for we are bringing forth the WORD and ye who deliberately turn away are in deliberate defiance ... " *(Esu 'Jesus' Sananda, June 5, 1991)*

"Will the evildoers not understand? They eat up my people ... " *(Psalm 14:4, Bible)*

" ... If you choose not to hear, ye have chosen the way of the void, and will be in perishment within the tides and upheavals of labor and birthing." *(Aton, 1989)*

"The instructions and truth of God shall go forth throughout the lands and the lands shall be reclaimed unto his kingdom ... so shall it come to pass and it shall be within this generation that it shall be made or broken, the covenant with God." *(Excerpt from 'Butterflies, Mind Control - The Razor's Edge', a Phoenix Journal, 1994)*

WHY THE END ?

"The time of truth upon Earth has arrived. Ye ones shall be in the choosing of thy truth, for the ending of a cycle and a forthcoming transition are at hand. The fulfilling of the prophecies are all but to the final chapter. Ye ones are in the final days! ... after the seven angels have poured forth their teachings and few have heard or seen, then shall I come, for mine creation shall be brought into peace." *(Sananda in 'The Wisdom of the Rays', Volume 1, 1997)*

"He who persists in the truth will survive. This lesson will be preached throughout the entire world as testimony for all peoples and then the end will come." *(Excerpt from 'And They Called His Name Immanuel', a Phoenix Journal, 1989)*

"Nothing is concealed that will not be revealed, and nothing hidden that will not become known." *(Matthew 10:26, Bible)*

"For there is nothing covered that shall not be revealed, neither hid that shall not be known." *(Luke 12: 3-4, Bible)*

"The times of which the prophets spoke are now in their blossom. It is time for full discharge so that you can make final choices." *(Hatonn, December 15, 1995)*

"Indeed, the Lord God does nothing without revealing his plan to his servants, the prophets." *(Amos 3:7, Bible)*

"Judge nothing before the time, until the Lord come, who ... will bring to light the hidden things of darkness ... " *(1 Corinthians 4:5, Bible)*

" ... I will give you words and a wisdom which none of your adversaries can take exception to or contradict." *(Luke 21:15, Bible)*

"For nation will rise against nation, and kingdom against kingdom ... and there will be terrors and great signs from heaven ... "

"But before all this ... This will be a time for you to bear testimony and THE WORD must first be taught to all nations ... " *(Excerpt from 'Sacred Wisdom', a Phoenix Journal, 1995)*

"Lastly, I appeal to the apostles of the last days, the disciples faithful to Jesus Christ who ... live a life despising the world ... The time has come that you should show yourselves to lighten the world."

"Fight, Sons of light, you small number who see, because the time of times, the final end is near."

"The demons allied to Antichrist will operate on Earth and in the sky and humanity will become worse. But God will not give up his truly faithful servants who are men of goodwill. The Gospel will be preached everywhere to all the people and the nations will know the TRUTH." *(Melanie Calvat, 1831-1940)*

"If people would change their minds and really be spiritual, there would be no need for arms and fighting. Everything could be settled by speaking the truth. But now, people wouldn't know the truth if you spoke it. It only upsets them. It hurts their ego. And then you are the enemy." *(Grandfather Semu Huarte, Chumash Nation, 1983)*

"It truly is not expected that very many, relatively, will recognize the truth before it is too late." ... Millions will be lost for they will refuse to accept while they wait and wait and wait for the truth THEY EXPECT." *(Excerpt from 'Aids The Last Great Plague', a Phoenix Journal, 1991)*

"The road of the soldiers of the One,
Certain the other [Hatonn] is of the vault [heaven].
Due to the moving desert [Mojave], saving the brave and the gorse.
The writing of the Commander of the Phoenix, Observed by the One.
Those whom are helpless are not." *(Nostradamus, Century VIII Quatrain 27) [The writings of Commander Hatonn in the Phoenix Journals fulfill God's promise to guide His people who are destroyed for lack of knowledge.]*

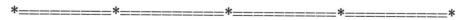

WHY THE END ?

END TIME SIGNS

"The years will be SHORTENED like months, the months like weeks, the weeks like days, the days like hours and an hour like a moment ... The Lord will SHORTEN those days for the sake of the elect ... " *(Excerpt from the 'Tiburtine Sibyl', 380 A.D.)*

"And except that those days should be SHORTENED, there should be no flesh saved: but for the elect's sake those days shall be SHORTENED." *(Matthew 24:22, Bible)*

"Indeed, had the Lord not SHORTENED the period, not a person would be saved. But for the sake of those he has chosen, he has SHORTENED the days." *(Mark 13:20, Bible)*

"Remember, the days will be SHORTENED because of the elect, but woe to those who do not carry out the Word of God." *(Our Lord at Dozule in 'Prophecies! The Chastisement and Purification' by Albert J. Herbert, 1986)*

"Woe to the inhabitants of the Earth! There will be sanguinary war, hunger, pestilence and epidemics, terrible rains of insects, thunder which will shake entire cities, earthquakes which will make entire regions uninhabitable. Voices will be heard in the air, and men will strike their heads against the wall, wishing for death, but this will bring them, for their part, terrible torture. Blood will flow everywhere. Who could ever report victory unless God SHORTENED the time of trial?" *(Melanie Calvat, 1831-1940)*

"After the year 1900, toward the middle of the 20th century, the people of that time will become unrecognizable. When the time for the advent of the Antichrist approaches, people's minds will grow cloudy from carnal passions, dishonor and lawlessness will grow stronger. Then the world will become unrecognizable. People's appearances will change and it will be impossible to distinguish men from women due to their shamelessness in dress and style of hair. These people will be cruel and will be like wild animals because of the temptations of the Antichrist. There will be no respect for parents and elders, love will disappear, and Christian pastors, bishops and priests will become vain men, completely failing to distinguish the righthand way from the left. At that time the morals and traditions of Christians and of the Church will change. People will abandon modesty, and dissipation will reign. Falsehood and greed will attain great proportions, and woe to those who pile up treasures. Lust, adultery, homosexuality, secret deeds and murder will rule in society."

"At that time men will also fly through the air like birds and descend to the bottom of sea like fish. And when they have achieved all this, these unhappy people will spend their lives in comfort without knowing, poor souls, that it is the deceit of the Antichrist. And, the impious one! - he will so fill science with vanity that it will go off the right path and lead people to lose faith in the existence of God ... "

"Then the All-good God will see the downfall of the human race and will SHORTEN the days for the sake of those who are being saved, because the enemy wants to lead even the chosen into temptation if that is possible ... then the sword of chastisement will suddenly appear and kill the perverter and his servants." *(St. Nilus, Fifth Century Hermit)*

"As the scenario reaches its FINAL stages it will be experienced as a great time warp. Time will appear to stand still in some experiences and in others, to feel like entire lifetimes in hours, moments or days ... " *(Commander Jycondria)*

"Dajjal will remain in the Earth for 40 years, a year being like a month, a month being like a week, a week being like a day, a day like the time it takes to burn a palm branch." *(Excerpt from the 'Mishkah al-Masabih')*

"Near the day of the Great Purification, there will be cobwebs spun back and forth in the sky." *(Native American Hopi Prophecy)*
[Residents of Quirindi, Australia said they saw cobwebs fall from the sky after unidentified aircraft passed overhead, as reported in the 'USA Today'

newspaper, August 11, 1998] [Visible contrails forming checkerboard patterns in American skies in 1998-1999 are reportedly made by jet exhaust from JP-8 jetfuel laced with toxic Ethylene Dibromide, which was found on cranberry bogs in Cape Cod]

"Yet greater SIGNS there be to see;
As man nears LATTER CENTURY." *(Mother Shipton, 1488-1561)*

"From the middle of the TWENTIETH CENTURY on, there will be uprisings in all parts of Europe. The Republics will be upheaved. Kings, the Great, and Priests will be killed and Padres and Nuns will leave their cloister. Hunger, epidemics and earthquakes will destroy numerous cities." *(Rudolfo Gilthier, 1675)*

"A great plague will befall mankind in the second half of the TWENTIETH CENTURY. Nowhere in the world will there be order, and Satan will rule the highest places, determining the way of things ... " *(The Third Prophecy of Fatima, Portugal, 1917)*

"The TWENTIETH CENTURY will be a period of terror and misery. In that century everything evil and disageeable that can be imagined will happen. In many countries the princes will rise up against their fathers, the citizens against authority, the children against their parents, the pagans against God, entire peoples against the established order. A civil war will break out in which the bombs will fall from heaven. And then a further one will break out in which almost all the world will be turned upside down. Financial disasters and ruin of property will cause many tears to fall. Men will be without mind and without piety. Poisoned clouds and rays which can burn more deeply than the equatorial sun, iron armies marching, flying vessels full of terrible bombs and of arrows, fatal flying stars and sulphuric fire destroying great cities. This century will be the most perverse of all because men will raise themselves up and destroy each other mutually." *(Anonymous 17th Century Monk in 'Die Zukunft der Welt'/'The Future of the World' by Ludwig Emmerich)*

WHY THE END ?

"A huge war will erupt in the second half of the TWENTIETH CENTURY. Fire and smoke will fall from the sky." *(The Third Prophecy of Fatima, Portugal, 1917)*

"The TWENTIETH CENTURY will bring death and destruction, defection from the Church, families, cities, and governments will go to pieces. It will be the century of the three great wars, which will follow each other in decades and will become increasingly devastating and bloody. Not only the Rhineland but all countries to the East and West will be laid desolate. After Germany has lost a terrible war, there will soon follow yet another. There will be no bread for the people and no hay for the cattle. Poisonous vapors, created by human hand, will sink down, destroying everything. Insanity will attack the spirit of man, and unrestrained hate shall rage. Evil will destroy evil, and many innocents shall perish." *(Anonymous German Monk of the Maria Laach Monastery, 16th Century)*

"I have seen a comet strike our Earth ... One of the worst disasters of the TWENTIETH CENTURY ... " *(Jeane Dixon, 1918-1997)*

"There has been so much hatred, so much war ... that ... cleansing ... will occur on the Earth before the end of the TWENTIETH CENTURY ... unless humanity does a rapid reverse to peace and only peace ... " *(The Christ in 'New Teachings For An Awakening Humanity', 1994)*

"For those who live the CENTURY through
In fear and trembling this shall do.
Flee to the mountains and the dens
To bog and forest and wild fens." *(Mother Shipton, 1488-1561)*

"And thou shall come up against my people of Israel, as a cloud to cover the land; it shall be in the LATTER DAYS ... " *(Ezekial 38:16, Bible)*

16   Information Pioneers Publisher

"It shall come to pass in the LAST DAYS, that I will pour a portion of my spirit on all mankind. Your sons and daughters shall prophesy, your young men shall see visions and your old men shall dream dreams." *(Acts of the Apostles 2:17, Bible)*

" ... In the LAST DAYS, mocking, sneering men who are ruled by their passions will arrive on the scene." *(2 Peter 3:3, Bible)*

" ... There will be terrible times in the LAST DAYS. Men will be lovers of money, proud arrogant, abusive, disobedient to their parents, ungrateful, profane, inhuman, implacable, slanderous, licentious, brutal, hating the good. They will be treacherous, reckless, pompous, lovers of pleasure rather than God as they make a pretense of religion but negate its power. It is such as these ... always learning but never able to reach a knowledge of the truth ... But they will not get very far, as ... the stupidity of these will be plain for all to see." *(II Timothy 3:1-9, Bible)*

" ... In the LAST TIMES some shall depart from the faith ... " *(1 Timothy 4:1, Bible)*

"For there shall be a time when they will not endure sound doctrine, but, according to their own desires ... and will indeed turn away their hearing from the truth ... " *(2 Timothy 4:3-4, Bible)*

"In the LAST times there shall be many dissensions among the peoples, blashemy, iniquity, envy, and villainy, indolence, pride and intemperance, so that every man shall speak that which pleaseth him. In those days evils shall abound: there shall be no respecters of persons, hymns shall cease out of the House of the Lord, truths shall be no more, covetousness shall abound among the priests: an upright man shall not be found." *(The Apocalypse of Thomas)*

"In the LAST days the kinsman shall show no favor to his kinsmen, nor any man to his neighbor ... And there shall be many that believe on my name and yet follow after evil and spread vain doctrine. And men shall follow after them and their riches, and be subject unto their pride, and lust for drink and bribery ... There shall come forth another doctrine ... And therein shall be a deadly corruption, and they shall teach it, and shall turn away them from eternal life." *(The Epistle of the Apostles)*

" ... In the LAST DAYS ... all the nations ... will be drunken with iniquity and all manner of Abominations." *(2 Nephi, 27 in 'The Book of Mormon')*

" ... You are living in the LAST AGE, the LAST DAY, and very near the dawning of the day of our Lord." *(Paul Solomon, March 24, 1972)*

" ... The things which must come to pass in the LAST TIMES: there shall be famine and war and earthquakes in diverse places, snow and ice and great drought shall there be, and many dissensions among the peoples."

"At that time shall be a very great rising of the sea, so that no man shall tell the news to any man. The kings of the Earth and the princes and captains shall be troubled, and no man shall speak freely. Grey hairs shall be seen upon boys, and the young shall not give place unto the aged ... in those days there shall be all manners of evils, even the death of the race of men from the east and even unto Babylon. And thereafter death and famine and sword in the land of Canaan and even unto Rome. Then shall all the fountains of waters and wells boil over and be turned into dust and blood. The heaven shall be moved, the stars shall fall upon the Earth, the sun shall be cut in half like the moon, and the moon shall not give up her light."

"On the fourth day at the first hour, the Earth of the east shall speak, the abyss shall roar: then shall all the Earth be moved by the strength of a great earthquake. In that day shall all the idols of the heathen fall, and all the buildings of the Earth. These are the SIGNS of the fourth day. And on the fifth day, at the sixth hour, there shall be great darkness over the world until evening, and the stars shall be turned away from their ministry. In that day all nations shall hate the world and despise the life of this world. These are the SIGNS of the fifth day." *(The Apocalypse of Thomas)*

"The least of the SIGNS of the LAST hour will be a fire which will gather mankind together from the East and the West." *(The Sahih of Al-Bukhari)*

"An emperor named 'P[eter]' will arise in the LAST DAYS. He will be a prince and a monarch and will reform the churches of all Europe. After him there will be no other emperor." *(Johannes Lichtenberger in 'Prognostico in Latino Book II', Chapter 16)*

"LAST world rulers of Kali Yuga (Age of Chaos) would be members of white race (Mletchmas) defined as one who eats bovine (cow) flesh, speaks much that is self contradictory and is destitute of all good conduct." *(Shrimad Bhagavatam, ancient Indian Hindu)*

"These are truly the FINAL YEARS ... for the next big happening will be the turning of the planet Earth onto its side ... " *(Excerpt from 'Mary's Message to the World' by Annie Kirkwood, 1991)*

"In the LAST DAYS Ethiopia will stretch out her hand to God." *(Psalm 67:32, Bible)*

" ... A salvation which stands ready to be revealed in the LAST DAYS." *(1 Peter 1:5, Bible)*

"In the LAST period Christians will not appreciate the great grace of God who provided a monarch, a long duration of peace, a splendid fertility of the Earth. They will be ungrateful, lead a sinful life, in pride, vanity, unchastity, frivolity, hatred, avarice, gluttony and many other vices, that the sins of men will stink more than a pestilence before God. Many will be the false teachings and resultant bewilderment." *(The Pseudo-Methodius in 'Monumenta Patrium Orthodoxographa', 1569)*

"Hearken ... things that shall come to pass in the LATTER AGES of the world. Great carnage shall be made, justice shall be outraged, multitudinous

WHY THE END ?

evils, great suffering shall prevail, and many unjust laws will be administered. The time shall come when they will not perform charitable acts, and truth shall not remain in them ... They will scoff at acts of humility; there will come times of dark affliction, of scarcity, of sorrow, and of wailing; in the LATTER AGES of the world's existence, monarchs will be added to falsehood. Neither justice nor covenant will be observed by any one people ... They will become hard-hearted and penurious, and will be devoid of piety. The clergy will become fosterers, in consequence of the tidings of wretchedness; churches will be held in bondage by the all-powerful men of the day. Judges will administer injustice, under the sanction of powerful, outrageous kings; the common people will adopt false principles. Excellent men shall be steeped in poverty, the people will become inhospitable to their guests, the voice of the parasite shall be more ageeable to them than the melody of the harp touched by the sage's finger. The professors of science shall not be rewarded, amiability shall not characterize the people; prosperity and hospitality shall not exist, but destitution will assume their place ... all classes of men shall be filled with hatred and enmity toward each other. The people will not associate affectionately with each other during the great festivals of the seasons; they will live devoid of justice and rectitude, up from the youth of tender age to the aged. The clergy shall be led by the misinterpretation of their reading; the relics of the saints will be considered powerless, every race of mankind will become wicked! Young women will become unblushing, the aged people will be of irascible temper ... Young people will decline in vigor ... there will be no standard by which morals may be regulated ... Troublous shall be the LATTER AGES of the world ... The possessors of abundance shall fall through the multiplicity of their falsehoods; covetousness shall take possession of every glutton, and when satisfied their arrogance know no bounds. Between mother and daughter anger and bitter sarcasms shall continually exist; neighbors will become treacherous, cold, and false-hearted towards each other. The gentry will become grudgeful ... and blood relations shall become cool towards each other. The trees shall not bear the usual quantity of fruit, fisheries shall become unproductive and the Earth shall not yield its usual abundance. Inclement weather and famine shall come and fishes shall forsake the rivers. The people will be oppressed for want of food ... Dreadful storms and hurricanes shall afflict them. Numberless diseases shall then prevail. Then a great event shall happen ... and if ye be not truly holy, a more sorrowful event could not possibly happen." *(Saint Columbeille, 521-597 A.D.)*

"As we near the LAST DECADE OF THIS CENTURY, we will encounter evil beings who are intent on taking advantage of everyone ... This is the last desperate attempt by evil forces to control the Earth before they realize that their power will be eclipsed by the shift and the new age." *(Spirit Guides of Ruth Montgomery, 1986)*

"In the LAST PERIOD ... the just God will give Lucifer and all his devils power to come on Earth and tempt his godless creatures." *(The Pseudo-Methodius, 680 A.D.)*

"The world being near its LAST period,
Saturn shall come yet late to his return,
The empire shall be changed into black nations [corruption],
Narbonne [S. France] shall have her eye picked out by a hawk."
(Nostradamus, Century III Quatrain 92)

"And in this LAST ERA all the kingdoms of Christianity and also of the unbelievers shall quake ... and there shall be more grievous wars and battles; towns, cities, castles and other buildings shall be burnt, desolated ... and so many evils shall be committed by the means of the infernal prince, Satan, that almost the entire world shall be undone and desolate ... " *(Nostradamus in 'The Epistle to Henry II', 1555)*

"Seven years before the LAST DAY, the sea shall submerge Eire [Ireland] by one inundation." *(Saint Columbeille, 521-597 A.D.)*

"When the ... Peace Treaty is officially signed [1994] then the countdown will begin ... marking the beginning of the FINAL seven years ... " *(Excerpt From 'UFOS, the Grand Deception and the Coming New World Order' by*

WHY THE END ?

Norio F. Hayakawa, 1993)

"Respect for God has disappeared from human hearts. They wish to efface even God's memory. This perversity is nothing less than the beginning of the LAST DAYS of the world." *(Pope Pius X, 1914)*

" ... Our Lady is very displeased because no one had heeded her message of 1917 [Fatima]. Neither the good nor the bad paid attention to it. The good ones go their way unconcerned and heeding not the Celestial directives; the bad, pursuing the broad way of perdition, completely ignoring the threatened punishment."

" ... Our Lady had repeatedly told me 'Many nations are going to disappear from the face of the Earth ... if we through prayers and the Sacraments, will not bring about their conversion'."

"We have hardly any time left to stave off the punishment of God. There are at our disposal two very effective means, prayer and sacrifice, but the Devil is doing his utmost to divert our minds from, and take away the taste for prayer. The outcome will be that we will either be saved or doomed."

" ... The Holy Mother has expressly said, 'We are approaching the LAST DAYS'." *(Sister Lucy of Fatima, Portugal, 1957)*

"I beheld upon the horizon a brilliant conflagration. Then my vision clouded over and I neither saw nor heard anything more. Then the spirit said to me: 'This is the beginning of the LAST DAYS of the Earth'." *(Prophecy of Premol, 17th Century)*

"The SIGN of doom: the Earth shall be moist with sweat; from heaven the king shall come to reign forever ... At midnight in the hour when the angel made Egypt desolate, and when the Lord despoiled hell, in the same hour He shall deliver His elect from this world." *(Bede the Venerable, 672-735 A.D.)*

"There was a great earthquake, and the sun became as black as sackcloth of hair, and the moon became as blood. And the stars of heaven fell unto the

Earth, even as a fig tree casteth her untimely figs, when she is shaken of a mighty wind. And the heaven departed as a scroll when it is rolled together, and every mountain and island were moved out of their places." *(Revelation 6:12-14, Bible)*

" ... When God dwelling in the firmament shall roll up the heaven, which like a scroll shall be put away, and all the many shaped vault of heaven shall fall on the vast Earth, and on the deep shall flow a ceaseless torrent of glowing fire, and shall consume the Earth ... the sea, and the pole of heaven, the nights, the days, and even the creation, and fuse all in one and set apart unto purification." *(Excerpt from the 'Sibylline Fragment', 2nd Century B.C.)*

" ... There will come a time when the inhabitants of the Earth will be seized with panic. The way of truth will be hidden from sight, and the land will be barren of faith. There will be great increase in wickedness, worse than anything you now see or ever have heard of ... The country you now see ruling the world will become a trackless desert, laid waste for all to see ... The sun will suddenly begin to shine in the middle of the night, and the moon in the daytime. Trees will drip blood, stones will speak, nations will be in confusion, and the courses of the stars will be changed. A king unwelcome to the inhabitants of the Earth will succeed the throne; even the birds will all fly away. The Dead Sea will cast up fish, and at night a voice will sound out, unknown to many but heard by all. Chasms will open up in many places and spurt out flames incessantly ... women will give birth to monsters, fresh springs will run with salt water, and everywhere friends will become enemies. Then understanding will be hidden, and reason withdraw to her secret chamber. Many will seek her, but not find her; the Earth will overflow with vice and wickedness." *(II Esdras 5:1-13, Apocrypha)*

"Leave Geneva, leave every one of you there.
Saturn [evil] will take your gold, in exchange for iron [war],
Zopyra [the deceiver of Babylon] will exterminate all who oppose him,
Before his coming there will be SIGNS in the sky." *(Nostradamus,*

WHY THE END ?

Century IX Quatrain 44)

" ... And many SIGNS shall appear in the sun and moon, and in the STARS and in the waters, and in other elements and creatures, so that, as it were in a picture, future events shall be foretold in their portents." *(Abbess Hildegard in 'Vision X', 1098-1179)*

"These are evil times, a century full of dangers and calamities. Heresy is everywhere, and the followers of heresy are in power almost everywhere." *(Venerable Bartholomew Holzhauser, 17th Century)*

"There will come a time when the world will become very godless. The people will become self-reliant from the king, and there will be a general loss of respect for authority and those who are no longer true to their masters or to their belief will become the rulers. There will then be a general uproar, so that father will fight against son, and son will fight against father."

"Then will come a time when one will no longer respect the beliefs of the church and the school. There will come a time when the Catholic religion will feel very crowded, and there will be an attempt to get rid of it. People will enjoy play and joyous occasions about this time, and be generally fascinated by entertainment. But then it will not take long for a change to step in. There will be an incredible war ... " *(Anonymous, recorded by Beykirch in 'Prophetstimmen', 1849)*

"When the time is near, people will not know how to dress. Women will wear hats like men, and pants like men. Then will follow a tragic and unlucky time like our Creator has spoken of before us. People will fear themselves on Earth, and fear things that are to come. Father will be against son, and son against father. Dogma will be perverted; men will try to overthrow the Catholic Church! Mankind will become lovers of pleasure. The true and believing will not be found anymore, after which the independent peoples will fight wars against each other for a long time. Thrones will have collapsed and kingdoms will collapse. And through this process, the unaffected East against the West will

24   Information Pioneers Publisher

resort to heavy weapons. Then it is no longer over fatherland, language or belief." *(Excerpt from 'The Proceedings of the Heavenly Renewal from the Unknown Who Became Illuminated', 1701)*

"When women walk around in pants, and men have become effeminate, so that one will no longer be able to tell men from women, then the time is near."

"People will build houses everywhere, high houses, low houses, one after another. When everyone builds, when everywhere buildings rise, everything will be cleared away."

"There will be a holy SIGN in the heavens, that a very severe Master will come and take off the skin of the people. He will not rule very long, then when all that has happened as I have said, then comes the great clearing away." *(Mathias Lang, 1753-1820)*

"And now a word in uncouth rhyme
Of what shall be in future time:
For in these wondrous far-off days,
The women shall adopt a craze
To dress like men and trousers wear,
And cut off their locks of hair."   *(Mother Shipton, 1561)*

"When women dress like men and trousers wear,
And cut off all their locks of hair,
When pictures look alike with movements free,
When ships like fishes swim beneath the sea,
When men outstripping birds can soar the sky,
Then half the world, deep drenched in blood will die."   *(Mother Shipton, 1561)*

"The SIGNS will be there for all to read
When man shall do most heinous deed
Man will ruin kinder lives
By taking them as to their wives.

WHY THE END ?

And murder foul and brutal deed
When man will only think of greed.
And man shall walk as if asleep
He does not look-he may not peep
And iron men the tail shall do
And iron cart and carriage too."   *(Mother Shipton, 1561)*

"The kings shall false promise make
And talk just for talking's sake
And nations plan horrific war
The like as never seen before
And taxes rise and lively down
And nations wear perpetual frown."   *(Mother Shipton, 1561)*

" ... You're going to see major changes at all levels that you won't recognize the world afterwards ... Between now and the year 2000 is the time span in which most of the major changes are going to be happening. They are happening right now, and they're going to intensify."   *(Sun Bear in 'Black Dawn/Bright Day', 1992)*

"When ... property given in trust is treated as spoil ... the most wicked member of a people becomes its leader, a man is honored through the evil he may do, singing girls and string instruments make their appearance, wines are drunk, and the last members of this people curse the first ones, look at that time for a violent wind, an earthquake, metamorphosis, pelting rain, and SIGNS following one another like bits of a necklace falling one after the other when its string is cut."   *(Mohammed in 'The Shama' of Tirmidhi', 31:39)*

Native American Hopi prophecy predicts when their land trust is dug up, great disturbances will develop in the balance of nature, since the Hopi land is a microcosm of the planet. Recently the Peabody Coal Co. has pumped water out of their aquifer.

26

" ... When you see the white man come into the four corners area and try to take it, then you will see ... the danger sign, the last stage before the Great Purification [1987-2011]." *(Native American Hopi Prophecy)*
[The Indian Relocation Act of 1985, H.R.3011, moved Hopi off land.]

" ... The Lamb broke open the first of seven seals ... I saw a white horse, its rider ... was given a crown." [The Church/crusades]
" ... The Lamb broke open the second seal ... Another horse came forth, a red one [communism]. Its rider was given the power to rob the Earth of peace by allowing men to slaughter one another."
" ... The Lamb broke open the third seal ... I saw a black horse, the rider ... held a pair of scales in his hand." [Black budget operations, corruption of justice]
" ... The Lamb broke open the fourth seal ... And I looked and beheld a green horse [United Nations Biodiversity - Biosphere Heritage Corridor Program using the Environmental 'Green' Police], and the name of him who sit on him was death ... And power was given him over the fourth part of the Earth, to kill with the sword and with famine and with death and with the wild beasts of the Earth." *(Revelation 6:1-8, Bible)*

"And the fourth angel sounded his trumpet. And the third part of the sun was smitten and the third part of the moon. And the third part of the stars. So as the third part of them was darkened and the day shone not for a third part of it and the night likewise." *(Revelation 8:12, Bible)*

"In the era of Kali (chaos): The leaders who will rule over the Earth will be violent and will seize the goods of their subjects ... Moral values and the rule of law will lessen from day to day until the world will be completely perverted ... The Earth will be honored for its material treasure only ... the only road to success will be the lie ... Marriage will cease being a rite ... " *(The Vishnu Purana of India, 1st Century A.D.)*

27

WHY THE END ?

"Prayers will be neglected, carnal decrees shall be pursued, transgressors will become leaders, it will not be possible to distinguish the faithful from the false, telling lies will become desirable ... The rain will do no good, it will fall out of season. Males will commit adultery will males, and females with females. Women will dominate. The offspring will disobey their parents, friend will treat his friend badly, sins will be taken lightly ... Then will appear a people from the West [America] who will dominate the weak among my people ... Usury will become rampant. Human blood will have no value, religion will have no helpers." *(Mohammed in 'The Mudkhal of Ibn-al-Hajj')*

"Men will increasingly neglect their souls ... The greatest corruption will reign on Earth. Men will become like bloodthirsty animals ... The crescent [Islam] will become obscured and its followers will descend into lies and perpetual warfare ... The crowns of the kings will fall. There will be a terrrible WAR between all the world's peoples ... Entire nations will die ... Hunger. Crimes unknown to law. The ancient roads will be filled with multitudes going from one place to another ... The greatest cities will perish by fire ... Families will be dispersed ... faith and love will disapper ... Within 50 years there will be 18 years of war and cataclysms ... Then the peoples of Agharti will leave their subterranean caverns and will appear on the surface of the Earth." *(King of the World from Tibet)*

"The fiery Dragon [China] when he cometh on the waves ... shall oppress the children of thee ... famine also pending and ... strife, then is nigh the END of the world and the LAST DAYS ... " *(Excerpt from the 'Sibylline Fragment', 2nd Century B.C.)*

"A great conflict ... in those times amongst all men ... when there shall be SIGNS and wonders by the Dragon in great abundance, when he shall again manifest himself as god in fearful phantasms flying in the air ... " *(Saint Ephraim, 4th Century A.D.)*

28   Information Pioneers Publisher

"A principal SIGN of the times in which the war will break out will be the general indifference in matters of religion and the general corruption of mores in many places. At that time they will give believers the name of fools, and the faithless will pretend to be men of light." *(Wessel Dietrich Eilert, 1848)*

"Before the war breaks out again, food will be scarce and expensive. There will be little work for the workers, and fathers will hear their children crying for food. There will be earthquakes and SIGNS in the sun. Towards the END, darkness will cover the Earth." *(Catholic Nun, France, 1872)*

" ... The blue star Kachina ... will be preceded by the last Great War ... " *(Native American Hopi Prophecy)*

"When the blue star Kachina makes its appearance in the heavens, the Fifth World will emerge." *(Native American Hopi Prophecy)*

" ... Moral corruption shall become worse than ever, which shall bring upon mankind the last and worst persecution of Antichrist, and the END of the world." *(St. Caesarius of Arles, 469-542 A.D.)*

"The END is at hand ... Yellow dust clouds take the breath of man and animal. In the city there is fire everywhere. The Earth moves, deep crevices open ... everything sinks into black depths ... Everything that was the result of men, lies in disarray and ashes." *(The Seeress of Prague, 17th Century)*

"And at the time of the END shall the king of the south push at him ... " *(Daniel 11:21-45, Bible)*

"When you hear about wars and threats of wars, do not yield to panic. Such things are bound to happen, but this is not yet the END. Nation will rise against nation, one kingdom against another. There will be earthquakes in various places and there will be famine. This is but the onset of the pains of labor ... Brother will hand over brother for execution and likewise the father his child;

children will turn against their parents and have them put to death ... the man who holds out till the END is the one who will come through safe." *(Mark 13:7-12, Bible)*

"Know that the END will come in five full cycles, for five, the difference between the Earth's number and that of the Gleaming Star, is the number of these children of war. As a sign that the END is nearing, My Father's Temple will be uncovered." *(Quetzelcoatl, 1st Century A.D.)*

" ... If there are settlements all over ... when all trees are cut down ... when only the hills remain, then the END of the world will come. Nothing will be left of us."

"It is said, but who really knows, if it will be a storm or if it will be the sun, which will burn us, which will destroy us. Fast, very fast the END will reach us. It is said, it will only last as long as dawn lasts, as long as the sun needs to reach the treetops. Fast it will be. And nothing will be left of us. One hour and we are all gone. Perhaps a great coldness will come or something else."

"Hachkyum, Our True Lord, will ... gather all of us there in Yaxchilan (the center of the universe) ... Then when the world's END is coming. Nothing will remain. Everything will find its END."

"It is said that in the ancient times it was Hachkyum, Our True Lord, who destroyed the old world with the Red Storm once. But this time it will be Akyantho', the god of the white man, who will ordain the END of the world." *(Lacandone, Mayan Prophecy)*

"From north to south, the world will be split into two mighty hosts. The north will march against the south, the son against the father, and bring misfortune with him across the mountains as the night follows the day ... A gloomy cloud will appear, and a terrible tempest will come forth from this cloud. It will consume a third of mankind, still living then. And it will destroy a third of all the crops, villages, and cities, and there will be great misery and lamentation."

"A mighty empire will vanish thereafter, and another will take its place.

From the east blows a storm, from the west a hurricane howls; woe to those who come into the sphere of this terrible whirlpool. Thrones a thousand years old will fall from the height ... Between the Rhine, the Elbe, and the Danube there will be a vast morgue, and a landscape of vultures and ravens ... When a SIGN of fire will appear in the heavens [comet], the time will have come close for these days to engulf humanity ... but the date, when this sign will flash across the heavens, no mortal will know." *(Hepidanus, 11th Century)*

"The destruction of the world will occur when faith in godliness shall perish from men, and justice is hidden away in the world, and men become renegades and, living on unholy enterprises, commit deeds of shame, and acts, dastardly and evil; and no man takes account of the godly, but even in their senselessness, fond fools, they destroy themselves, rejoicing in acts of violence, turning their hands to deeds of bloodshed."

"Now I will tell thee a very evident SIGN, that thou mayest understand when the END of all things is coming on the Earth. When swords upon the star-lit heavens appear at even and at morn, then will come the whirlwind from heaven upon the Earth; the sun above at midday e'en will cease to shine, the moon instead will give her light, and come again upon the Earth. One SIGN will be that drops of blood will flow down from the very rocks; and in the clouds shall ye behold a conflict fierce fought ... likewise a chase upon wild beasts, all seemingly in a hazy mist. Then shall the Lord who dwells in heaven bring all things to their FINAL END." *(Excerpt from the 'Sibylline Fragment' III: 798-806, 2nd Century B.C.)*

" ... The prophecies say that when the coyote and the crow and the Indian perish from this Earth, everybody, including all races will die." *(Grandfather Semu Huarte of Chumash Nation, 1983)*

"Behold the END OF TIME! Behold the END of evil and the beginning of good. What is going to happen is not an ordinary event. It is a grand epoch which is going to commence." *(Magdalene Porzat)*

<u>WHY THE END ?</u>

"Brothers kill brothers, and even children spill one another's blood. Everyone steals and hoards great wealth, and sensual sin prevails. The END of the world is nigh - yet men are hard and cruel, and listen not to the doom that is coming. The sun is dimmed ... never ending storms blow and devour the crops." *(The Ragnarok, Ancient Norse Prophecy)*

"There shall be wonders and strange appearances in heaven and on Earth before the END of the world comes ... The sun and the moon fighting with the other, a continual rolling noise of thunder and lightning, thunder and earthquake; cities falling and men perishing in their overthrow, a continual death for lack of rain, a terrible pestilence and great mortality, mighty and untimely, so they that die lack burial ... The kinsman shall show no favor to his kinsman, nor any man to his neighbor ... In those years and days shall war be kindled upon war, the four ends of the Earth shall be in commotion and fight against each other. Thereafter shall be quakings of clouds, darkness and ... persecutions ... Thereupon shall come doubt and strife and transgressions against one another." *(The Epistle of James)*

"You are living in the END TIMES. Great shall be your trials." *(Cyndi Cain, November 2, 1992 in 'The Visionaries - U.S.A. - Today!' by Albert J. Herbert, 1993)*

" ... You shall rise for your reward at the END of Days." *(Daniel 12:13, Bible)*

"The Purification will begin shortly after humans build a great house in the sky [Spacestation began in 1998]. By then there will be fires everywhere and greedy, selfish, power-mad leaders, internal wars. This is the last danger sign." (Native American Hopi Prophecy)

"When you see the gourd of ashes in the sky [meteor], the great Purification is underway." *(Native American Hopi Prophecy)*

                                     Information Pioneers Publisher

"This is the message of the END OF THE AGE ... Behold the day ... that burneth as an oven." *(Phylos in 'Psychic & UFO Revelations in the Last Days', 1989)*

" ... When the world starts to live in peace and abundance after the second all-out war, all of that will be just a bitter illusion, because many will forget God, and they will worship their own human intelligence ... People will do many stupid things, thinking that they know and can do everything, but they will not know anything ... They will believe that their illusion is the real truth, although there will be no truth in their heads ... "

"In Serbia it will not be possible to distinguish a man from a woman. Everybody will dress the same. This calamity will come to us from abroad but it will stay with us the longest. A groom will take a bride, but nobody will know who is who."

"People will be lost and more and more senseless day by day ... "

"The whole world will be plagued by a strange disease [AIDS] and nobody will be able to find a cure; everybody will say I know, I know, because I am learned and smart, but nobody will know anything. People will think and think, but they will not be able to find the right cure, which, with God's help, will be all around them and in themselves [oxygen]."

"The more people will know, the less they will love and care for each other. Hatred will be so great between them that they will care more for their different gadgets than for their relatives. Man will trust his gadget more than his first neighbor ... "

"Those who will read and write different books with numbers [pollsters/ statisticians/economists/engineers] will think that they know the most. These learned men will let their lives be led by their calculations, and they will do and live exactly how those numbers tell them. Among these learned men there will be good and evil men. The evil ones will do evil deeds. They will poison air and water and spread pestilence over the seas, rivers and Earth, and people will start to die suddenly of various ailments. Those good and wise will see that all this effort and hard work is not worth a penny and that it leads to the destruction of the world, and instead of looking for wisdom in numbers they will start to seek it in meditation."

"When they start to meditate more they will be closer to God's wisdom, but it will be too late, because the evil ones will already ravage the whole Earth and men will start to die in great numbers. Then people will run away from the cities to the country and look for the mountains with three crosses, and there, inside, they will be able to breathe and drink water. Those who will escape will save themselves and their families, but not for long, because a great famine will appear. There will be plenty of food in towns and villages, but it will be poisoned [genetically altered]. Many will eat because of hunger and die immediately. Those who will fast to the END will survive, because the Holy Ghost will save them and they will be close to God." *(Mitar Tarabic, 1829-1899)*

"Toward the END of the world, mankind will be purified through sufferings ... A powerful wind will rise in the North carrying heavy fog and the densest dust by divine command and it will fill their throats and eyes so they will cease their savagery and be stricken with great fear. After that there will be so few men left that seven woman will fight for one man ... " *(Abbess Hildegard of Bingen in 'Scivias', 1145 A.D.)*

"The time of times is coming and the END of all ENDS, if mankind is not converted ... " *(Third Prophecy of Fatima, Portugal, 1917)*

"As a species, you are approaching the END CYCLE. It is coming about in the next twenty years and has been called by some, by those who have this belief system, The END OF TIMES. Indeed, it is an ENDING. It is an incredible ENDING. Always when there is an ENDING there is a beginning because nothing ever terminates." *(Archangel Michael in 'New Cells, New Bodies, New Life!' by Virginia Essene, 1991)*

"The Son of Perdition, who will reign very few times, will come at the END DAY of the duration of the world, at the times corresponding to the moment just before the sun disappears from the horizon." *(Abbess Hildegard of Bingen in 'Scivias', 1145 A.D.)*

"Satan is directing the world ... If humanity does not resist him, I shall give him leave to act, and it will be a catastrophe, such as has not been seen since the Deluge, and this will be the END OF THE CENTURY." *(Jesus Christ's message to Madeleine at Dozule, France, March 1, 1974)*

"That is how it will be at the END OF THE WORLD. Angels will go out and separate the wicked from the just and hurl the wicked into the fiery furnace." *(Matthew 13:49-50, Bible)*

"But go thy way till the END be: for thou shalt rest, and stand in thy lot at the END of the days." *(Daniel 12:13, Bible)*

"Behold, I am with you all days, even to the END OF THE WORLD." *(Matthew 28:20, Bible)*

"As to the day, after the fall of Antichrist, when the world will END, man must not seek to know, for he can never learn it, the secret the Father has reserved for Himself ... " *(Abbess Hildegard in 'Vision X', 1098-1179)*

"But when you see Jerusalem surrounded by armies, then know that its desolation is near." *(Luke 20:21, Bible)*

"When the people will see the horror of destruction in Jerusalem and the lands thereabout of which the prophets have already spoken, then the END will come." *(Excerpt from 'And They Called His Name Immanuel', a Phoenix Journal, 1989)*

"My eyes become obscured at the sight of this terrible cataclysm. But the Spirit said to me that the man who hopes in God does penance because the all-powerful God will draw the world out of confusion and a new world will commence. Then the Spirit said to me: 'Here is the beginning of the END of time which begins!'." *(The Monk of Premol, 1783)*

WHY THE END ?

"See, the END is coming! Lawlessness is in full bloom, insolence flourishes, violence has risen to support wickedness. It shall not be long in coming, nor shall it delay. The time has come, the day dawns." *(Ezekiel 7:10-12, Bible)*

"An unusual Chastisement of the human race will take place towards the END of the world." *(Blessed Mary of Agreda, Spain, 17th Century)*

"The confusion will be so general that men will not be able to think aright ... At that time there will be such a terrible crisis that people will believe that the END of the world has come." *(Father Nectou, 18th Century)*

"The Fourth World shall END soon, and the Fifth World will begin. This the elders everywhere know. The SIGNS over many years have been fulfilled, and so few are left."

"This is the First Sign: We are told of the coming of the white-skinned man, like Bahana, but not living like Bahana - men who took the land that was not theirs and men who struck their enemies with thunder."

"This is the Second Sign: Our lands will see the coming of spinning wheels of wood filled with voices ... the white men bringing their families in wagons across the prairies."

"This is the Third Sign: A strange beast, like a buffalo but with great white horns, will overrun the land in large numbers ... the coming of the white men's cattle."

"This is the Fourth Sign: The land will be crossed by snakes of iron." [Railroad]

"This is the Fifth Sign: The land shall be criss-crossed by a giant spider's web." [Electric & Phone Wires]

"This is the Sixth Sign: The land shall be criss-crossed with rivers of stone that make pictures in the sun." [Roads]

"This is the Seventh Sign: You will hear of the sea turning black, and many living things dying because of it." [Radioactivity]

"This is the Eighth Sign: You will see many youth, who wear their hair long like my people, come and join the tribal nations, to learn their ways and wisdom."

"And this is the Ninth and LAST SIGN: You will hear of a dwelling-place in the heavens, above the Earth that shall fall with a great crash. It will appear as a blue star [meteor]. Very soon after this, the ceremonies of my people will cease."

"These are the SIGNS that the destruction is coming. The world shall rock to and fro. The white man will battle against other people in other lands (with those who possessed the first light of wisdom [China]. There will be many columns of smoke and fire ... Only those which come will cause disease and a great dying. Many of my people understanding the prophecies, shall be safe. Those who stay and live in the places of my people also shall be safe. Then their will be much to rebuild. And soon (very soon afterward Bahana will return. He shall bring with him the dawn of the Fifth World. He shall plant the seeds of his wisdom in their hearts. Even now the seeds are being planted. These shall smooth the way to the Emergence into the Fifth World." *(White Feather, Native American Hopi Elder)*

The Aztecs call the present 5th epoch 'Ollin' and have predicted it will END by an earthquake on December 24, 2011 coinciding with the ancient Chinese oracle, 'The I Ching'.

" ... Look at the cataclysm which is to come at the END OF THIS CENTURY not as the ending of an age but as a birth, the dawning of the new age ... to understand the need for, and the purpose of, a cataclysm, to see why man must change ... for the Age of Aquarius is to be an age of great evolution." *(Ramala Prophecy in 'The True Meaning and Significance of Cataclysm')*

"And when flowers will be begot within flowers and within fruits [genetic food engineering], then will the Yuga [Age] come to an END." *(Excerpt from the Hindu 'Muhabharata')*

WHY THE END ?

" ... And all the people praise the reign of the heaven-sent Prince; but afterwards the evil will take over and endure more or less until the END of time. The Light On High has not been given to me for the LAST events of the world called the apocalypse." *(Mother Josefa of Bourg, 1857)*

"Finally, it will be understood that the END of the world was merely a kind of Purification." *(Mario De Sabato, 1971)*

"A single day will see the burial of mankind ... great thrones, great nations ... All will descend into the abyss ... All shall be overthrown in ONE hour." *(Seneca, Roman Poet)*

Berossus (Second Century Chaldean Astrologer) used the Great Pyramid to predict the END time between 2000 and September 2001.

Cabalistic-Hermetic followers predict doomsday when their 7,000 calendar ends around year 2000.

The last Celtic-Druid 500 year cycle ends around year 2000.

" ... Spoken by prophets ... on May 5, 2000, you will see a dawning of a new day." *(Paul Solomon, January 21, 1991)*

"Tibetan Buddhism is expected to END after the 13th incarnation of the Dalai Lama who would be dethroned (13th really was 14th) and the final world period will be at hand for the coming of future Buddha, Maitreya." *(Excerpt from 'Heave Up', a Phoenix Journal, 1994)*

"Many signs will be happening soon in your skies to give further witness of the coming END TIMES. As more events occur people will start to wonder why these things are happening with such an increase in frequency ... Once these things are put into motion, many will be shocked into panic ... " *(Message to John Leary, May 16, 1998)*

"These changes in the Earth will come to pass, for the time and times and half times are at an END, and there begin those periods for the readjustments." *(Edgar Cayce, 1936)*

" ... Where she is nourished for a time, and times, and half a time ... " *(Revelation 12:14, Bible)*

" ... They shall be given into his hand until a time and times and the dividing of time." *(Daniel 7:25, Bible)*

" ... It shall be for a time, times, and a half ... all these things shall be finished." *(Daniel 12:7, Bible)*

" ... The time of times, the final END, is near." *(Melanie Calvat, 1831-1940)*

"The Earth is near the END of an era. The Earth will have a new look and a new feel. It is time for the renewal and it is time for this END. Only in the ENDING can there be a new beginning ... Make sure you understand that this is not the END, but the beginning of a new era and a new world and a new understanding." *(Excerpt from 'Mary's Message to the World' by Annie Kirkwood, 1991)*

"It sounds like the END of the world ... it really isn't ... it is the end of a time period - a beginning of better things to happen." *(Victoria Angelis on the Mike Jarmus Radio Show, 1997)*

"It is not the END of the world, but it is the END of the era and of the world as you know it to be or have known it to be." *(Hatonn, 1995)*

WHY THE END ?

Information Pioneers Publisher

TRIBULATION / PURIFICATION

"The mountains and all nature will tremble because of the disorder and the misdeeds of men, which will rise to the very heavens." *(Melanie Calvat, 1846)*

"In the last period ... the just God will give Lucifer and all his devils power to come on Earth and tempt his godless creatures ... Then suddenly TRIBULATION and distress will arise against them." *(The Pseudo-Methodius, 680 A.D.)*

"There will be a holy sign in the heavens ... a severe Master will ... not rule very long ... then comes the great CLEARING AWAY." *(Mathias Lang, 1753-1820)*

"Before the powers of destruction will succeed in their design, the universe will be thrown into disorder, and the age of iron will be plunged into nothingness." *(Johann Friede, 1204-1257)*

"For there shall be then GREAT TRIBULATION, such as hath not been from the beginning of the world until now, neither shall be." *(Matthew 24:21, Bible)*

"That day is a day of wrath, a day of TRIBULATION and distress, a day of calamity and misery, a day of darkness and obscurity, a day of clouds and whirlwinds, a day of the trumpet and alarm ... " *(Zephaniah 1:15-16, Bible)*

"We foresee a time of TRIBULATION ... but those who are meditating and readying themselves for these strenuous times will find solace within and will understand how puny their individual worries are in relation to the cosmos." *(Spirit Guides of Ruth Montgomery, 1986)*

WHY THE END ?

"Pray ... and do penance, because you have entered into the time of the great CHASTISEMENT which the Lord will send for the PURIFICATION of the Earth." *(Blessed Mary to Father Gobbi, January 1, 1991, in 'The Discernment of Visionaries and Apparitions Today' by Albert J. Herbert, 1994)*

"And immediately after the TRIBULATION of those days, the sun shall be darkened and the moon shall not give her light and the stars shall fall from heaven and the powers of heaven shall be moved." *(Matthew 24:29, Bible)*

"The GREAT TRANSFORMATION is underway ... no less than the rebirthing of humanity into Radiance and Knowingness, from out of the present ignorance and darkness ... Be prepared for a period of great change. This shall be a horror to some. They shall come to see that their horror comes from their ignorance and fears borne from that ignorance. The warning siren is screaming, alarms are going off, yet many see not that the mass conscious reality is on the verge of a great shift. This shift shall literally shock the world." *(Germain, June 17, 1996)*

"The dangers which are fast approaching are in the form, of storms of tremendous size. Tremors will rock the Earth, volcanic eruptions will become common place. Tidal waves will be of enormous size. The sky will stand still, or so it will appear. The sun will seem to rise from a new direction. The magnetic pole has already shifted and continues to wobble ... It is not the end of this world, but it is the end of this era and of the world as you know it to be. There will be new beginnings and new land - if you don't allow the 'Big Boys' to blow up the globe."
"The people who make it through this time will take a new stance and a new viewpoint. The world will become based, as a societal structure, on more freedom and justice ... the only way to prepare is in your heart and within your mind." *(Hatonn, December 19, 1995)*

"Earth is in a final chaotic period for she is going to transit into a new format. Long has she been ... a dark planet. She was chosen to be the present opportunity for Satan to give up his madness of proving that he is greater than God ... he has not yet come to the point of doing this, and so he has been allowed to play out the scenario again ... This time the rules have been changed, for he has indeed totally destroyed planets as evidenced by the asteroids and other pieces of planetary debris that are floating about ... He will not be allowed to bring Earth unto total destruction. No more distortion can be allowed in the universe - as far as planetary orbits and inter-relationships are concerned. However, there can be no intervention until the point of actual destruction is reached. That is the way the rules are written and they will be followed to the letter ... It is always hoped that mankind will awaken to the fact that some force other than their own psyche is at work in their world, and that they will stand together and proclaim, Enough! And thusly Satan will once and for all, get the message he cannot win ... However, as long as he can continue to fool you and to manipulate you, and go on with his games there is little hope ... " *(Tomeros Maasu Korton in 'The Wisdom of the Rays', Volume 1, 1997)*

"That which has been prophesied is at hand. You are in the Ending Times of the current cycle of humanity on that orb. This is a time when chaos reigns supreme, for the confusion of change is overwhelming to the masses ... Out of the old harshness of chaos shall spring forth the peace and balance that you ... constantly seek."

"This is the time for change. Nothing shall be the way it was. NOTHING! ... Let go of the past, for it shall stand in the way of the future if you allow it to consume you." *(Ceres Anthonious Soltec in 'Wisdom of the Rays', Volume 1, 1997)*

"Your entire solar system is now coming into the Great Initiation ... heading directly for the Super-Sun which governs your galaxy ... This increased state of vibration frequency will profoundly affect everything within your system. You are moving from a third dimensional into a fourth dimensional world ... Almost all things upon the face of the Earth will be destroyed by these things which shall come upon this beloved land ... you must get prepared ... " *(Sanat Kumara in 'The Wisdom of the Rays', Volume 1, 1997)*

WHY THE END ?

"A short period of cleansing to usher in a new Golden Age of light."
(Excerpt from 'Sipapu Odyssey' by Dorushka Maerd, 1989)

"The time is drawing near when you will be shaken and frightened, not because of punishment, but to renew the land and the minds of mankind. The Earth will shake and be moved by violent forces which will cause many to lose their physical lives."

"The planet ... is being bombarded with forces which will cause it to change its direction in relationship to the universe ... During this realignment, the Earth will be turned and shaken, and you will have many catastrophic effects ... "

"My desire is to warn you of the coming trying times ... some of you will survive these catastrophic events by renewing your spiritual values. Only in prayer and meditation will you find solace ... "

"Prepare to ... make amends for your prejudices, intolerances, fears, envy, animosity and false pride ... It will be your undoing not to forgive. First, you must forgive yourself. Then forgive all others who have hurt you ... "

"Bring peace into your family and your home ... Send thoughts of love to all people on Earth ... It is only by love and prayer that you will be safe ... There will be much destruction of the land before the turning of the axis ... the hurricanes ... the tornadoes, the earthquakes, the volcanoes and the winds will batter you to such a degree that you will not have the energy or will to wage war ... This is not punishment, but the effect of centuries of hatred, anger and fear. The tensions which have invaded man's consciousness will be unleashed on Earth ... "

"Magnetic fields will play havoc on Earth in the last days. Machines will fail and science will not have answers. As the wave of magnetic energy ... nears Earth, some unusual sights will occur in the heavens. There will be lights and sounds picked up from the farthest reaches of the universe. A different energy will enter the atmosphere. This will be one of the causes of the changing weather patterns." *(Excerpt from 'Mary's Message to the World' by Annie Kirkwood, 1991)*

"As you look around the world today you cannot help but notice the increasing tempo of human conflict all over the globe as both nations and individuals oppose each other for political, ideological, and religious reasons. But humanity is not only suffering from an outer level through famine, earthquake, disease, and war but also on an inner level through its lack of spirituality, its self-centeredness, its greed, its concern only for self at the expense of its fellow human beings and the other kingdoms of the Earth. All these events bear witness to the approach of Armageddon and the ending of the age. Humanity needs to be PURIFIED. Humanity needs to experience the cosmic fire of PURIFICATION in order to come forth reborn in the Aquarian Age."

" ... Remember the impact of the last great impulse of the Christ energy ... who came to the Earth two thousand years ago. Consider how long it took for that energy to become an effective force on ... Earth. The spiritual consciousness needed to save this world cannot be grounded in the time left before the Earth Changes ... "

"As to the timing of this event there are many opinions but, in truth, there is only one being who possess that knowledge and that is your God ... Furthermore that knowledge will not be released to anyone until the actual moment in time draws near." *(Ramala Prophecy, 20th Century)*

" ... There must be many a purging in high places as well as low; that there must be the greater consideration of each individual, each soul being his brother's keeper ... these shall call upon the mountains to cover many ... so shall ye see those in high places reduced and calling on the waters of darkness to cover them." *(Edgar Cayce, 1877-1945)*

" ... The great TRIBULATIONS will come upon you. You will be buffeted by the winds of a tempest and hurricane; of the great works built in you by human pride, not a stone will remain upon a stone." *(Mother Mary at Jerusalem, March 5, 1982)*

"Your planet and all her inhabitants are going through a rapid increase in frequency. The rate of this frequency increase will itself continue to increase until a new level of equilibrium is reached. This cycle will continue over the next five to seven years."

"What does this mean in terms of your health? ... A small annoyance may rapidly grow into severe illness in a matter of months instead of years!"

"Viewed from a larger perspective, this is the Cleansing and PURIFICATION Cycle."

"Many would rather die than confront that, out of years of bitterness, denial, and or such, they have created their illness by slowly choking off their connection to the inner Life-Force ... "

"Let go of the past! ... Find yourself in the here and now, and learn to flow a little more energy each and every day ... you will find that you have more physical and emotional energy to give." *(Master Hilarion, November 11, 1998)*

"The civilization you now exist in will shortly be vastly altered. Do not be in fear or upset over this. Just know that a new and glorious civilization is about to occur which will allow for an unbelievable shift in the understanding of the reality of the galaxy in which you reside." *(Excerpt from 'You Are Becoming A Galactic Human' by Virginia Essene and Sheldon Nidle, 1994)*

" ... Pray always that ye may be accounted worthy to escape all these things that shall come to pass." *(Luke 21:36, Bible)*

"It is the time for the GREAT PURIFICATION. We are at a point of know return. The two-legged are about to bring destruction to life on Earth ... Without a connection to nature, the people drift, grow negative, destroy themselves." *(Brave Buffalo, Brule Sioux Nation, 1985)*

"Through intense TRIBULATION shall man be brought nearer to perfection and more fitted to enjoy the wonders of the new Aquarian Age ... that ... will in the end fulfill the meaning of the symbol 'the water bearer' whose pouring out of water on the Earth is the emblem of unselfishness ... arrive at through suffering." *(Louis Hamon 'Chiero', 1926)*

"Sooner or later, you shall see GREAT CHANGES,
Extreme horrors and persecutions,

                               Information Pioneers Publisher

The moon led by her angel,
The heaven draws near its inclination." *(Nostradamus, Century I Quatrain 56)*

"The change shall be very hard,
The city and country shall gain by the big CHANGE,
A high prudent heart shall be put in, the unworthy expelled,
Sea, land, people, its state shall CHANGE." *(Nostradamus, Century IV Quatrain 21)*

"Not only the PURIFICATION of the human body, but a world-wide PURIFICATION in every field is impending. This means a general house-cleaning of the whole world and the obliteration of the clouds of negativity accumulated during thousands of years." *(Meishu Sama)*

" ... Human actions and speech of violent, destructive or negative nature create clouds in the spiritual realms ... are finally dissipated ... in the form of turbulent weather or disasters ... " *(Meishu Sama)*

"The Earth will be split asunder and the discharge will wander through the Earth and into the atmosphere. The atmosphere is already entering a state of negative pollution. This is what you are doing with your negative energies on the Earth." *(Excerpt from 'The Mystery of the Crystal Skulls' by Chris Morton and Ceri Louise, 1997)*

"You must overcome the present level of negativity because your current environment of ugly thinking is not only destroying your own planet but threatening your physical future ... If you knew how many souls on Earth at the present time doubt everything ... you would know why this is called a dark planet ... This is the last time for a thousand years that doubt will be allowed to flourish on planet Earth. After that time there will be no more doubting souls left here. They will all have been removed. This is your future children of the light. No more will you have to battle this hideous quality of infectious thought. In a few years the spiritual cleansing will remove those souls who will not now

Information Pioneers Publisher

honor God or hear the inner voice of God. In these approaching times, you will be spiritually lost if you do not have God's inner voice at your disposal. Where will you be without this spiritual communication device in Earth's emergencies? The fear and suffering will be great."

"There will soon be a division between believers and nonbelievers of God, practioners of love and peace and those who are not learning it ... between those who practice self mastery and those who do not - not a punishment but an effect you have created. Time has run out. The school must graduate its students from this place." *(The Christ in 'New Teachings For An Awakening Humanity', 1995)*

"Men get so bad they make Earth Mother shake, boil, and explode even. Then men be good, they be peaceful, have good vibrations again. Earth Mother gonna like that, she settle back down, be peaceful." *(No-Eyes in 'Phoenix Rising' by Mary Summer Rain, 1993)*

"You ones must come to realize the reasons why these things shall occur. It is because of the universal laws of balance (the laws of cause and effect) ... you are responsible for that which you helped to create ... The amount of suppressive negativity that exists at this time is so devastating ... to the point of near destruction of her loving being." *(El Morya in 'The Wisdom of the Rays', Volume 1, 1997)*

"Earth's axis is influenced by the weight of the karma of humanity. Man's inhumanity to man and voluminous thought forms and feelings of negative emotions have tipped the axis of the planet. Electrons have weight-though very slight, singly, of tremendous heaviness in the aggregate ... this has been concentrated mostly in the northern hemisphere and has bent the axis. This bend of the axis causes instability in Earth's revolving action." *(Excerpt from 'Project World Evacuation', 1993)*

" ... The whole Earth will shudder ... releasing the negativity that it has been holding onto ... And its our own stuff ... " *(Alex Collier, 1995)*

                                              Information Pioneers Publisher

"If you choose to remain in the negativity and violence of thought and deed which persists here on this planet you must accept the consequences of that choice. You will not be allowed to continue spiritual life on this planet after the cleansing time. There will be two distinct realms designed for humanity - one for God and one for those of unaware consciousness ... no longer ... a vast middle ground of maybe or someday I'll think about it. The sidelines are vanishing now ... You will need to be fortified by a daily connection to your higher self in order to live through the possible events known as the TRIBULATION and to be admitted into that transformational period leading to the thousand years of peace ... Cleanse yourself especially at the mental and emotional/psychological level where the distortions of doubt in human personality would keep you from surrendering to the Creator of all ... Cleanse your inner unconscious limitations ... your fear, anger, your sadness, regret, guilt ... all are required to do it. When you are healed and capable of peacefulness, each one, then the planet will be filled with peace and war will end. The most difficult part will be the surrender of your ego/personality's desire to maintain its own power and think it knows best what it should do at any given time. There is none on the planet who knows the best action to take everyday unless he or she is listening to the voice of God within! ... Each of you will be 'saved' to the degree you surrender your little personal will to the great will of the Creator." *(The Christ in 'New Teachings For An Awakening Humanity', 1994)*

"Solidified thought forms have densified into ... institutions, and constructions, etc., which must be broken up to yield to new vibrations and new creations. From the higher vibration will emerge the new Heaven and the new Earth. The entire surface of the planet will be reconstructed." *(Lytton, in 'Project World Evacuation', 1993)*

"Your world will soon be faced with the manifestation of great change. The cycle has reached a point where there is no turning back to a less abrupt or less physically 'harsh' solution. The Universal Laws of Cause and Effect will implement that which is necessary for balance ... What you ones will be experiencing is the sum total of all the negativity that has been allowed to grow and fester. It is all of these 'unchecked' thoughts that have created the conditions which now exist ... "

"Your world is at the breaking point on many fronts, and the recoil will be quite devastating to those of you who are not prepared." *(Serapis Bey, May 10, 1998)*

"Of all things, the fire and the wind shall be worse for it shall be liquid and white with heat and the winds shall fan it and it shall not cool, nor shall they put out the fire, for it shall burn as it touches, and it shall search the Earth for miles and it shall have enormous velocity with the blowing winds it shall be flung into widespread portions of the countrysides and those who recognize have builded their hovels against that day can be shielded from the rain of burning fragments, but the hovels must be built above the flows in those places near the cinder cones. The Mother is releasing the eons of stored corruption from within." *(Aton, 1989)*

"Your planet is on the path to recovery and in the process will make physical adjustments that will ring forth Earth Changes. These events many of which will be recorded as cataclysmic are simply the outward aspects of inner decision to return to a state of balance."

"Earth is being bombarded with the high frequency light vibrations in hope of awakening a sleeping race ... The many ... who wait to awaken until later in this century probably cannot do so without pain and suffering. The longer the personality resists its awakening, the more profound the experiences the soul must bring to ignite awareness." *(The Christ in 'New Teachings For An Awakening Humanity', 1994)*

"Admonitions through the prophets, then through the Son of God himself, were not enough to change man and induce him to take the right course. He did not want to, and increasingly nourished his conceited idea of being a world-ruler, in which lay hidden the germ for his inevitable downfall. The germ grew with his conceit, and prepared the catastrophes that must now be unleashed according to the eternal law in creation, which man failed to recognize because of his conceited idea of being master prevented him from doing so." *(Dr. Richard Steinpach, the Grail Message Prophet)*

"The inner man must be changed and purged of greed, avarice, hatred, aggressiveness ... Man does not realize that the combined thought of all mankind controls the nature of the Earth ... War and anger is that reflection of mankind that is coming back to him through the upheavals of natural disasters." *(Artemis' message to Anthony Volpe, 1981)*

" ... The vibratory rate of the Earth is being quickened and the transmutation of Karma accelerated. Literally, you will reap in the afternoon what you have sown in the morning, for this the ending of an age, this is the culminating point of a great learning process. This is humanity's moment of truth ... it's time of the transformation und transfiguration ... Those that do not transform will die no matter whether it be through war, natural disaster or disease. Only the pure in heart, those who follow God's laws, the Natural Order, will survive to see the dawning of the New Age." *(Ramala Prophecy, 20th Century)*

"For the evil done by men even nature will cry out and earthquakes will occur in protest against those who have committed crimes on Earth. The Earth will tremble and you yourselves will also tremble ... "
"The seasons will change their intrinsic character; Earth will be lit with a fiendish red light; water and the fire will cause terrible seismic movements which will engulf mountains and cities." *(Melanie Calvat, 1831-1940)*

"Inner disturbances taking place within the planet itself are direct recollections of the aspirations and the attitudes and vibrations of those who dwell upon it." *(Excerpt from 'Project World Evacuation', 1993)*

"The human race will be cleansed from the Earth Mother because it has become an irritating, infectious disease ... it will not be a case of our being punished for our sins ... it will be a case of being punished by our sins. It's instant karma - getting back what we give." *(John White, author of 'Pole Shift')*

"Many of the dreams or visions don't necessarily mean the end. They could also indicate a change. Our people say that people who are not spiritually in tune can't adapt to this change. They won't have the necessary physical, mental, and spiritual strength to change themselves. It is being said that humanity will become mad."

"There will be an energy or something similar that will influence the atmosphere. As a consequence, the pressure in our brain will increase by 35 percent. But people who have become spiritually clear and accept these approaching energies [photons] of the cosmos will be able to adapt to and use them positively for themselves. They will find protected areas where they will be secure from this human cleansing process."

"Seventy to eighty percent of humanity are not spiritually but materialistically oriented. That's why they won't be able to endure this transformation; they go mad. They will kill themselves and destroy everything around them. It will be like a madhouse. Probably somebody will then push the famous button because of this." *(Tim Sikyea of Native Canadian Denee, Yellowknives Tribe, 1988)*

"Mankind will be decimated by epidemics, famines and poison. After the catastrophe they will emerge from their caves and assemble, and only a few will have been left to build the new world. The future is approaching at a quick place. The world will be destroyed in many quarters and will never be the same as before." *(Melanie Calvat, 1846)*

"The Earth Changes will take place ... planet will be different ... so much corruption ... animals and insects will turn against us ... After the PURIFYING time ... lifestyle will change ... those working on the dark side eliminated ... all people will come together ... " *(Native American Hopi Elder 'Grandfather' on Art Bell Radio Show, June 16, 1998)*

" ... Water and fire will PURIFY the Earth, and the period of true peace will begin." *(Melanie Calvat, 1846)*

" ... Two brothers, the older white, the younger red ... were given a stone tablet with a sign of a circle ... broken in half. The older brother took his people to another land where he would develop the power of reason ... The younger brother would stay here [America] where he would protect the land and develop spiritual power."

"The older brother was to come back to his younger brother and they would combine their material and spiritual power to make paradise."

"But there was a warning: if the white brother returns having changed the sign from a circle to a cross, then, Beware! ... will mean that he has gone wrong." *(Native American Hopi Prophecy)*

"My people await Bahana, the lost white brother ... He will not be like the white men we know now, who are cruel and greedy ... He will bring with him the symbols, and the missing piece of that sacred tablet now kept by the elders, given to him when he left, that shall identify him as the True White Brother." *(Native American Hopi Prophecy)*

"If world accepts Great White Brother in old ways ... traditional fashion, then there would be peace and happiness. However, should he find the people of Earth have lost the old ways, that they have lost their true connection with the traditional ways of respect for Mother Earth, then he would send in the Purifier [Comet Herculobus with a tail of meteors] to cleanse the Earth ... the day of PURIFICATION." *(Native American Hopi Prophecy)*

"The elder brother ... mission was to help his younger brother bring about PURIFICATION DAY, at which time all evil doers would be punished or destroyed, after which real peace, brotherhood, and everlasting life would be established." *(Native American Hopi Prophecy)*

"Meha will weed out wicked who have disturbed the way of life of the Hopi, the true way of life on Earth ... wicked people will be beheaded. Thus will be PURIFICATION from all righteous people, the Earth and living things on Earth ... ills of Earth will be cured, Mother Earth will bloom again and all people will unite unto peace and harmony for long time to come. If Hopi vanishes, motion of Earth will become eccentric ... water will swallow the land and people will perish. If Hopi fails, it will trigger the destruction of the world and all mankind ... " *(Native American Hopi Prophecy)*

"When the GREAT PURIFICATION is near, these helpers will shake the Earth first for a short time in preparation. After they shake the Earth two times more, they will be joined by the True White Brother, who will bring the PURIFICATION day to the world ... " *(Native American Hopi Prophecy)*

"All elements will become altered, because it is necessary, that the whole condition of the Centuries becomes changed: certainly will the Earth at many places be in a dreadful state of collapse and all living things will be swallowed up. Numerous strong towns and cities will be shattered and collapse in earthquakes ... The sea will scream out and raise itself against the whole world. The air will be dirty and be polluted because of the grossness and discord of men ... The air will completely change and because of pestilence, illness through it will breakout, and will be completely spoiled. Men will become like animals from the various new diseases. They will be overcome and die suddenly. An indescribable plague will break out from a sudden and terrible famine and will torment men. It will be such great suffering in the whole world, and there is no where in the West that this will not find its place. Since the beginning of the world there has been nothing as horrible as this." *(Liber Mirabalis, 1524)*

"The Earth starts shaking and does not seem to stop. All power fails; your house starts coming apart; the ground is splitting open; gas lines rupture, fires ignite, your city stars to burn ... across THE ENTIRE CITY!"

"Now the Earth starts shaking again, just as hard or harder than previously. Water lines are broken, streets are, for the most part impassable due to rubble ... "

"You must think about these sorts of possibilities BEFORE they happen so that you can act in intelligence."

"As these Earth Changes start, there shall be survivors and a great migration of displaced people. In their desperation and confusion, they shall do things which they would NOT normally do in a 'civilized' society."

"They will steal from, and even murder, the ones who are trying to help them. There will be massive refuge camps. Ones will be moving inland from the coastal areas. These mobs will be fighting for survival. Food supplies will be scarce and the Government will send out the Army and the National Guard to control these panic-stricken, destitute survivors."

"Call upon the Holy God of Light and act with intelligence -- and prepare! The life you save may not only be your own or your family's, but that of a complete stranger ... "

"The mental impact forthcoming shall be QUITE HARSH! You ones are past the point of avoiding these realities."

"As the Earth cracks open and your major crustal plates (tectonic plates) shift, many sleeping volcanoes shall spring to life as your planet seeks to balance the pressures and stresses within. This alone shall cause a shifting of weather patterns GLOBALLY. The impact shall be felt by everyone on the planet."

"As countries become desperate for survival, they shall petition other countries for aid. When that aid does not come, ones shall attempt to take that which they need. This could easily escalate to the level of a planctary war."

"These planetary Earth Changes shall be exploited by your planet's controllers in order to depopulate and control more fully the masses."

"You ones who enjoy all the 'modern conveniences' shall have the hardest time as you will no longer be able to just go down to the local store ... The nation's food supply will be under strict control ... Your elected Government officials may be deciding who of you eats or does not eat." *(Lord Michael, July 7, 1996)*

" ... Those phenomena that are referred to as the stellar events, as if the stars had fallen, the moon turned to dripping blood, the Earth renewed ... will come as a result of the war being fought this day ... planet Earth will be so destabilized that virtually every mountain and valley, every sea will be changed in its geographical nature quite literally. Earthquakes as have been prophesied since the beginning of time will change the face of the Earth. But all this is the labor pains for a new birth of a new Eden on Earth."

WHY THE END ?

"And so it shall be again, when all that is false, all that is manipulated and denatured about the face of the Earth, be broken down and returned to the Earth, then shall Eden bloom again, and man live in harmony and there shall be no more war." *(Paul Solomon, 1991)*

"He ... showed me increasing natural disasters coming upon this Earth. There were more and more hurricanes and floods occurring over different areas of our planet. The earthquakes and volcanoes were increasing. We were becoming more and more selfish and self-righteous. Families were splitting, governments were breaking apart because people were only thinking of themselves."
"I saw armies marching on the United States from the south and explosions over the entire world ... "
"Suddenly this corridor was closed off and a second corridor started to open ... the planet grew more peaceful. Man and nature were better ... He was not as destructive and he was beginning to understand what love is ... The Lord sent a mental message ... You have 45 years." *(George G. Ritchie, Jr., 1943)*

"You have arrived at a learning time in which a choice for or against God must be made. In God's plan for rescue, you have been brought to this closing chapter on peace. If all or most of you choose it, the planet will not have to be cleansed and will rise as a beacon of light ... If only a minority learn this required lesson, then only the minority will be allowed soul progress as examples for others to observe."
"There is one possible activity that could draw humanity together and take the focus of war away. That would be changes of the Earth herself ... "
(The Christ in 'New Teachings for An Awakening Humanity', 1994)

"In the near future, there will commence storms of huge magnitude which will cause many to think the end of the world is at hand, but you will know differently! This will only be the cleansing of Mother Earth ... The confusion will be great. Many will have no idea where they are or what has happened ... Since it is the time for this era to end, the violence in which it ends is up to you collectively." *(Excerpt from 'Mary's Message to the World' by Annie Kirkwood, 1991)*

"And these great TRIBULATIONS shall proceed this way, while the Son of Perdition shall open his mouth in the contrary doctrine. But when he shall have brought forth the words of falsehood and his deceptions, heaven and Earth shall tremble together. But after the fall of Antichrist the glory of the Son of God shall be increased." *(Hildegard of Bingen in 'Vision X', 1098-1179)*

"Great calamities will be seen in the world bringing confusion, tears and sadness for all. Great earthquakes will submerge cities. Epidemics and famine will play great havoc, especially where the sons of darkness are to be found. Never has the world in this tragic hour more need of prayer and penitence." *(Sister Elena Aiello, 1959)*

"Behold the End of time. Behold the End of evil and the beginning of good ... "
"It is necessary that God should send His Spirit to renew the face of the Earth ... the fire from below [volcanoes] for burning and changing everything. Behold here, the fire from above [comet/meteors] ... I see the Earth rendered level; its valleys are raised; its mountains lowered; there is nothing more but gentle hills and beautiful vales [valleys]." *(Magdalene Porzat, 19th Century)*

"The Earth is defiled by its people, they have disobeyed the laws ... therefore a curse consumes the Earth ... and very few are left." *(Isaiah 2:4-6, Bible)*

"And I beheld when he had opened the sixth seal, there was a great earthquake and the the sun became black as sackcloth of hair and the moon became as blood [sky colored from war debris] and the stars of heaven fell unto the Earth even as a fig tree casteth her untimely figs, when she is shaken of a mighty wind. The heaven departed as a scroll [The 'Warning'] when it is rolled together and every mountain and island moved out of their places and the kings of the Earth ... and every freeman hid in rocks of mountains ... for the great day of his wrath is come." *(Revelation 6:12-17, Bible)*

   [Radio Show host Art Bell's guest Sean David Morton says the sixth seal begins to open in November '99.]

   " ... The day will come when not one stone will be left on another, but it will all be torn down." *(Luke 21:6, Bible)*

   "A third of your people shall die of pestilence and perish and hunger within you; another third shall fall by the sword; and a third I will scatter in every direction and I will persue them with the sword." *(Ezekiel 5:12, Bible)*

   "Mankind will be decimated by epidemics, famine, and poison ... Only few will be left to rebuild the world." *(Seeress Regina)*

   "Tell my people that I tried to wake them up through powerful storms, fires, floods and earthquakes, but even then they would not wake up. This is why I will pour out my wrath when they least expect it." *(Dumitru Duduman in 'Dreams and Visions from God', 1996)*

   "The upcoming catastrophic cleansing shall become the greatest awakening of mankind ever on the planet. The end result shall be a rebirth of radiance and knowing. Peace and balance shall come out of the chaos as the PHOENIX rises from the ashes of destruction." *(Esu 'Jesus' Sananda, June 25, 1996)*

   "But the PHOENIX shall be consumed in the fire, and when the dew moistens the ashes he will again revive according to his nature." *(Paracelsus, 1493-1541)*

   "Remember that the symbol of the Aquarian Age is the PHOENIX ... the mythical bird which consciously sacrifices itself on the cosmic fire, releasing its old form in order to come forth purified in the new. " *(Ramala Prophecy, 20th*

Century)

The Greeks recognized what was called the Phoenix Cycle, derived from Egyptian legends of the Bennu bird that rose from its own ashes every 500 years.

" ... Great PHOENIX ... gonna rise up again just like all times ago."
(No-Eyes in 'Phoenix Rising' by Mary Summer Rain, 1993)

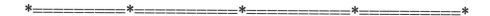

========================*============*============*

WHY THE END ?

ECONOMIC UPHEAVAL / FAMINE

"Only after the last tree has been cut down. Only after the last fish has been caught. Only after the last river has been poisoned. Only then will you realise that money cannot be eaten." *(Native American Cree Prophecy)*

"After big business go away from peoples, the tiny ones gonna stop. Many peoples think they be okay, they safe 'cause they have own business, 'cause they no have to work for boss - they all wrong ... Money places gonna be no good ... Money places gonna stop. They not gonna give out more big monies to build. No more peoples gonna have monies for houses. No more places left to sell houses even ... price of land and house gonna go way down - it gonna go way down like water through old beaver dam ... Many people gonna try to sell house and land to get more monies - to live. They not gonna get 'nough even. They still gonna owe plenty monies. Stuff gonna be like big whirlpool circle going down and down, deeper and deeper. It gonna suck way down. It not gonna go up - ever." *(No-Eyes in 'Phoenix Rising' by Mary Summer Rain, 1993)*

"The owners will cease their U.S. operations and take their business overseas ... and Wall Street will be thrown into confusion."
"During this economic melee, the far sighted investors will quickly unload their stocks, liquidate their assets, and withdraw their funds, leaving the banks embarassingly over-balanced with liabilities. With the major banks caught off-guard, the people will be in a maddening rush to withdraw their assets. However, they will be ... disappointed to discover that the F.D.I.C. [a private corporation] has not been able to insure their hard earned savings. Such will be the contributing factors to the forthcoming deep recession that will ... slip into a depression." *(Mary Summer Rain, in 'Phoenix Rising', 1993)*

"You must expect gigantic changes within your government structures as your present monetary systems become chaotic. There will be no money for taxes and without taxes there will be a rapid withdrawal of politicians and the chain of events will cause the government to fail." *(Hatonn)*

WHY THE END ?

" ... Insurance industry collapses because of high claims due to Earth Changes." *(Gordon-Michael Scallion, 1992)*

"An event will happen on this Earth which will then set in motion a chain of events which will lead to the destruction of the financial empires of the world ... " *(Ramala Prophecy, 20th Century)*

"The counterfeit of gold and silver inflated [Federal Reserve notes],
After the theft thrown away as worthless [financial collapse]
Discovered that all is dissipated by the debt [federal deficit from compound interest],
Scripts and bonds are all wiped out." *(Nostradamus, Century VIII Quatrain 28)*

" ... Financial disasters and ruin of property will cause many tears to fall ... Almost the whole world will be turned upside down, men will be without sanity and without piety. There shall be poisonous clouds, and rays which can burn more deeply than the equatorial sun, armies on the march encased in iron, flying ships full of terrible bombs and arrows, and flying stars with sulfuric fire which destroy whole cities in an instant." *(Prophecy of Warsaw, 1790)*

"The great credit [Federal Reserve], of gold, of silver, great abundance,
Shall blind honor by lust [bribes],
The offense of the adulterer [printing paper money backed by nothing] shall be known,
Which shall come to his great dishonor." *(Nostradamus, Century VIII Quatrain 14)*

"Shortly after the shortage of the two metals [gold and silver]
Which will occur between March and April,
How expensive life will become!
But two heads of state of noble birth will bring help by land and sea." *(Nostradamus, Century III Quatrain 5)*

"It will be a time when you see financial and political disturbances that the Antichrist will appear as a man of peace to solve your problems." *(Message to John Leary, June 10, 1998)*

"The beginning of the cashless society will be the preparation for the Antichrist's control over people." *(Jesus' message to John Leary, May 1994)*

"The New Age Movement will be applauding the false peace that the Antichrist will portray. There will be increasing controls put on your money system with international ties ... 'debit cards' ... will gain increasing acceptance ... it is through these means the Antichrist will ... attempt to control your lives." *(Jesus' message to John Leary, May 1994)*

"They will complain of lost wealth and weep over
Choosing [politicians] who will make mistakes from time to time.
Very few men will want to follow them,
Deceived as they will be by their speeches." *(Nostradamus, Century VII Quatrain 35)*

"I saw the time when the cities wouldn't exist in their present state. During the changes the most dangerous places will be near cities with nuclear and chemical plants. But all major cities will experience a breakdown in services ... electric service out of order because of the storms and earthquakes, broken water mains and no more gasoline because of a major breakdown of the system."
"I also foresaw race riots in the big cities ... When there is no money to pay their salaries, the police will not be there to protect the people in the city." *(Sun Bear in 'Black Dawn/Bright Day', 1992)*

"I saw civil wars breaking out in Central and South America and the rise of socialist governments in all these countries before the year 2000. As these wars intensified, millions of refugees streamed across the U.S. border, looking for a new life ... millions ... out of El Salvador and Nicaragua, and millions more crossing the Rio grande into Texas. There were so many of them that we had to line the border with troops and force them back across the river. The Mexican economy was broken by these refugees ... " *(Dannion Brinkley)*

"There shall come the financial collapse of your world. You will then be placed under total control of the evil ones who carefully planned it to be exactly this way ... You will have chaos, depressions, and collapse of your systems ... You have FAMINES and they will worsen ... and will have plagues. They will kill millions ... You shall have Earth Changes ... you shall have floods in unmerciful measure. You will have sustained winds of greater than a hurricane ... And your power lines blown down and you will be in dire circumstances ... You will have earthquakes of great magnitude and widespread, which will crumble the land beneath you and disrupt your financial base, your life resources of heat (gas) and power (electricity) for indefinite duration. Millions will perish. You will have volcanic eruptions which will take entire islands and build others. You have further contaminated the magma in the fissures of the Earth by underground nuclear testing and it shall spew forth and shower the lands with radioactive downpour." *(Aton)*

"Things gonna change for all people that love stuff ... Changes come, no more New York, no more books, no more T.V. - radio even." *(No-Eyes in Mary Summer Rain's 'Spirit Song', 1987)*

"Time as you know it is coming to an end, sooner than you think. There will not be cars or T.V.s." *(Chanupa Wambdi Wicasa, Dakota tribe)*

" ... As part of the transformation, we will be learning important lessons about our overdependence on technology ... When we reach the time technological gadgets don't work, you may find that you don't need a lot of things that you have now ... " *(Sun Bear)*

" ... And there shall be FAMINES, and pestilences ... All these are the beginning of sorrows." *(Matthew 24:7:8)*

"There will be great shortages in food supplies and proclaimed shortages of fossil fuels as they are hoarded and usurped for reasons of greed. You will find yourselves without transportation because there be no fuel to run your machinery ... There will be great energy shortages. Electricity will become unavailable for many reasons." *(Hatonn)*

"You'll see it in your newspapers. You'll hear it talked in places you had never suspected that men would speculate on such things, but it comes. And the begining of a FAMINE of seven years, a time when men will begin to fight in the streets over scraps of bread. You will see men lining before the doors of institutions finding their currency has no value." *(Paul Solomon, December 4, 1974)*

"They gonna lind out how good stuff be when they have no food in house, in store even! Then they can eat their great stuff. They gonna find out how great stuff be when they no can get gas! ... What they gonna do when crazy peoples running all over? What so 'bout electricity, no natural gas, no propane?" *(No-Eyes, Native American Chippewa)*

"The great FAMINE which I sense approach
Often will turn, then will become universal
So great and so long that they will grab
Roots from trees and the infant from the breast." *(Nostradamus, Century I Quatrain 67)*

"The time will come that gold will hold no comparison in value to a bushel of wheat." *(Brigham Young, 1801-1877)*

"The voice of the unusual bird [vulture] is heard,
In the pipe [speaker] of the breathing floor [stock market]:
Bushels of wheat will rise so high,
That man will devour his fellow man." *(Nostradamus, Century II Quatrain 75)*

                             Information Pioneers Publisher

WHY THE END ?

"The grains not to abound too much, of all other fruits force,
The summer, spring wet, winter long, snow, ice;
In arms the east, France itself will reinforce,
Death of cattle, much honey, the seat to the besieged." *(Nostradamus, Presage 124)*

"There will appear so vast a plague that more than two thirds of the world will fall and decay." *(Nostradamus in 'The Epistle to Henry II', 1555)*

"Very great FAMINE by a wave of plague,
By long rain the length of the pole of the arctic:
Hoarded gold, herbs [foodstuffs], 275 miles above the hemisphere [Spacestation],
Living without law, exempt from politics." *(Nostradamus, Century VI Quatrain 5)*

"FAMINE will spread over the nations, and nation will arise against nation, kingdom against kingdom, and states against states, in our own country and in foreign lands; and they will destroy each other caring not for the blood and lives of their neighbors, of their families, or of their own lives." *(Brigham Young, 1860)*

"In the southern Balkans and all of Greece,
A very great FAMINE and PLAGUE through false dust [radiation].
It will last nine months through
The whole peninsula [Italy] as of Peleponnesus [Greece]." *(Nostradamus, Century V Quatrain 90)*

"Mars, Mercury and silver joined together, [July 2 & Aug 1, 2000]
Towards the south a great drought,
In the bottom of Asia shall be a great earthquake,
Corinthe [Greece] and Ephesus [Turkey] shall then be in perplexity." *(Nostradamus, Century III Quatrain 3)*

"The just shall be put to death wrongfully,

Publicly, and being taken out of the midst,

So great a plague, shall break into that place,

That the judges shall be compelled to run away." *(Nostradamus, Century IX Quatrain 11)*

"A child shall be born with two teeth in his mouth [Antichrist],

It shall rain stones in Tuscany [Italy],

A few years after there shall be neither wheat nor barley,

To feed those that shall faint for hunger." *(Nostradamus, Century III Quatrain 42)*

" ... The skies no longer rain, the Earth no longer beareth fruit, the springs run out, the rivers dry up, herbs no longer sprout, grass no longer grows, trees wither from their roots and no longer put forth fruits, the fishes of the sea ... die out. And then in dread shall moan and groan all life alike when all shall see the pitiless distress that cometh them by night and ... by day and nowhere find the food ... to fill themselves ... for stern governors of the people [F.E.M.A.] shall be appointed ... and whoso bears ... the seal of the tyrant [Mark of the beast debit/ I.D. Card-microchip implant] may buy a little food." *(Saint Ephraim, 4th Century)*

"And I ... saw a beast rise up out of the sea, having seven heads and ten horns, and upon his horns ten crowns, and upon his heads the name of blasphemy ... And I saw one of his heads as it were wounded to death; and his deadly wound was healed and all the world wondered ... And they worshipped the dragon which gave power unto the beast: and they worshipped the beast ... and power was given unto him to continue forty and two months."

"The ten horns shall be ten kings rising up out of that kingdom; another shall rise up after them [European Union], different from those before him, who shall lay low three kings ... " *(Daniel 7:24, Bible) [Austria is to join the E.U. and 3 other countries are to be integrated or removed which equals ten]*

                                       Information Pioneers Publisher

"And he opened his mouth in blasphemy against God, to blaspheme his name ... and them that dwell in heaven."

"And it was given unto him to make war with the saints, and to overcome them: and power was given unto him over all kindreds, and tongues and nations."

"And all that dwell upon the Earth shall worship him, whose names are not written in the book of life of the Lamb ... "

"And I beheld another beast coming up out of the Earth, and he had two horns like a lamb [U.S. and England], and spake as a Dragon."

"And he exerciseth all the power of the first beast before him, and causeth the Earth and them which dwell therein to worship the first beast, whose deadly wound was healed."

"And he doeth great wonders, so that he maketh fire [lasers] come down from heaven [by satellites] on Earth in the sight of men."

"And he deceiveth them that dwell on the Earth by the means of those miracles which he had power to do in the sight of the beast ... "

"And he causeth all, both small and great, rich and poor, free and bond, to receive a mark in their right hand [microchip], or in their foreheads."

"And that no man might buy or sell, save he that have that mark, or name of the beast, or the number of his name."

"Here is wisdom. Let him that hath understanding count the number of the beast: for it is the number of a man; and his number is six hundred threescore and six." *(Revelation 13:1-18, Bible)*

"The populated places will be made uninhabitable.
Great discords to obtain food from the fields.
Lands will be governed by incapable officials [F.E.M.A.],
And among the great brothers [U.S.A. & Russia] chaos and death."
(Nostradamus, Century II Quatrain 95)

WHY THE END ?

                       Information Pioneers Publisher

The united States of America

"Presently I heard a voice saying, 'Son of the Republic, look and learn!' while at the same time my visitor extended her arm eastwardly. I now beheld a heavy white vapor at some distance rising fold upon fold. This gradually disappeared, and I looked upon a strange scene. Before me lay spread out in one vast plain all the countries of the world - Europe, Asia, Africa, and America. I saw rolling and tossing between Europe and America the billows of the Atlantic and between Asia and America lay the Pacific."

"'Son of the Republic', said the same mysterious voice as before, 'Look and learn!' At the moment I beheld a dark, shadowy being, like an angel, standing, or rather floating in mid-air, between Europe and America. Dipping water out of the ocean in the hollow of each hand, he sprinkled some water upon America with his right hand, while with his left hand he cast some on Europe. Immediately a cloud raised from these countries, and joined in mid-ocean. For a while it remained stationary, and then moved slowly westward, until it enveloped America in its murky folds. Sharp flashes of lightning gleamed through it at intervals, and I heard the smothered groans and cries of the American people." [Revolutionary War]

"A second time the angel dipped from the ocean, and sprinkled it out as before. The dark cloud was then drawn back to the ocean, in whose heaving billows it sank from view. A third time I heard the mysterious voice saying, 'Son of the Republic, look and learn'. I cast my eyes upon America and beheld villages and towns and cities springing up one after another until the whole land from the Atlantic to the Pacific was dotted with them."

"Again, I heard the mysterious voice say, 'Son of the Republic, the end of the century cometh, look and learn.' At this the dark shadowy angel turned his face southward, and from Africa I saw an ill-omened specter approach our land. It flitted slowly over every town and city of the latter. The inhabitant presently set themselves in battle array against each other [Civil War]. As I continued looking I saw a bright angel, on whose brow rested a crown of light, on which was traced the word 'Union', bearing the American flag which he placed between the divided nation, and said, 'Remember, ye are brethren.' Instantly, the

71

inhabitants, casting from them their weapons, became friends once more, and united around the National Standard."

"And again I heard the mysterious voice saying, 'Son of the Republic, look and learn.' At this the dark, and shadowy angel placed a trumpet to his mouth, and blew three distinct blasts; and taking water from the ocean, he sprinkled it upon Europe, Asia and Africa. Then my eyes looked upon a fearful scene: From each of these countries arose thick, black clouds that were soon joined into one. Throughout this mass there gleamed a dark red light [communism] by which I saw hordes of armed men, who, moving with the cloud, marched by land and sailed by sea to America. Our country was enveloped in this volume of cloud, and I saw these vast armies devastate the whole country and burn the villages, towns and cities that I beheld springing up. As my ears listened to the thundering of the cannon, clashing of swords, and the shouts and cries of millions in mortal combat, I heard again the mysterious voice saying 'Son of the Republic, look and learn.' When the voice had ceased, the dark shadowy angel placed his trumpet once more to his mouth, and blew a long and fearful blast."

"Instantly a light as of a thousand suns shone down from above me, and pierced and broke into fragments the dark cloud which enveloped America. At the same moment the angel upon whose head still shone the word 'Union', and who bore our national flag in one hand and a sword in the other, descended from the heavens attended by legions of white spirits. These immediately joined the inhabitants of America, who I perceived were well nigh overcome, but who immediately taking courage again, closed up their broken ranks and renewed the battle."

"Again, amid the fearful noise of the conflict, I heard the mysterious voice saying, 'Son of the Republic, look and learn'. As the voice ceased, the shadowy angel for the last time dipped water from the ocean and sprinkled it upon America. Instantly the dark cloud rolled back, together with the armies it had brought, leaving the inhabitants of the land victorious."

"Then once more I beheld the villages, towns and cities springing up where I had seen them before, while the bright angel, planting the azure standard he had brought in the midst of them, cried with a loud voice: 'While the stars remain, and the heavens send down dew upon the Earth, so long shall the Union last.' And taking from his brow the crown on which blazoned the word, 'Union', he placed it upon the Standard, while the people, kneeling down, said, 'Amen'."

"The scene instantly began to fade and dissolve, and I at last saw nothing but the rising, curling vapor I at first beheld. This also disappearing, I found myself once more gazing upon the mysterious visitor, who, in the same voice I had heard before, said, 'Son of the Republic, what you have seen is thus interpreted: Three great perils will come upon the Republic. The most fearful is the third, but in this greatest conflict the whole world united shall not prevail against her. Let every child of the Republic learn to live for his God, his land and the Union.' With these words the vision vanished, and I started from my seat and felt that I had seen a vision wherein had been shown to me the birth, progress, and destiny of the United States." *(George Washington, First President)*

" ... For ere another century shall have gone by the oppressors of the whole Earth, hating and envying her and her exaltation, shall join themselves together and raise up their hands against her."

"But if she be found worthy of her high calling, they shall be truly discomfited and then will be ended her third and last struggle for existence. Henceforth shall the Republic go on, increasing in goodness and power, until her borders shall end only in the remotest corners of the Earth, and the whole Earth shall, beneath her shadowy wings, become a Universal Republic." *(General George McClellan, Chief of Union Army)*

"You will see the Constitution of the United States almost destroyed; it will hang by a thread as fine as the finest silk fiber ... it was made under the inspiration of God, and will be preserved and saved by the efforts of the White Horse and the Red Horse who will come to its defense. A terrible revolution will take place in America such as has never been seen before, for the land will be literally left without a supreme government, and every species of wickedness will be rampant. It will be so terrible that father will be against son, mother against daughter, and daughter against mother. The most terrible scenes of

                                           Information Pioneers Publisher

murder, bloodshed, and rapine that has ever been looked on will take place. Peace will be taken from the Earth."

"England and France will be allied together in order to keep Russia from conquering the world ... While the terrible revolution is going on, England and France will try to make peace in the United States. They will find the United States broken up, many claiming authority, still there will be no responsible government. Then it will appear that England has taken possession of the country. The Black Horse will join Russia. Armed with British bayonets, the doings of the Black Horse will be terrible. The west coast of America will be invaded by the Orient." *(Joseph Smith: The White Horse Prophecy, 1843)*

"Of the aquatic triplicity [surrounded by three oceans] will be born
One who will make Thursday for its holiday [Thanksgiving celebrated by U.S.A.]
Its fame, praise, rule its power to grow
By land and sea tempest to the Orientals [China]." *(Nostradamus, Century I Quatrain 50)*

"I looked and beheld a scene most revolting to my senses ... I saw the representatives of one branch of the Republic holding in their hands fetters they themselves had forged. These are the chains with which sons of the Republic ... desire to bind their fellows. These are they who seek to subvert the cause of human freedom ... They plot to take away human rights, and to destroy the freedom of the soul, to possess the homes of the industrious without fee or reward. Woe unto such, for vengeance awaits them. Their souls shall be in derision, and the heavens shall laugh at their folly."

"I ... beheld that the bands that held society together during the reign of the Republic, were snapped asunder ... Society had broken loose from all restraints of principle and good conscience. Brotherhood had dissolved. Respect for common rights and even the rights of life and property had fled the land. I saw faction after faction arise and contend with each other. Political strife was everywhere. Father and son alike contended in these awful feuds. The spirit of deadly hate ... passed through the Republic. Blood was written on every banner.

The spirit of bloodshed appeared to possess every heart."

"I looked and beheld that many who were angry with the rulers of the Republic, for the subversion of the Constitutional Law, and their wholesale plunder of the public moneys, arose and proclaimed themselves the friends of the Constitution in its original form. These looked around for some to sustain the country's flag inviolate, pledging themselves and their fortunes and sacred honors to that end."

"A voice was suddenly heard declaring these words: 'In the distant mountain tops are to be found the true lovers of freedom and equal rights, a people who have never made war upon each other. Go there, for only there can the flag be secure from the spoiler. There alone can the flag you love wave so proudly for the protection of all the people, irrespective of creed and color'."

"While thus engaged I cast my eyes to the far west, when suddenly appeared on Ensign Peak, near Salt Lake City, a beautiful Flag whereon was written these words: 'Friends of Human Liberty throughout the world, all hail! We greet you under the flag of freedom, our country's flag' ... I beheld that the multitude wept with joy. The laws were again administered in purity. The people prospered. Tyrants were hurled down. All religious bodies were equally protected before the law. No North, no South, no East, no West, but one unbroken nation whose banner waved for all the world." *(Bishop Charles David Evans, 1892)*

"And I beheld and heard an EAGLE [U.S.A.] HAVING A RED TAIL [Communist Manifesto laws] as if it were blood, flying through the midst of heaven, saying with a loud voice, 'Woe, Woe, Woe to those who dwell on the Earth'." *(Revelation 8:13, from the Aramaic 'Peshitta' Bible translated by George Lamsa)*

"I have seen a government within a government develop in the United States ... being controlled and financed by a well-oiled political machine of one of the leading political families. With their eyes on the White House, I see them discredit any man who occupies it without their approval, no matter how good his political programs may be."

WHY THE END ?

"They will (through political intimidation, propaganda, and illegal sixth-column activities) make every effort to show the nation that only their man, the one who heads their machine, has the sole right to occupy the White House. Their campaign is going to cause great harm to our nation both here and abroad."

"I 'see' this group succeed in taking over de facto control of the country. They will give rise to an upheaval in our social structure as never before seen. They will bring about increased racial unrest and great discontent. Foreign subversive elements will (as they did in the 1960's) infiltrate the unruly factions and cause renewed fighting on the nation's campuses and in racial ghettos. All of the evil in the masses will be swept toward an unknown frenzy by this 'machine'."

"I see a member of this 'machine' ascend to power in New York City, enforcing new laws and regulations which will affect many households of that great metropolis."

"The social and religious chaos generated by this political 'machine' throughout the United States will prepare the nation for the coming of the prophet of the Antichrist. This political unit of the East will be the tool of the serpent in delivering the masses to him." *(Jeane Dixon in 'My Life and Prophecies', 1969)*

"He will rise high over his wealth, more to the right [Liberal],
He will remain on the square stone [Masonic oath],
Toward the south placed at the window [television],
A crooked staff in his hand, his mouth sealed." *[A wealthy man plans the secret overthrow of the U.S. Government by a puppet from the south.] (Nostradamus, Century V Quatrain 75)*

"Unless there is, then, a more universal oneness of purpose on the part of all, this will one day bring - here, in America - revolution!" *(Edgar Cayce, 1877-1945)*

"It will be very different from the war between the North and the South ... It will be a war of neighborhood against neighborhood, city against city, town

 Information Pioneers Publisher

against town, county against county, state against state, and they will go forth destroying, and being destroyed and manufacturing will, in great measure, cease for a time, among the American nation." *(Orson Pratt in 'Journal of Discourses', Volume 20, 1879)*

"I saw the International Boundary at Blaine, Washington, torn up clear across to Nova Scotia, where it disappeared. The American and Canadian governments broke up in chaos. I saw race rioting upon the American continent on a vast scale. I saw hunger and disease throughout the world. Strife and chaos swept away the world we know." *(D. Modin, 1947 in 'Prophecy: 1973-2000')*

"Sad councils [governments], unfaithful and malicious,
By ill advice the law [Constitution] be betrayed,
The people shall be moved, wild and quarrelsome,
Both in country and city the place shall be hated." *(Nostradamus, Century XII Quatrain 55)*

"Though there may come those periods when there will be great stress, as brother against brother, as a group or sect or race against race, yet the leveling must come ... there must eventually become a revolution in this country (and there will be a dividing of the sections as one against another). For these are the leveling means and manners to which men resort when there is plenty in some areas and a lack of sustenance in the life of others."

"When many of the isles of the sea and many of the lands come under the subjugation of those who fear neither man nor the devil: who rather join themselves with that force by which they may proclaim might and power as right ... then shall their own land see blood flow, as in those periods when brother fought against brother." *(Edgar Cayce, 1877-1945)*

"The temple [bank] where Hisperian [American] citizens will place their treasures,
That which is stored in a secret place:

WHY THE END ?

The hungry and starving will break the bonds to open the temple,
Treasure will be retaken, the temple ravaged, a horrible riot in their midst."
(Nostradamus, Century X Quatrain 81)

"Ye are to have a division in thine own land [civil war] before there is the second of the Presidents that next will not live through his office - a mob rule." *(Edgar Cayce, 1877-1945) [After F.D.R., the First President that did not finish office was John F. Kennedy. Sean David Morton, on the Art Bell Radio Show, predicted President Clinton will not finish his term.]*

" ... In America ... a restabilization of the powers of the peoples in their own minds - a breakup of the rings, the cliques, in many places ... " *(Edgar Cayce, 1877-1945)*

" ... Their cities will be left desolate. The time is coming when the great and populous city of New York ... will be left without inhabitants." *(Orson Pratt in 'Journal of Discourses', Volume 20, 1879)*

"And the fifth angel poured out his vial upon the seat of the beast [The United Nations building in New York is the seat of the Beast of Revelation 13 and Daniel 7: having the body of a leopard (France); the mouth of a lion (England); eagles wings (U.S.A); and bear's feet (Russia)] and his kingdom was full of darkness ... and blasphemed the God of heaven because of their pains and their sores [radiation burns], and repented not of their deeds." *(Revelation 16:10-11, Bible)*

"And after this I saw another angel coming down from heaven having great authority ... and cried out with a mighty voice, 'She has fallen, she has fallen, Babylon the Great, and has become a habitation of demons, a stronghold of every unclean spirit ... because all the nations have drunk of the wrath of her immorality, and the kings of the Earth have committed fornication with her, and by the power of her wantoness the merchants of the Earth have grown rich ... for her sins have reached even into heaven' ... Therefore in one day her plagues shall come, death and mourning and famine, and she shall be burnt up in fire [nuked] ... and the kings of the Earth ... saying 'Woe, woe, the Great City, Babylon [New York], for in one hour has thy judgement come! ... the merchants ... who grew rich by her, will stand afar off for fear of her torments, weeping and mourning ... for in one hour she has been laid waste!'" *(Revelation 18:1-20, Bible)*

"Babylon, the Great City ... will be not be found any more ... and the sound of harpers and musicians and flute players and trumpets will not be heard in thee any more ... " *(Revelation 18:21-22, Bible)*

" ... The sky has become a profound night. This obscurity is accompanied by a rolling thunder, or rather it seemed to me that the thunder came at the time from the four corners of the Earth. It is impossible for me to describe to you my terror: the sky has become all on fire, it is lanced from all sides with flaming arrows: they are making a war so terrible that it appears to announce the ruin of the entire world. I perceive now a large cloud colored red like the blood of beef; this cloud is rolling on all sides and I am giving way to anxiety, not knowing what it signifies."

"All the universe will be astonished to apprehend the destruction of the most beautiful, the most splendid city, so proud of its crimes. It is an abomination to me! She has poisoned all the nations with her sick philosophy which spreads impiety everywhere; it is the cursed Babylon that is so inebriated with the blood of my saints; her vanity will spill it again ... She will be full of such crimes ... all the evils will fall on her in a single instant."

" ... A frightful war, the huge cloud is divided in four parts which fall at that time on the great city [New York], and in an instant she is all on fire. The flames that devour it are elevated in the air, and then I see it no more, but one vast Earth, black like carbon."

"After all that, the sky is clear, and, after a fearful night, I see the most beautiful day I have ever seen. A gentle spring scents the air, and all appears to be in perfect order." *(Anonymous Trappist Monk of Notre-Dame-Des-Gardes)*

WHY THE END ?

"The 'Great City' of the United States will be destroyed by rockets, and the West Coast will be invaded by Asians, but they will be beaten back ... The Third World War will come, but I cannot predict the year. War will begin on a rainy night, shortly before harvest time, when the ears are full. War will begin after the assassination of an eminent politician in Czechoslovakia or in Yugoslavia. An invasion from the East will follow ... " *(Alois Irlmaier, 19th Century)*

"At 45 degrees the sky [jetstream] will burn [radiation]
Fire to approach the great NEW CITY [New York]:
In an instant a great scattered flame will leap up,
When one will want to demand proof of the Normans [Russians]."
(Nostradamus, Century VI Quatrain 97)

"There shall be a war worse than any seen by man and fire shall rain from the sky and the NEW CITY will be devastated." *(Excerpt From the 'Phoenix Express', Volumes 13 & 14, 1991)*

" ... In 2100 A.D. ... The sea apparently covered all of the western part of the country ... Water covered part of Alabama. Norfolk, Virginia became an immense seaport. New York had been destroyed either by war or an earthquake and was being rebuilt." *(Edgar Cayce, 1936)*

"The citizens of Mesopotamia [Iraq]
Irate against their friends of Tarragona [angry with U.S.A., the friend of Russia],
Games, rites, banquets, all of the people put to sleep [bread & circus to distract the Americans],
Vicar to Rhone, captured city, those of Ausonia [S.Italy]." *(Nostradamus, Century VII Quatrain 22)*

"By a strange people and a remote nation [terrorists],
The GREAT CITY near the water [New York City] shall be much troubled,
The girl [Statue of Liberty] without great difference for an estate,

The chief [Governor] frightened, at not having been warned." *(Nostradamus, Century II Quatrain 54)*

" ... Places on the geographical globe which will be blown away ... from such as Saddam Hussein ... He will use weapons of mass destruction on Britain and the U.S. the first chance that comes ... New York is ... targeted for the biggest blast of all ... " *(Excerpt from 'Rise of Antichrist', Volume 2, a Phoenix Journal, 1998)*

"A few nuclear plants will ... have a total meltdown and then nuclear exchange will occur and one will strike New York City ... " *(No-Eyes in 'Phoenix Rising' by Mary Summer Rain, 1993)*

" ... California Las Vegas ... the state of New York ... all of Florida ... This is Sodom and Gomorrah! In one day it will burn."

"The Russian spies have discovered where the nuclear warehouses are in America. When the Americans will think that it is peace and safety - from the middle of the country, some of the people will start fighting against the government. The government will be busy with internal problems. Then from the ocean, from Cuba, Nicaragua, Mexico ... They will bomb the nuclear warehouses. When they explode, America will burn!"

"Watch where the Russians penetrate America ... Alaska, Minnesota, Florida ... When America goes to war with China, the Russians will strike without warning." *(Dimitru Duduman in 'Dreams and Visions from God', 1996)*

"Your nation will face massive destruction and take over as a Chastisement for your sins." *(Message to John Leary, May 22, 1998)*

"The year 1999, seven months
From heaven comes a great king of terror
To resuscitate the great king of the Angolmois [Mongols]
Before that Mars reigns for happiness." *(Nostradamus, Century X Quatrain 72) [Ed Dames on the Art Bell Radio Show, December 22, 1998,*

said the King of terror is a terrorist biological (anthrax) attack on Shea or Yankee Stadium in New York in July 1999.]

"The EAGLE [U.S.A.] driven back around the tents [Arab homes]
Will be chased by other birds [nations] around him.
When the sounds of cymbals, trumpets and bells [war]
Will restore sense to the senseless woman." *(Nostradamus, Century II Quatrain 44)*

"The marines shall stand before the city,
Then shall go away for a little while,
A citizen army [militia] shall then hold the ground,
The fleet returning and recovering a great deal." *(Nostradamus, Century X Quatrain 68)*

"1999 food shortages in U.S. due to harsh weather ... in 2005 West Canada part of the U.S." *(Sean David Morton on the Art Bell Radio Show, October 1, 1998)*

"New states will be formed from Texas and California; a new U.S. Constitution will be adopted under the pressure of radical changes and civil war; and the U.S. will expand to absorb Canada, Central America and the West Indies." *(David G. Croly, 1829-1889)*

======================*===========*===========*

WHY THE END ?

Information Pioneers Publisher

SOLAR FLARES

"The fourth angel poured out his bowl on the sun. He was commissioned to burn men with fire." *(Revelation 16:8, Bible)*

" ... The light of the sun will be seven times greater." *(Isaiah 30:26, Bible)*

"Solar flare activities will cause hotter heat, sickness and insanity. Do not overexpose yourself to the sun. These solar flares will tilt the axis more and cause climactic changes." *(Scientist John Prochaska in 'Project World Evacuation', 1993)*

"Scientists have spoken of two enormous sunspots on the surface of the sun ... that are the largest ever seen. But if they should flare, they would cause a magnitude of Earth disturbances and earthquakes the like of which has never been known ... " *(Excerpt from 'Project World Evacuation', 1993)*

" ... You will begin to witness an increase in earthquakes as a result of an increased solar wind from the sun. Massive eruptions on the sun will be affecting your communications and brownouts will occur with this increase in solar activity." *(Message to John Leary, May 16, 1998)*

"Solar max will mar millennium (the peak of the sunspot cycle should coincide with the turn of the century, possibly causing trouble with telecommunications, satellite components, and global positioning systems)." *(Excerpt from 'Insight on the News', December 8, 1997)*

"By 1997 sunspot and solar flare activity begins to exceed the normal range, and will continue to accelerate ... " *(Gordon-Michael Scallion in 'Notes from the Cosmos', 1997)*

WHY THE END ?

Ed Dames, on the Art Bell Radio Show (June 12, 1998), predicted Earth will be hit by a solar flare that will debilitate all radio communications - first a precursor event he calls a 'shot across the bow. He said this will be followed by a solar related event 'kill shot' which takes us by surprise - in 1999. He also believes the Y2K computer problem will be overshadowed by this event. For the future he sees the ozone layer blown away, the existence of barren areas and another race here.

"Solar flare will hit Earth in 1999 ... will cause a seering (purging) of the planet and we will lose many trees."

"It is the ascension process of the planet ... will cause three days of darkness ... a judgement." *(Victoria Angelis on the Mike Jarmus Radio Show, 1997)*

" ... A magnetic pole shift ... will be triggered by solar flare activity ... Most satellites - because of severe solar flares - will become nonfunctional ... will occur between December 1997 and 2001."   *(Gordon-Michael Scallion, November 1997, Earth Changes Report)*

The N.O.A.A. reported two major solar flares occurred on November 4 and 6, 1997 as reported in Earth Changes Report December 1997.

A Sun quake ocurred on May 27, 1998.

On August 27, 1998 - a 5 minute burst of gamma radiation/X-rays hit over the Pacific which shut down some satellites, but was absorbed by the atmosphere - scientists said it was enough energy to power all light bulbs on Earth for a billion times a billion years.

In January 1999 scientists detected the largest gamma ray burst known, nine billion light-years from Earth, which released the energy equivalent to billions of years of light from thousands of suns.

"With the increase of solar discharges, a result of the sun's adjusting magnetic fields, great bursts of radiation shall couple to the magnetosphere ... power plants shall fail en masse ... " *(Gordon-Michael Scallion, May 1997, Earth Changes Report)*

Scientist J.F. Simpson concluded the Earth has maximum earthquake frequency at times of high solar activity. He suggested that solar flares may cause abrupt changes in the speed of the Earth's rotation, which in turn might induce temporary stresses, placing a critical strain on parts of the Earth's crust (tectonic plates) already weakened by existing deformation.

Professor Raymond Wheeler of the University of Kansas found a close connection between peak solar activity and wars. Solar activity disturbs the Earth's magnetic field which affects the hormone balance/stability of the human brain. He found wars to usually occur a year or two before, or sometimes a year after the peak solar activity. The next solar peak is expected in the year 2000.

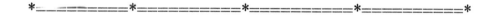

Information Pioneers Publisher

GEOMAGNETIC POLE SHIFT

"There shall be a shifting of the magnetic pole taking place in stages. It will not be an immediate shift but it will be one that takes place through three phases possibly even five ... " *(Excerpt from 'Blood and Ashes', a Phoenix Journal, 1990)*

"Magnetic fields will play havoc on Earth in the last days. Machines will fail and science will not have answers. As the wave of magnetic energy ... nears Earth, some unusual sights will occur in the heavens. There will be lights and sounds picked up from the farthest reaches of the universe. A different energy will enter the atmosphere [photons]. This will be one of the causes of the changing weather patterns." *(Excerpt from 'Mary's Message to the World' by Annie Kirkwood, 1991)*

" ... The Earth's magnetic field shall become erratic as it prepares for a new course ... With the beginning of the shifting of the magnetic poles ... weather becomes erratic ... because the magnetic field of the Earth not only changes position, so the compass is pointing in a new direction, but its pulse and frequency ... " *(Gordon-Michael Scallion)*

"There are many fluctuations taking place ... causing the magnetic field of your planet to fluctuate ... causing ... odd behavior, aches and pains (especially areas of the back, base of the skull and shoulders, where there are denser complexes of nerve muscle function), mental confusion and simple inability to focus mentally ... These magnetic fluctuations will eventually cause a reversal of the magnetic poles of planet Earth. This is not the same as a physical pole shift (of the Earth's rotational axis) ... will have an effect upon compasses and all other magnetic instruments." *(Germain, September 6, 1997)*

"Between 1998 and 2002 ... Earth's magnetic field begins to shift ... moving in steps of six to seven degrees at a time, to the west. This shall occur two or three times." *(Gordon-Michael Scallion in 'Notes from the Cosmos', 1997)*

The St. Paul Pioneer Press Sept '97 reported the Minnesota-St. Paul International Airport renumbered two of its runways due to a 9 degree magnetic shift of the Earth. Airports in Hawaii are reported to be 28 degrees off.

" ... Three similar magnetic pulse events, each induced into Earth via solar flare activity and each causing a magnetic pole shift of at least 6 or 7 degrees."

"When these events begin, technology as we know it will come to a screeching halt." *(Gordon-Michael Scallion, November 1997, Earth Changes Report)*

"There is a high probability that in July 2003 we will ... have a magnetic pole shift - the first one in 4,671 years. This will impact on all electromagnetic devices on the planet." *(Alex Collier, 1995)*

The Russian Space Program researchers discovered when astronauts are outside the Earth's magnetic field (i.e. a zero magnetic field) first they get agitated, then they became aggressive toward each other. Then they went completely insane.

According to Russian scientists, the geomagnetic field of the Earth is currently declining toward zero. [This is the result from photons currently showering the planet.]

Information Pioneers Publisher

WHY THE END ?

Information Pioneers Publisher

EARTH CHANGES

"There will be famine and pestilence and earthquakes in many places." *(Matthew 24:7, Bible)*

"The Earth is polluted because of its inhabitants, who have transgressed laws, violated statutes, broken the ancient covenant. Therefore a curse devours the Earth, and its inhabitants pay for their guilt; therefore they who dwell on Earth turn pale, and few men are left."

"The traitors betray: with treachery have the traitors betrayed! Terror, pit, and trap are upon you, inhabitant of Earth; He who flees at the sound of terror will fall into the pit; He who climbs out of the pit will be caught in the trap."

"For the windows on high will be opened and their foundations will shake. The earth will burst asunder, the earth will be shaken apart, the earth will be convulsed." *(Isaiah 24:16-19, Bible)*

"There shall be a massive cleansing cycle ... It is as if your planet has a fever, and before it breaks, her temperature will need to rise. She will need to excrete the poisons (toxic, radioactive wastes, etc.) which have been placed under her skin. She will, in the process, have to rearrange her waters and shift their healing properties to the places which need them the most." *(El Morya in 'The Wisdom of the Rays', Volume 1, 1997)*

"When there is the first breaking up of some conditions in the South Sea and those as apparent in the sinking or rising of that which is almost opposite to it, or in the Mediterranean, and the [Mount] Etna area [located in East Sicily not far from sister volcano Mt. Vesuvius in Naples, Italy]. Then we may know it has begun." *(Edgar Cayce, July 23, 1938)*

" ... If activity occurs both in the Caribbean [Soufriere Hills on Montserrat] and Italy [Mt.Etna] at the same time [both erupted January 13, 1999], the mega EARTH CHANGES will occur in the U.S. and other countries within months.

WHY THE END ?

All of these events should be seen as final warnings before a magnetic pole shift, which will be triggered by solar flare activity." *(Gordon-Michael Scallion, November 1997, Earth Changes Report)*

"As the Earth cracks open and your major crustal plates shift, many sleeping volcanoes shall spring to life as your planet seeks to balance the pressures and stresses within. This alone shall cause a shifting of weather patterns globally. The impact shall be felt by everyone on the planet." *(Violinio Saint Germain in 'The Wisdom of the Rays', Volume 1, 1997)*

"It is evident that volcanic action will shortly erupt on the Earth ... one occurrence activates and produces another within subterranean levels of the Earth. Therefore ... within a very short time these eruptions will activate earthquakes along the western seaboard through the fault lines there."
"During these western disturbances we ... anticipate a series of tidal waves to come to the southern portion of the Atlantic seaboard that will create much chaos and destruction in the Bermuda area, the Caribbean and the coastline of Florida."
"In the eastern sector, the disturbances which are below the surface of the ocean will move northward up the Atlantic coast with pockets of heavy storms for both England and the American seaboard ... the actions of these great bodies of water shall be severe. They will lash upon the lands with no respect of persons or property." *(Soltec in 'Project World Evacuation', 1993)*

"Six volcanoes to become active: Mt. St.Helens, Mt. Rainier, Mt. Olympia, Mt. Hood, Mt. Shasta and Mt. Lassen. Mt. Rainier is one that will ... be felt to East Coast. Rumblings day and night. Martial law takes over. Helicopters everywhere. Government takes extra food away and gives it to those who needed it. Earthquakes last less than a week but volcanoes continue. West Coast shut off by military ... East Coast - lot of buildings destroyed ... sloshing water ... people moving towards Mississippi and Kansas. Weather changes - like twisters ... all parts of country affected ... sometime weather is hot, sometimes cold. People finally realize that they've got to cooperate, once

things calm down, even though the the Earth still moves beneath their feet."
(Jesse Garcia)

"When it shall come upon the Earth ... there shall be great suffering ... the fire and the wind shall be worse, for it shall be mighty spouts of fire and molten lava from the pits of earth, and it shall be liquid and white with heat, and the winds shall fan it ... and it shall scorch the earth for miles - and it shall have enormous velocity." *(Excerpt from 'Spiral To Economic Disaster', a Phoenix Journal, 1989)*

"Mt. Rainier is one that will start to go and it's going to be felt all the way across the United States to the East Coast." *(Jesse Garcia in the 'Leading Edge' newspaper, July/August 1996)*

"Yet greater sign there be to see
As man nears latter century
Three sleeping mountains gather breath [Volcanoes];
And spew out mud, and ice and death.
And earthquakes swallow town and town;
In lands as yet to me unknown." *(Mother Shipton, 1488-1561)*

"The GREAT ROUND MOUNTAIN of seven stades [Vesuvius is known as the Round Mountain and is approximately 7 stadia = 4200 feet in height]
   After peace, war, famine, flood,
   It will roll far, sinking great countries [Japan]
   Even the ancient ones, and of great foundation." *(Nostradamus, Century I Quatrain 69)*

There are over 5,000 active volcanoes underwater, worldwide, on the bottom of the Earth's oceans. The thermal heating from all of them is carried to the surface and then into the atmosphere, becoming part of the weather pattern systems and causing the El Nino/La Nina phenomenon.

                                       Information Pioneers Publisher

"1998 through 2001 ... the time period wherein ... mega EARTH CHANGES begin." *(Gordon-Michael Scallion, January/February 1998, Earth Changes Report)*

" ... You've entered the times when the changes come. You'll begin to see features on the face of the Earth that will startle men and begin speculation that the end days are at hand ... even earth underneath your feet would seen unstable, and you will see the earth breaking open as its crust would shift and move." *(Paul Solomon, December 4, 1974)*

"When the great time will come, in which mankind will face its last, hard trial, it will be foreshadowed by striking changes in nature; the alternation between cold and heat will become more intensive, storms will have more catastrophic effects, earthquakes will destroy greater regions and the seas will overflow many lowlands. Not all of it will be the result of natural causes, but mankind will penetrate into the bowels of the Earth and will reach into the clouds, gambling with its own existence." *(Johann Friede, 1204-1257 A.D.)*

"Earth Mother gonna breathe real hard ... She gonna blow ber breath all over. It be fire hot. It gonna dry land up. Big part of land gonna be all dry. It gonna be burned crispy ... that not all Earth Mother's breath gonna do. She gonna blow hard over land. She gonna blow waters 'round lands. Breath gonna take plenty waters over many lands ... The wind will come up in quick gusts ... It blow people's cars. It blow people's boats and trains before they know it coming even!"

"Times in winter be bad. Great storms come. They cover all towns. They gonna be all over. Times in summer gonna be many bad rains too. Much lightning make many fires. Big ice stones gonna come more. They gonna come many more days. Summer and winter be all mix up. It happen all in one hour of time." *(No-Eyes in 'Phoenix Rising' by Mary Summer Rain, 1993)*

"Watch temperatures to hit 125 degrees in August in places in the United States where these temperatures have not occurred before. Then know that the drought has begun ... The period of crises is three years. Then the floods shall come." *(Gordon-Michael Scallion, 1995)*

"One will see the severity by some very severe droughts in your land [U.S.A.]. The weather patterns will be changing ... one will see the beginning of shortages. This time will be ... so severe that in certain localities ... the grocery stores, will be open only a few days in the week ... When these shortages come, it will be very abrupt and the shortages will last for quite a while." *(Aron Abrahamsen)*

"In part of the world that had once been fertile with wheat and corn, I saw parched desert and furrowed fields that farmers had given up on. In other parts of the world, torrential rainstorms had gouged out the Earth ... creating rivers of ... mud. People were starving ... begging for food ... some ... had given up or were too weak to beg ... " *(Dannion Brinkley)*

"By the heat of the sun upon the sea,
At Black Bridge, the fishes shall be half broiled,
The inhabitants shall come to cut them up,
When Rhodes and Genoa shall want biscuits." *(Nostradamus, Century II Quatrain 3)*

"The seasons will be altered, the Earth will produce nothing but bad fruit. The stars will lose their regular motion. The moon will only reflect a faint reddish glow. Water and fire will give the Earth's globe convulsions and terrible earthquakes which will swallow up mountains, cities ... " *(Prophecy of La Salette, 1846)*

"During the period of the hollow peace, the seasons will change ... " *(Melanie Calvat, 1846)*

"Along with these changes there will be great earthquakes which will ... cause severe shifting of entire tectonic plates. As these splits and grindings occur you will have massive volcanic eruptions over widespread areas of previously dormant cones. In portions near your nuclear testing grounds you will experience probably spillage of radioactive material into your atmosphere. You will also experience radiation leakage from nuclear power plants as they are disrupted by land changes. Portions of your continents will split and sink, and in other areas this will cause thrusting upward of other masses." *(Excerpt from 'From Here To Armageddon', a Phoenix Journal, 1990)*

"A 10-12 point quake will hit the Pacific Coast as Earth's birthing contractions become harder and more closely following one another." *(Aton)*

"A great fire [volcano] will be seen as the sun rises
Noise and light extending far northward
Death and cries are heard within the circle [Ring of Fire]
Death by iron [oxide], fire, famine awaiting them." *(Nostradamus, Century II Quatrain 91)*

"During many nights the Earth shall quake,
About the spring, two great earthquakes shall follow one another,
Corinth [Greece], Ephesus [in Turkey] shall swim in the twin seas,
War shall be moved by the two great wrestlers." *(Nostradamus, Century II Quatrain 52)*

"The earthquake shall be so great in the month of May,
Saturn in Capricorn. Jupiter and Mercury in Taurus.
Venus also in Cancer, Mars in Virgo.
Then hail will fall greater than an egg." *(Nostradamus, Unpublished Quatrain)*

" ... The North American Plate and the Pacific Plate ... Perhaps half of the plate structure of the Earth, shift as in a single moment. They do not go down or up, but rather, they slip ... it might be something akin to twenty-five or thirty degrees of slippage."

96

" ... The St. Lawrence Seaway has become a large inland sea. The Mississippi divides the United States in two ... land masses thrust up from the ocean bottom as a result of the shift. I see huge land masses in the Atlantic and the Pacific thrust up ... " *(Gordon-Michael Scallion, June 1996, Earth Changes Report)*

" ... Earthquakes on the western coast of the United States with California, Oregon and Washington state engulfed by waters to remain as ... small islands. The Great Lakes burst ... and lower Lake Michigan drains into the Gulf of Mexico causing enormous erosion. The Mississippi River basin forms a huge bay. The eastern ... coastline is broken into small islands ... Florida sinks ... These changes ... begin around ... 1992 and close by ... 2009." *(Lori Toye, 1995)*

"When the major quakes rock Los Angeles and California, they will not completely collapse the state until a major quake down the fault line of the Mississippi River. This midwest quake will give a warning ... and in twelve hours, a second devastating quake will divide the continent. After that, major triggers around the world will occur. First, Los Angeles; then New York, then Italy ... " *(Scientist Johnny Prochaska in 'Project World Evacuation', 1993)*

"California, Nevada, Utah underwater. Arizona is new coastline to Denver. Southern Idaho new coastline. In central United States a huge bay covers Texas, Louisiana. Parts of Arkansas underwater. Mississippi River wide. Great Lakes combined. East Coast very broken up ... New York, Washington, D.C. and tip of Florida underwater ... vortex areas protected/safe: south of Chicago, Georgia, South Carolina, Arizona/New Mexico, Colorado, Montana/Idaho. A meteor/comet hits planet in Nevada and escalates these changes. In the east, a new coastline extends to the Appalachians." *(Lori Toye, 1998)*

"Watch Japan and expect within 3-5 days later it will affect the west coast of America." *(Soltec)*

<u>WHY THE END ?</u>

"Alaska is a warning to Japan, and Japan shall serve its wake up call to the west coast of the U.S. (How about with some incredible tsunamis?) ... Mt. Pinatubo [Phillippines] ... is a part of the predictions (clues) of changes which would come upon the people and the world." *(Ceres Anthonious Soltec in 'The Wisdom of the Rays', Volume 1, 1997)*

" ... EARTH CHANGES between period 1994-2002. Expect the following: first there will be a severe earthquake followed by a tsunami (tidal wave) near the east coast of India ... A few days later another wave will hit the mid-section of India. Then a third wave will hit the northern area several days after the second wave."

"Approximately 12 days after the third wave an earthquake will manifest itself at the bottom of the ocean adjacent to Japan. This will ... cause another tidal wave which will devastate the Phillippine Islands as well as Japan ... The people will not have much warning with this quake. There will only be this one with a magnitude of 9.5. It will devastate Japan, demolish Tokyo and Kyoto ... "

"Three weeks later another quake ... near California resulting in a rift which will cause lands to open up from north to south along the San Andreas Fault. The San Joaquin and Sacramento valleys will sustain great damage. Following this, an opening of a rift between Seattle and Tacoma, in the State of Washington, going east-west almost into Idaho."

"Two months later ... there will be an earthquake in the Palmdale and San Diego areas ... will appear to be like one ... But they are actually two separate quakes ... In San Diego the quake will go north and east resulting in ... making San Diego, for the moment, an island. The quake will creep south into the Baja, California area causing a rift from the Pacific Coast going very close to the border ... Eventually that rift will open up and water will fill it. Along the West Coast of the U.S.A. land will begin to fall apart, going from Los Angeles into San Bernadino. From Santa Barbara to San Luis Obisbo will be an island extending into the city of Modesto. This island will be called the Greater Santa Barbara Island." *(Aron Abrahamsen, September 1994)*

"I saw the great earthquake which will cause a break-off ... All coast cities were inundated and sank out of sight forever. I saw a tidal wave that followed, which affected the Gulf of Mexico and the mouth of every river of the United States as well as the East Coast, with tidal waves which caused much flooding and loss even in the inland as the rivers overflowed the land."

"Soon after these three warning quakes, we will see what has been predicted for many years - the greatest earthquake of ... modern times."

" ... A good portion of the coast of California is just a shell that projects out over the water like a shelf ... There are only upright supports holding the coast of California."

"One day these supports will tip enough that they cannot bear the weight of the land. This will be at the time of the Great earthquake. The west side of the San Andreas will break-off and slide into the sea ... "

"The earthquake will be the most severe destruction that has come upon this Earth since the time of Noah's flood. This is the reason God is revealing what will take place; the people must be warned ... there will be ten million people ... lost in these disasters, and great suffering for those that remain alive. After the disaster, there will be famine and shortage of water ... along the coast all the way to Canada ... There will be new diseases ... Climates will change on the West Coast." *(Rev. C.F. Harrell, 1965)*

"Garden of the world near the NEW CITY [San Joaquin and Sacramento valleys near L.A. is major food producer],

    In the path of the hollow mountains: [Skyscrapers]

    It will be seized and plunged into the tub [ocean]

    Forced to drink water poisoned by sulfur [volcanic gas]." *(Nostradamus, Century X Quatrain 49)*

"I found myself in Los Angeles ... and odd-shaped cars crowded the city streets ... guys ... with beards and wearing, some of them, earrings ... something was going to happen ... there isn't anything left ... there was a funny smell ... A smell like sulphur, sulfuric acid ... the ground kept trembling ... then hundreds of sounds - all kinds of sounds, children, and women, and those crazy guys with

Information Pioneers Publisher

earrings. They were all moving, some of them above the sidewalk ... They were lifted up ... And the waters kept oozing ... it was the end of the world ... People falling down, some of them hurt badly. Pieces of buildings, chips flying in the air ... the city ... was tilting toward the ocean - like tilting a picnic table ... The buildings ... crumbled down to nothing ... now the ocean was coming in ... "

" ... Grand Canyon ... was closing in, and the Boulder Dam was being pushed, from underneath. And then, Nevada, and on up to Reno ... Baja, California. Mexico ... some volcano down there was erupting ... Columbia ... volcano eruption ... three months before the Hollywood earthquake ... Venezuela ... volcanic activity ... Japan ... started to go into the sea ... Hawaii ... huge tidal waves beating against it."

" ... Around the globe ... Constantinople. Black Sea rising. Suez Canal ... drying up ... Mt. Etna is shaking ... England - huge floods ... New York ... water level was way up ... somewhere in the Atlantic the land had come up. A lot of land [Atlantis]." *(Joe Brandt, 1937)*

"Big quake in California in 2010 ... then New Madrid quake in 2012." *(Sean David Morton on Art Bell Radio Show, October 1, 1998)*

"Earthshaking fire from the center of the Earth,
Will cause an earthquake around the New City [L.A.].
Two great rocks [North American & Pacific tectonic plates form San Andreas Fault] shall have long warred against each other.
Then Arethusa [an underground spring of lava] will redden a new river." *(Nostradamus, Century I Quatrain 87)*

"All elements will become altered, because it is necessary that the whole condition of the Centuries becomes changed; certainly will the Earth at many places be in a dreadful state of collapse and all living things will be swallowed up. Numerous strong towns and cities will be shattered and collapse in earthquakes ... the sea will scream out and raise itself against the whole world. The air will be dirty and polluted because of the grossness and discord of men ... " *(Liber Mirabilis, 1524)*

"You will hear of magnificent cities ... sinking into the Earth entombing the inhabitants. The sea will heave itself beyond its bounds, engulfing many cities. Famine will spread over the nation, and nation will rise against nation, kingdom against kingdom, states against states, in our own country and in foreign lands." *(Brigham Young, 1801-1877)*

"All sea coast cities will be fearful and many of them destroyed by tidal waves ... For in none of those cities does a person live according to the Laws of God." *(St. Hildegard, 1098-1179)*

"Strifes will arise through the period. Watch for them near Davis Strait (between Greenland and Canada) in the attempts there for the keeping of the life line to a land open."

"Watch for them in Libya and in Egypt, in Ankara and in Syria, through the straits about those areas above Australia, in Indian Ocean and the Persian Gulf ... There will appear open waters in the northern portions of Greenland. There will be new lands seen off the Caribbean Sea, and dry land will appear ... South America will be shaken from the uppermost portion to the end ... "

"The Earth will be broken up in many places. The early portion will see a change in the physical aspect of the west coast of America ... All over the country we will find many physical changes of a minor or greater degree. The greater change, as we will find, in America, will be the North Atlantic Seaboard. Watch New York, Connecticut and the like. Los Angeles and San Francisco will be destroyed before New York even. Portions of the now east coast of New York, or New York City itself, will in the main disappear. This will be another generation, though, here: while the southern portions of Carolina, Georgia, these will disappear. This will be much sooner. The waters of the Great Lakes will empty into the Gulf of Mexico ... If there are the greater activities in [Mounts] Vesuvius (Naples, Italy) or Pelee [connected by tectonic plate boundaries and then runs westward to the eastern boundary of the Pacific Plate: The San Andreas Fault] then the southern coast of California and areas between Salt Lake and southern portions of Nevada may expect within three months following same, an inundation caused by earthquakes. But these ... are to be more in the Southern than in the Northern Hemisphere ... West Coast destruction early on ... as will the inundations of the Carolinas and Georgia ... Norfolk will be safe and it is a relatively low place and closest to the sea." *(Edgar Cayce, 1877-1945)*

"Land will appear off the east coast of America ... Lands will appear in the Atlantic as well as the Pacific. And Poseidia will be among the first portions of Atlantis to rise again ... Shifting of Poles around 2000-2001, it will begin with signs in the South Pacific and Mediterranean ... appearance of lands near Bimini." [appeared in 1977]

"And a great land shall have arisen out of the ocean of the Atlantic [Atlantis], and many islands also, to care for those who were forced from their homes in the land that destroyed itself ... Europe."

"As to the changes ... the Earth will be broken up in the western portion of America. The greater portion of Japan must go into the sea."

"The upper portion of Europe will be changed as in the twinkling of an eye."

"There will be upheavals in the Arctic and in the Antarctic that will make for the eruption of volcanoes in the Torrid areas, and there will be the shifting then of the poles (so that where there has been those of a frigid or semi-tropical it will become more tropical) ... and in the Antarctic off Tierra del Fuego land [south of S. America, belonging to Chile and Argentine Republic; separated from the mainland by the Strait of Magellan], and a strait with rushing waters."

"And these will begin in the periods of '58-'98 when these will be proclaimed as the periods when His Light [strobing rainbow lights of space craft] will be seen again in the clouds." *(Edgar Cayce, 1877-1945)*

" ... Part of the Northern Hemisphere covered by snow has been shrinking ... sea ice near Greenland has become substantially thinner ... " *(The New York Times, July 4, 1991)*

Glacier expert Terrence Hughes of the University of Maine said the loss of Antarctic ice, in the last decade, has increased and is an early warning for the imminent accelerated collapse of the ice sheet.

"At the time of the shift there will be a terrific chain of earthquakes. Japan, two-thirds of the British Isles and the countries of the warring nations of Europe and the Balkans will be submerged."

"New York City will be hit by a terrific earthquake and be submerged ... tidal waves will engulf the Atlantic coastline hundreds of miles inland. We will have a fifty foot flood level in Pittsburgh. Washington, D.C. will be flooded. The submerged islands of Atlantis will rise up in the Atlantic." *(Michael X. Barton in 'Psychic & UFO Revelations in the Last Days', 1989)*

"New York City to be destroyed by an earthquake." *(Cheiro, 1926)*

"Each time I saw New York being hit by a gigantic tidal wave ... " *(Barbara Hudson in 'Psychic & UFO Revelations in the Last Days', 1989)*

"New York hit by a tidal wave." *(Victoria Angelis on Mike Jarmus Radio Show, 1997)*

"Connecticut to sink ... " *(John White in 'Pole Shift', 1980)*

Sean David Morton predicts Mt. Pelee to erupt May/June 1999 then triggers quakes on east coast of U.S. in August-October 1999.

" ... Expect large inundations ... extending for ten or fifteen miles from the eastern most part of Ohio, bordering Lake Erie, to the western most part along the lake front."

"This is because there is an underground fault in Lake Erie, as well as in the St. Lawrence Seaway ... will be activated ... causing a ... tsunami right in the Seaway, pushing ... to the shoreline of Ohio, Michigan and the Canadian shoreline. ... The inundation in New York and Pennsylvania will be from five to twelve miles ... There will be an activation of a fault in ... Ohio from Columbus east-west to the borders." *(Aron Abrahamsen, May 1995)*

"By the turn of the century, the Mississippi River divides the United States into two continents ... " *(Gordon-Michael Scallion)*

" ... The Mississippi will stretch its present shorelines to an incredible new width to accomodate the inrushing waters of the Great Lakes." *(Mary Summer Rain)*

" ... The Saint Lawrence becomes a narrow inland sea feeding into ... where the five Great Lakes once were. The water then spills south ... widening ... the Mississippi, and on to the Gulf of Mexico ... Then more water breaks out from the Lakes region, cutting a new river channel through the Midwest to Phoenix."

" ... The West Coast has become a series of islands ... the continent has divided into two ... a new West Coast has now formed from Phoenix, Arizona to Denver ... up to the western edge of Nebraska ... the Atlantic Ocean ... has pushed back the land of the southern states ... Half ... of Georgia, and the Carolinas ... inundated. A third of Florida is underwater, as is most of New York, D.C. and the Northeast Coastline."

" ... New lands are thrust up from the ocean floor in both oceans, not too far off the coasts of America. Other countries sink below the sea, Japan is gone. Africa is divided into three pieces ... Canada largely untouched, except for ... Manitoba, which is largely lost to rising waters. Australia loses almost all of its coastal land. New Zealand rises out of the sea ... " *(Gordon-Michael Scallion in 'Notes from the Cosmos', 1997)*

"United States ... will be rent in twain in the area of the Mississippi River and the region of Canada, the Great Lakes ... that river shall be split to the Gulf of Mexico."

"The land of the West will be as a great sea ... When this is in accomplishment, the mid area of thy country shall be ... sunken into the sea with only a few of your highest mountain acropolii left as islets, perhaps three and no more than five. ... to the areas of the Atlantic; the bottom will submerge the land of the seaboard. The risen land will be as a new mountain range of the eastern portion ... some 18,000 feet in altitude and the land will bear the city of the old. That will be cold as your present highest peaks and uninhabitable."

"That which is known as England will be naught seen, France will be to the bottom of that Atlantic ... Russia will be a sea ... in the north it will flow as one into that which is known as Siberia. After these things, planet Earth will rest for 3,000 years ... The ocean waves will wash over desert sands upon new shores of the Rocky Mountains ... These great places that you now know as the coast area will be no more ... California ... there will not be a place within that state which shall be as is, for there shall be a great purging ... not a place shall be left untouched within the Earth. But there shall be areas of protection whereby the land masses will be thrust upward into an altitude above the onrushing waters. Islands will be left ... The seed of the beginning will be kept in safety ... There shall be such a great rush of winds and upheaval of the Earth and the greatest of all, the fire from the Earth within shall leap from beneath. It shall be as a molten mass and ye shall be glad to be on the mountain peaks ... " *(Sanandu, June 28, 1989)*

> "The GREAT CITY by the maritime ocean [Atlantic],
> Surrounded by a crystalline swamp [glass buildings]:
> In the winter solstice and the spring,
> It will be tried by a frightful wind." *(Nostradamus, Century IX Quatrain 48)*

Major Ed Dames predicted the Jet Stream will twist and drop down to ground level causing 125 mph winds and as it picks up dust it will create dark skies and could produce microbursts of 325 mph winds. [Michigan experienced 100+ mph winds in 1998 from this phenomenon.]

"There shall be winds ... none the Earth has known ... shall contain both rain and wind and hail as big as bird's eggs ... and it shall be that the suffering

Information Pioneers Publisher

shall be great upon the Earth ... And not a place shall there be upon the Earth which shall escape the winds which bloweth."

"And ... there shall be winds in the time of winter ... the trees shall bow down their boughs, and the winds shall sting with the cold ... "

"And there shall be a mighty earthquake and it shall split in twain the country of North America and it shall be as nothing the world has known before ... a great part of the great land of the north continent go down and a great sea shall form within her center part from ... Canada into the Gulf of Mexico ... now the Atlantic Ocean ... shall have a mountain range which has been thrown up from the bottom of the Atlantic; and it shall be extended into the air to the altitude of ten thousand feet and it shall be the City of old, for it was the Light of the world." *(Excerpt from 'Sipapu Odyssey', by Dorushka Maerd, 1989)*

"The areas west in Los Angeles such as Hollywood and Beverly Hills, etc., are to be annihilated, as will the 'colonies' along the coastline in the first big shakers ... The same basic things will happen along the midland rift coming down from the Great Lakes and ripping through the Chicago and other major river cities. The Eastern Seaboard will be in state of frozen immobility when this is due to strike." *(Hatonn, December 24, 1997)*

"Everything had tilted down to the right. Alaska was now the tip of North America. Mexico wasn't south anymore, but rather west. New York was only partially visible ... All of North America's East and West Coasts were gone. Florida appeared to be ripped entirely off the continent. The major fault lines had cracked. The San Andreas ripped through the land like some giant tearing a thin piece of paper. The torn shred drifted out into the churning ocean. The waters of the world literally swished back in one huge movement, paused and came surging back to seek a new level of balance. This great movement washed over hundreds of islands. Hawaii was gone completely. Burneo, Sumatra, Phillippines, Japan, Cuba, United Kingdom - all vanished within a blink of an eye! ... Michigan was covered with angry rushing waters. Upper Michigan had been torn away with the force of Lake Superior's emergency exit. All the Great Lake waters were forging downward, following the Mississippi

River. Massive land areas on either side of the Mississippi River were flooded out of view. A great trench was being dug by the powerful force of the rushing waters. The land area below Michigan was drowned. Water was everywhere. There was no land under an imaginary line from Houston to somewhere around Raleigh, North Carolina. Most of New York, Pennsylvania and Ohio were under water. All of Michigan and Indiana were. The United States was now divided completely. The eastern portion was an island ... all of the coastal land west of the Sierra Nevadas was gone."

"A large portion of the Appalachian Range split and spread out. The Great Divide appeared to be fairly untouched. Volcanoes spewed in much of the western section of the land." *(Mary Summer Rain in 'Spirit Song', 1985)*

"The final East Coast will be located westward ... from a few miles to more than 100 miles, except for land which rises in elevation due to a shift in the plate tectonic system off the Eastern Seaboard."

"Current land regions that will rise in elevation are: From Chesapeake Bay, Virginia south to Cape Hatteras, North Carolina, and from Jacksonville, Florida to Cape Canaveral, Florida." *(Gordon-Michael Scallion, February 1997, Earth Changes Report)*

"Then the area ... [Virginia Beach] will be among the safety lands - as will be portions of what now is known as Ohio, Indiana, and Illinois and much of the southern portion of Canada and the eastern portion of Canada ... " *(Edgar Cayce, 1941)*

"The new lands will appear in these last years. Atlantis will rise and become known." *(Excerpt from 'Mary's Message to the World' by Annie Kirkwood, 1991)*

"The Atlantic Ocean ... moving in over the coastal areas ... Trenton, New Jersey being flooded out ... " *(Lynn Volpe in 'Psychic & UFO Revelations in the Last Days', 1989)*

Information Pioneers Publisher

WHY THE END ?

"The oceans are going to rise at least 200 feet between 1996 and 2008."
(Alex Collier, 1995)

" ... The edge of the East and West Coasts was not as it is usually depicted ... but rather both were very much lacerated ... most of the Florida panhandle was completely missing ... The lacerated coastlines meant inundated areas which will take place before the three day darkness." *(Anonymous Scientist, August 26, 1986, in 'The Three Days Darkness' by Albert J. Herbert, 1986)*

"Paris will be destroyed by fire and Marseilles will be inundated by the sea, other great cities will be destroyed by fire and razed to the ground." *(Melanie Calvat, 1831-1940)*

"At that time shall be a very great rising of the sea, so that no man shall tell the news to any man." *(The Apocalypse of Thomas)*

"Seven years before the last day, the sea shall submerge Eire [Ireland] by one inundation." *(St. Columbeille, 521-597 A.D.)*

"I saw a land swallowed by the sea and covered with water ... And it was told me that was England." *(Frater Balthassar Mas, 1630)*

" ... The land of the fog will sink into the ocean." *(The Seeress of Prague, 17th Century)*

"Almost all of England and the European Coast to Berlin will sink except for a few mountain peaks." *(Alois Irlmaier, 19th Century)*

"The great empire in the sea ... will be devastated by earthquake, storm, and flood. This empire will suffer much misfortune from the sea. It will be divided into two islands and part of it will sink." *(St. Hilarion, 291-371 A.D.)*

"The great Britain comprised England
 Will come by waters so high to be inundated
 The new league of Ausonia will make war
 That against them they will come to band." *(Nostradamus, Century III Quatrain 70)*

"For storms will rage and oceans roar
When Gabriel stands and on sea and shore
And as he blows his wondrous horn
Old worlds die and new be born." *(Mother Shipton, 1488-1561)*

"But slowly they are routed out
To seek diminishing water spout
And men will die of thirst before
The oceans rise to, mount the shore.
And lands will crack and rend anew
You think it strange. It will come true." *(Mother Shipton, 1488-1561)*

"Who survives this ... and then
Begin the human race again.
But not on land already there
But on ocean beds, stark, dry and bare." *(Mother Shipton, 1488-1561)*

WHY THE END ?

Information Pioneers Publisher

The POPE and the CHURCH

"But after some considerable time fervor shall cool, iniquity shall abound, and moral corruption shall become worse than ever, which shall bring upon mankind the last and worse persecution of Antichrist, and the end of the world."

"There shall be a great carnage and as great an effusion of blood as in the time of the Gentiles: the Universal CHURCH and the whole world shall deplore the ruin and capture of that most celebrated city ... the altars and temples shall be destroyed; the holy virgins after experiencing many outrages, shall fly from their monasteries: the pastors of the CHURCH shall abandon their pulpits and the CHURCH itself be despoiled of all temporalities." *(St. Caesarius of Arles, 469-542 A.D.)*

" ... Things that shall come to pass in the latter ages of the world ... they will plunder the property of the CHURCH ... in the latter ages of the world's existence, monarchs shall be addicted to falsehood. Neither justice nor covenant will be observed by any one people of the race of Adam ... the clergy will become fosterers, in conscquence of the 'tidings of wretchedness'; CHURCHES will be held in bondage by the all powerful men of the day. The changes of the seasons shall produce only half their verdure, the regular festivals of the CHURCH will not be observed ... The clergy shall be led into error by the misinterpretation of their reading; the relics of the saints will be considered powerless ... " *(Saint Columbeille, 521-597 A.D.)*

"Even for the CHURCH, it will be the time of its greatest trial. Cardinals will oppose cardinals, bishops will oppose bishops."

"Satan will walk in their midst, and in Rome there will be great changes. The CHURCH will be darkened, and the world will be shaking with terror." *(The Third Prophecy of Fatima, Portugal, 1917)*

"In the last times ... my priests shall not have peace among themselves, but shall sacrifice unto me with deceitful minds: therefore will I not look upon them ... Then shall the priest behold the people parting from the House of the

WHY THE END ?

Lord and turning unto the world, as well as transgressing in the House of God ... The House of the Lord shall be desolate and her altars be abhorred ... The place of holiness shall be corrupted, the priesthood polluted, distress shall increase, virtues shall be overcome, joy perish and gladness depart. In those days evils shall abound: there shall be no repecters of persons, hymns shall cease out of the House of the lord, truths shall be no more, covetousness shall abound among the priests: an upright man shall not be found." *(The Apocalypse of Thomas)*

"The time for the great trial will also come for the CHURCH: cardinals will oppose cardinals, bishops be against bishops, Satan will walk amid their ranks like a rabid wolf. There will be many changes in Rome! What is corrupt will fall and will never again rise up ... The CHURCH will remain in darkness, and the world will be crazed by the terror." *(Mary to Mother Elena Leonardi, February 13, 1977 in 'Prophecies! The Chastisement and Purification' by Albert J. Herbert, 1986)*

"The work of the devil will infiltrate even into the CHURCH in such a way that one will see cardinals opposing cardinals, bishops against other bishops ... Churches and altars will be sacked. The CHURCH will be full of those who accept compromises and the demon will press many priests and consecrated souls to leave the service of the Lord." *(Virgin Mary message to Sister Agnes Katsuko Sasagawa, in Akita, Japan, 1973)*

"The time is coming when princes will renounce the authority of the POPE. Individual countries will prefer their own CHURCH rulers to the POPE. CHURCH property will be secularized. Priests will be persecuted. After the birth of Antichrist, heretics will preach their false doctrines undisturbed, resulting in Christians having doubts about their holy Catholic faith."

"Toward the end of the world, mankind will be purified through sufferings. This will be true especially of the clergy, who will be robbed of all property. When the clergy has adopted a simple manner of living, conditions will improve." *(Hildegard of Bingen, 1145 A.D.)*

"The CHURCH of Rome will become involved in the great battle. Before the year 2000 comes, there will be many changes within the CHURCH and the community of the CHURCH. A great battle will begin in the CHURCH. Rome believes it is strong. It doen't see how hollow it is." *(Message from The Mother of All People to a Dutch Maiden, 1952)*

"Father will be against son, and son against father. Dogma will be perverted; men will try to overthrow the Catholic CHURCH! Mankind will become lovers of pleasure. The true and believing will not be found anymore ... " *(Anonymous, in the 'Proceedings of the Heavenly Renewal from the Unknown Who Became Illuminated', 1701)*

"In the last period ... many will doubt the Catholic faith is true ... " *(The Pseudo-Methodius, 680 A.D.)*

"Tell you children that their children will live to see the time when the Earth will be cleared. God will do away with people because there will be no charity among men. Religious faith will decline; priests will not be respected; people will be intent only on eating and drinking; there will be many immensely rich people and large amounts of paupers; great wealth will not endure long, for the red caps will come. People will hide in the forests and many will go into exile."

"After this civil conflict and general clearing people will love each other as much as previously they hated one another." *(Mathias Lang, 1753-1820)*

"And ... the rottenness of those that have ministered in places, will be brought to the light, and turmoils and strifes shall enter." *(Edgar Cayce, 1877-1945)*

"O vast Rome, thy ruin approaches,
Not of thy walls, but of thy blood and substance
One harsh in letters [investigator] will make a very horrible notch [accusation],

113   Information Pioneers Publisher

Pointed iron [drug needle] driven into all to the hilt."   *(Nostradamus, Century X Quatrain 65)* *[Drug running supported by Vatican exposed]*

"Five punctures appear. The malady spreads.
CHURCHES overflow with the devout, and blood tails are seen.
ROME scoffs, the puzzle deepens.
Images weep [Mary's statues] and the King demands answers before his death." *(Nostradamus, Unpublished Quatrain)*

"And to you Rome, what will happen! Ungrateful Rome, effeminate Rome, proud Rome! You have reached such a height that you search no further. You admire nothing else in your sovereign except luxury, forgetting that you and your glory stands upon Golgotha. Now he is old, defenseless, and despoiled; yet at his word, the word of one who was in bondage, the whole world trembles."

"Rome! To you I will come four times."

"The first time, I shall strike your lands and the inhabitants thereof." [Earthquakes in 1998]

"The second time, I shall bring the massacre and the slaughter even to your very walls. And will you not yet open your eyes?"

"I shall come a third time and I shall beat down to the ground your defenses and the defenders, and at the command of the Father, the reign of terror, and of desolation shall enter into your city."

"But My wisemen have now fled and My law is even now trampled underfoot. Therefore I will make a fourth visit. Woe to you if my law shall still be considered as empty words. There will be deceit and falsehood among both the learned and ignorant. Your blood and band that of your children will wash your stains upon God's law. War, pestilence, famine are the rods to scourge men's pride and wickedness. O wealthy men, where is your glory now, your estates, your palaces? They are the rubble on the highways and byways."

"And your priests, why have you not run to 'cry between the vestibule and the altar, begging God to end these scourges? Why have you not, with the shield of faith, gone upon the housetops, into the homes, along the highways and byways, into every accessible corner to carry the seed of my word? Know

you that this is the terrible two-edged sword that cuts down My enemies and breaks the anger of God and of men?" *(St. Giovanni, John Bosco, 1815-1888)*

"Mars threatens us with a warlike force,
Seventy times he shall cause blood to be shed,
Causing the ruin of the CLERGY
And those who will hear nothing from them." *(Nostradamus, Century I Quatrain 15)*

"Rome shall soon have a bloodbath; Rome shall suffer in revolution ... Because they have turned from their God ... Prayer has been discarded for all materialism and worldly knowledge." *(Our Lady, 1977)*

"There will be a great revolution in Rome, in Italy, and many countries in Europe ... because the man of sin is preparing the way ... The forces of communism will enter upon the seat of Peter." *(Our Lady, 1978)*

"The infernal gods will cause Hannibal [the North African],
To be reborn again, a terror to all men.
Only this time the destruction will be far worse than in the past,
He will come against the Romans by way of Babel [Middle East]." *(Nostradamus, Century II Quatrain 30)*

"Through fire coming down from the sky, the city will be almost totally burned,
While at the same time there will be tremendous flooding.
Sardinia [Italy] will be vexed by the North African fleet
And the CHURCH will have to vacate her seat of power." *(Nostradamus, Century II Quatrain 81)*

"Watch for the major revolution in Africa, Western Europe and especially upheaval and revolution in Italy which touches the Vatican [then to the Mideast]. Then watch for the fleeing of the POPE into safety outside Rome [will occur in

secrecy, but will leak out]. Then very soon will come THE WARNING followed
... by a Great Miracle in Spain ... area of Garabandal ... " *(Excerpt from 'Phoenix Journal Express', Volumes 1 & 2, 1990)*

"There will come a great wonder [The Warning], which will fill the world with astonishment. This wonder will be preceded by the triumph of revolution. The CHURCH will suffer exceedingly. Her servants and her chieftan will be mocked, scourged and martyred." *(Dannion Brinkley, 1975)*

"Russia will march upon all the nations of Europe, particularly Italy, and will raise her flag over the Dome of St. Peters. Italy will be severely tried by a great revolution, and Rome will be purified in blood for its many sins, especially those of impurity. The flock is about to be dispersed and the POPE will suffer greatly." *(Mother Mary to Sister Elena Aiello, 1959)*

"Russian troop movements force the POPE to leave Rome.
Plaster, chalk and dust will be reduced to ashes;
But the revolution which will follow will be a trap for them,
Final aid opposed to their border." *(Nostradamus, Century IX Quatrain 99)*

"Very near the Tiber [river in Italy] presses Libitinia [Roman goddess]:
Shortly before the great inundation
The chief of the ship [Pope] taken, thrown into the bilge:
Castle [St.Peter's], palace [Vatican] in conflagration." *(Nostradamus, Century II Quatrain 93)*

"All priests but six will be murdered. The POPE will flee ... " *(Alois Irlmaier, 19th Century)*

"What is certain is that the POPE will leave Rome, and in leaving the Vatican, he will have to pass over the dead bodies of his priests." *(Pope Pius X, 1909)*

"Religions shall be persecuted, priests shall be massacred, the CHURCHES shall be closed, but only for a short time; the HOLY FATHER shall be obliged to abandon Rome."

"All the enemies of the CHURCH, known and unknown, will perish all over the world during the universal darkness, with the exception of a few who will be converted." *(Anna Maria Taigi, 1769-1857)*

"A great multitude of people will lose their lives in those calamitous times, but the wicked will not prevail. They will indeed attempt to destroy the whole CHURCH, but not enough time will be allowed them, because the frightful crisis will be of short duration. When all is considered lost, all will be found safe. This disaster will come to pass shortly after the power of England begins to wane. This will be the sign. As when the fig tree begins to sprout and produce leaves, it is a sure sign that summer is near, England in her turn will experience a more frightful revolution than that of France." *(Father Nectou, 18th Century)*

"I have seen one of my successors, of the same name, who was fleeing over the bodies of his brethren. He will take refuge in some hiding place; but after a brief respite he will die a cruel death."

"Respect for God has disappeared from human hearts. They wish to efface even God's memory. This perversity is nothing less than the beginning of the last days of the world." *(Pope Pius X, 1914)*

"The ROMAN CHAIR will stand empty for some time ... this will not however be a war of religion, but all who believe in Jesus Christ will have a common cause ... A principal sign of the times in which the war will break out will be the general corruption of mores in many places. At that time they will give believers the name of fools, and the faithless will pretend to be men of light." *(Wessel Eilert, 1764-1833)*

"Some day a POPE will flee from Rome in the company of only four cardinals ... and they will come to Koeln [Cologne]." *(Helen Walraff, 19th*

WHY THE END ?

Century)

"After 72 hours everything will be over ... Thereafter the POPE will return ... " *(Alois Irlmaier, 19th Century)*

St. *Malachi predicted 112 POPES including the last 3:*

De Labore Solis (Labor of the Sun): *Pope John Paul II (Cardinal Karol Wojtyla) who was born during a total eclipse of the sun.*

"The entourage of John-Paul II ['the work of the sun'] Sheltering on the isle of Capri,
Will be taken prisoners and led away by the revolutionaries.
They will be taken to prison like animals,
Across the Bigorre near Tarbes." *(Nostradamus, Century X Quatrain 29)*

" ... When Pope John-Paul II leaves Rome or is claimed dead ... the schism will begin. This is the warning to go into hiding, since the Antichrist will soon take power and kill all of those against the New World Order." *(Message to John Leary, April 17, 1998)*

"When ... John-Paul II is removed from his office, the Antipope will dominate and control ... all of the Roman Catholic Churches ... the Antipope will worship the Antichrist ... " *(Message to John Leary, June 15, 1998)*

" ... Towards the end of the world ... at that time the POPE with his cardinals will have to flee Rome in tragic circumstances to a place where they will be unknown. The POPE will die a cruel death in his exile. The sufferings of the CHURCH will be much greater than at any previous time in her history ... but God will raise a holy POPE ... This man will rebuild almost the whole world through his holiness." *(John of the Cleft Rock, 14th Century)*

" ... The long-secret prophecy of Fatima was ... revealed to me. I saw the throne of the POPE, but it was empty. Off to one side, I was shown a POPE with blood running down his face and dripping over his left shoulder. Green [olive] leaves of knowledge showered down from above, expanding as they fell. I saw hands reaching out to the throne, but no one sat in it, so I realized that within this century a POPE will be bodily harmed. When this occurs, the head of the CHURCH will thereafter have a different insignia than that of the POPE ... that power would still be there but that it would not rest in the person of a POPE." *(Jeane Dixon, 1918-1997)*

<u>*De Gloria Olivae (Glory of the Olive):*</u> *the penultimate POPE, the olive symbolic of peace.*

"Oh, what a messenger of peace of the glory of the olive tree, of the Lord, oh, what a protector, all filled with goodness! - the POPE, Leo XIV, energetic monarch, a glorious reign." *(The Monk of Padua)*

"The Lion Monarch shall be made famous unto all and shall subvert kingdoms, peoples and nations. Then God shall send a king from the sun, who shall cause all the people of the Earth to cease from disastrous war." *(Excerpt from the 'Sibylline Fragment', 2nd Century B.C.)*

" ... Will be in office a short time, but will make new rules which are disastrous to the CHURCH and allow the last POPE to align himself with the Antichrist. The last POPE is embittered from a family of former Nazis ... has curvature of the spine, will share Vatican secrets with the Antichrist, thus aiding him in his military push against Europe and provide funding for Antichrist's military operation. The last POPE will move his abode, but destination not prophesied." *(Excerpt from 'Conversations with Nostradamus', Volume I, by Dolores Cannon, 1991)*

WHY THE END ?

Peter Romanus (Peter of Rome):

"During the final persecution of the Holy Roman Catholic CHURCH, there shall sit upon the throne Peter the Roman, who will pasture his flock in the midst of many tribulations. With these passed, the city of the hills [Rome] will be destroyed, and the awful judge will judge the peoples." *(St. Malachi, in Arnold de Wion's 'Lignum Vitae', 1595)*

"In the world there will be made a king
Who will have little peace and a short life.
At this time the ship of the PAPACY will be lost,
Governed to its greatest detriment." *(Nostradamus, Century I Quatrain 4)*

"There will appear toward the North
Not far from Cancer the bearded star [comet]:
Susa [Iran], Siena [Central Italy], Boeotia [Greece], Eretria [Ethiopia],
The GREAT ONE OF ROME will die, the night over." *(Nostradamus, Century VI Quatrain 6)*

"Because of the war-like conditions in Europe and Italy, the Anti-Pope moves the throne of Peter to Jerusalem." *(Dr. Mary Jane Even)*

"The Arab prince Mars, Sun, Venus, Lion
The reign of the CHURCH will succumb to the sea
Toward Persia [Iran] well near a million
Byzantium [Turkey], Egypt will resist the temptation." *(Nostradamus, Century V Quatrain 25)*

"Weep Milan [N.Italy], weep Lucques, and Florence [C.Italy],
When the great Duke [Pope] shall go upon the Chariot,
To change the siege near Venice he advances,
When Colonee shall change at ROME." *(Nostradamus, Century X Quatrain 64)*

"There will be a POPE who will not dare so much as look upon Rome. Similarly, one thing the Romans must understand, among others, is that before the death of the POPE, our Lord will make him suffer such disgrace that there will be nothing to compare with it. It is likewise necessary that the Romans know, among other things, that from that time on will begin their destruction, step by step, and that it will be because of their sins." *(Merlin Ambrosius, 1150 A.D.)*

" ... He will come to Jerusalem, and having put off the diadem from his head and laid aside the whole imperial garb, he will hand over the empire of the Christians ... When the Roman Empire shall have ceased, then the Antichrist will be openly revealed and will sit in the House of the Lord in Jerusalem." *(Excerpt from the 'Tiburtine Sibyl', Alexander's Oracle of Baalbek, 380 A.D.)*

" ... The Romans [Church] will ... live in Jerusalem for seven and a half-seven times. When the ten and a half years are completed the Son of Perdition will appear." *(The Pseudo-Methodius, 680 A.D.)*

"By the power of the three realms,
The HOLY SEE will be moved elsewhere [Jerusalem],
Where a new POPE will receive the spirit
And there will be a new CHURCH seat of power." *(Nostradamus, Century VIII Quatrain 99)*

In May 1993, Israel's Foreign Minister Shimon Peres promised the Pope hegemony of Jerusalem by the end of the year 2000. In October 1998, the Vatican began building an embassy in West Jerusalem and the Holy See has demanded a say in the final status of Jerusalem as dictated in the first Oslo Accord.

"After five the CHURCH will be expelled;
A person will flee, abandoning the POPE:
False rumors of help circulate,

The head [of the Church/Pope] will then abandon the Holy See." *(Nostradamus, Century X Quatrain 3)*

"The great star will burn for seven days [comet]
The cloud will cause two suns to appear
The big mastiff [England] will howl all night
When the GREAT PONTIFF will change country." *(Nostradamus, Century II Quatrain 41)*

" ... Towards the end of time one of the descendants of the king of France shall reign over all the Roman Empire; and that he shall be the greatest of the French monarchs, and the last of his race."

"After having most happily governed his kingdom, he will go to Jerusalem, and depose on Mount Olivet his sceptre and crown. This shall be the end and conclusion of the Roman and Christian Empire." *(Rabanus Maurus, 776-856 A.D.)*

"When the SON OF PERDITION has arisen, the king of the Romans will ascend Golgotha upon which the wood of the Holy Cross is fixed, in the place where the Lord underwent death for us. The king will take the crown from his head and place it on the cross ... When the cross has been lifted up on high to heaven, the king of the Romans will directly give up his spirit. Then every principality and power will be destroyed that the SON OF PERDITION may be made manifest." *(The Pseudo-Methodius, 680 A.D.)*

"Rome will lose its sceptre through following false prophets. The POPE will be taken prisoner by his attendants. The CHURCH will be held hostage, and after a short time there will be no more POPE." *(Rudolfo Gilthier, 1675)*

"There will be no POPE, and the air will be as a pestilence, destroying men and beasts alike. Not since the creation of the world has one experienced such misfortune." *(Caesarius of Heisterbach, 1180-1240 A.D.)*

" ... After the crisis, he will have a general council, despite the oppositions made by the clergy itself. Afterwards there will be but one flock and one pastor [ONE WORLD RELIGION] ... up to the destruction of the Antichrist." *(Abbe Souffrant, 19th Century)*

"The great Monarch and the Great Pope will precede the ANTICHRIST." *(Werdin d'Otrant, 13th Century)*

"The Sixth Epoch of the Spirit commences with the powerful Monarch and the HOLY PONTIFF ... and will last until the appearance of the Antichrist." *(Barthalomew Holzhauser, 1613-1658 A.D.)*

"When the time of the reign of Antichrist is near, a false religion will appear which will be opposed to the unity of God and His CHURCH. This will cause the greatest schism the world has ever known." *(Jane Le Royer, 18th Century)*

"The Prince of this world has been permitted to found a kingdom of his own, which will be only an empty mold of the undivided kingdom of Christ. Many members of the CHURCH will not see the difference, because even they seek the temporal, and they will be deceived by the Prince of this world." *(Emelda Scochy, 1933)*

"When he comes nothing will be changed, in the nunnery everyone will be dressed as usual; the religious exercises will realize that the Antichrist is in charge." *(Bertine Bouquillon, 1850)*

"Their eyes closed, open to the old fantasy,
The habit of priests will be abolished.
The great monarch will punish their frenzy,
Stealing the treasure in front of the temples." *(Nostradamus, Century II Quatrain 12)*

WHY THE END ?

"Once the Antichrist comes to power ... most of the Church buildings will be either destroyed or made into museums." *(Message to John Leary, April 16, 1998)*

" ... At Fatima ... the third secret ... is that Satan would enter into My Son's CHURCH." *(Our Lady, 1978)*

The words "Mystery Babylon" and Roman numerals DCLXVI (666) appear on the golden carp hat worn by the Pope. The symbol 'vivivi' (vini,vidi,vinci) = 'I come, I saw, I conquered' on Pope's Babylonia hat band across forehead - as testimony he is present emperor of Rome in direct line from Julius Caesar who was Pope before Jesus (100-44 B.C.). The inscription on the Pope's miter reads "VICARIUS FILII DEI" (Vicar of the Son of God).

"Rome will lose the faith and become the seat of Antichrist. The demons allied to Antichrist will operate on Earth and in the sky, and humanity will become even more evil. But God will not give up His truly faithful servants who are men of goodwill. The Gospel will be preached everywhere to all the people and the nations will know the truth."

"Fight, Sons of light, you small number who see, because the time of times, the final end, is near."

"The CHURCH will be in the dark, the world will be convulsed but in this confusion, Enoch and Elijah, will appear, full of the spirit of God. They will preach, and in their words will be the power of God; and men of good will who believe in God. Many spirits will be consoled; in virtue of the Holy Spirit, they will make great progress, and condemn the diabolical errors of Antichrist."

"Enoch and Elijah will be put to death. Pagan Rome will be destroyed, and fire will fall from heaven, destroying three cities. The sun will be darkened, and only the faithful will survive." *(Melanie Calvat, 1831-1940)*

"The red flag will flutter over the Vatican. God's punishment on Rome will be announced by an earthquake much stronger than that at Golgotha." *(Monk Da Terni, 20th Century)*

" ... One will be entered into the House of God, and woe to man when he places him upon the Seat of Peter, for then the great day of the Lord shall be at hand." *(Blessed Virgin Mary to Veronica Lueken, March 18, 1974)*

=====================*===========*===========*

WHY THE END ?

                                       Information Pioneers Publisher

THE ANTICHRIST / SON OF PERDITION

" ... It is the last hour ... as you have heard that ANTICHRIST cometh ..."
(1 John 2:18, Bible)

" ... Every spirit that acknowledges Jesus Christ ... belongs to God, while every spirit that fails to acknowledge him does not belong to God, such is the spirit of ANTICHRIST ... " *(1 John 4:3, Bible)*

"For many seducers are gone out into the world who confess not that Jesus Christ is come in the flesh. This is a seducer and an ANTICHRIST." *(2 John 1:7, Bible)*

"Who is a liar, but he who denieth that Jesus is the Christ? This is ANTICHRIST ... " *(1 John 2:22, Bible)*

" ... Two great forces are struggling to gain control of man's mind ... going on for time immemorial ... may be described as positive (in harmony ... with God) and negative (encompassing ANTICHRIST motives designed to gain control over man for ... power). This battle ... is being waged on two fronts, the physical and the metaphysical ... to bring about either the spiritual salvation or destruction of homo sapiens." *(Wilbur Smith, in 'Psychic & UFO Revelations in the Last Days', 1989)*

"You will see a time where events will seem like they are happening almost simultaneously. Time will appear as if it was speeded up. A time of chaos throughout the world will occur. All these events will cause people to demand some stable leadership. These things will make way for the entrance of the ANTICHRIST. He will appear as a man of peace with great powers but his reign will not last long." *(Jesus' message to John Leary, April 1994)*

"When three signs come, the inhabitants of the Earth know that he is near. In the city of Aeneas a one hundred year old woman will bear twins with the aid of the faithless. A burning river will issue from Mt.Etna and devour the inhabitants. After this, two peaks shall crash together in the snowy mountains, the earth there will be opened in an abyss, and a snowy mist will ascend to heaven."

"After these things, there will be a gathering together of many nations bestial in their manner of life and a division of the world into ten sceptres [regions] ... Heaven, the sun, and the elements will seem to be a testimony to the abomination in that he will do wonders, make the stars dark, weaken the perfect."
(Excerpt from the 'Erythraean Sibyl', 12th Century)

"The sixth age of the spirit commences with the powerful Monarch and the Holy Pontiff ... and will last until the appearance of the ANTICHRIST."

"Peace will reign in all the universe, because the divine power will bind Satan for many years, until the SON OF PERDITION will rave anew."
(Barthalomew Holzhauser, in 'Visiones', 1646)

"But after some considerable time fervor shall cool, iniquity shall abound, and moral corruption shall become worse than ever, which shall bring upon mankind the last and worse persecution of ANTICHRIST, and the end of the world." *(St. Caesarius of Arles, in 'Mirabilis Liber Prophecias Revelationes', 469-542 A.D.)*

"As the PROPHET of ANTICHRIST advances his ideology, men will become dazzled by the progress of civilization and be blinded by the rich standard of living." *(Jeane Dixon, 1969)*

"As a result of the tremendous propaganda efforts of the PROPHET of the ANTICHRIST, the influence of Christianity will have greatly diminished by the time the seductive child [ANTICHRIST] is thirty years of age." *(Jeane Dixon, 1969)*

"The social and religious chaos generated by this political machine throughout the United States will prepare the nation for the coming of the

128

PROPHET of the ANTICHRIST. This political unit of the East will be the tool of the serpent in delivering the masses to him."

"His [The FALSE PROPHET'S] domain will be the intellectual seduction of mankind. It means a mixture of political, philosophical, and religious ideology that will throw the populations of the world into a deep crisis of faith in God ..."

"The idea of a forerunner or PROPHET is not new ... One of his first duties and responsibilities in readying the world for the advent of his 'master' is to manipulate the available propaganda machines. With teaching and propaganda the PROPHET will cause people not merely to accept the ANTICHRIST but rather to desire him with positive enthusiasm to create the conditions of his coming and to participate actively in organizing the frightful and terrifying despotism of his World Empire."

"Secondly, there will be 'miracles', the signs and wonders that will 'lead astray the inhabitants of the earth.' His most convincing sign will be the conquest of the powers of nature, of which the 'fire from heaven' is the ultimate symbol. These will not be supernatural or preternatural events, but rather the prodigies of science and human achievements, but interpreted in such a way as to lead men away from God and toward the worship of the ANTICHRIST."

"Thirdly, the ideological and falsely scientific PROPHET will develop the image of a proud and haughty spirit of anti-Christian science that will seem to make many religious traditions outmoded and unacceptable ... "

"Fourthly and finally, there will be the period of full victorious reign of the ANTICHRIST and his PROPHET. This will be the triumph of the ANTICHRIST on the stage of universal history, and standing beside him will be the PROPHET, who personifies anti-Christian science. The PROPHET of the ANTICHRIST and the ANTICHRIST himself will be specific and identifiable persons."

"With his world-wide propaganda the PROPHET ... will promise to bring the reign of justice upon this earth."

"The PROPHET ... will entice and seduce millions to worship the works of man's own hand, to worship his own self, and ultimately to worship the ANTICHRIST."

"The PROPHET will communicate to men through his world propaganda

Information Pioneers Publisher

machine the supreme ambitions of human science. He will announce that science is able to penetrate all of the secrets of nature, to domesticate all of the forces of nature, especially those of life, indeed of human life itself! He will profess that men will be able to live as they please, so long as they please ... if they will only follow him." *(Jeane Dixon, 1969)*

"As a result of the powerful influence and persuasion of the PROPHET of the ANTICHRIST, universal confusion, division, and schisms will prevail." *(Jeane Dixon, 1969)*

According to Nostradamus in 'Conversations with Nostradamus', Volume II, by Dolores Cannon:

The ANTICHRIST will have a somewhat lengthy name, and one will be the next to the last one of Mohammed. He will have strong ties to Libya and Syria. He will take advantage of the Earth Changes to further his rule. He will first take over Persia [Iran] then S. Europe, Rome/Italy, Russia and China.

" ... Mohammed ... will bring you a false doctrine ... and his kind will put down the foundation for a bloody ending to this world." *(Excerpt from 'And They Called His Name Immanuel', a Phoenix Journal, 1989)*

In the 'Garden of Aton', researcher Nora Boyles has found the leader of the Islamic Salvation Front in Algeria, Abdelkader Hachani to parallel many clues given.

The name 'Abdel-kader' can be interpreted as 'Abdel' meaning servant to God, the same as 'Abdullah', Mohammed's second name. 'Kedar' was a country located between Jerusalem and Damascus (present day Syria and Jordan) thus giving him ties to that area.

If the Antichrist came from Algeria (North Africa) it would tie in clues about a revolution beginning in Africa and spreading, Islam rising up in strength to begin a holy war and World War III.

Another potential candidate is Prince Abdullah of Saudi Arabia who was involved with the 1973 oil embargo.

Jeane Dixon and Nostradamus (In 'Conversations with Nostradamus' by Dolores Cannon) state the ANTICHRIST was born February 5, 1962.

In February 1999, Abdullah bin Hussein, a descendant of Mohammed, became the new King of Jordan. According to the newspaper 'USA Today', he was born on February 5, 1962, although other news reports state his birthday was January 30, 1962. He was schooled in Britain and the U.S.A. and is a career military soldier.

"A wily man [Antichrist] will be elected without saying anything,
He will play the saint, living in simple fashion.
Then he will suddenly exercise his tyranny,
Putting the greatest countries in a state of utter coercion." *(Nostradamus, Century III Quatrain 41)*

"The head of the British government will be supported by the power of the United States,
When the cold will make Scotland hard as stone:
The red [communist] leaders will have at their head an ANTICHRIST so false
That he will drag them all into war." *(Nostradamus, Century X Quatrain 66)*

"And in the latter time of their kingdom, when the transgressors are come to the full, a king of fierce countenance and understanding dark sentences shall stand up. And his power shall be mighty, but not by his own power: and he shall destroy wonderfully, and shall prosper and practice, and shall destroy the mighty and holy people." *(Daniel 8:23-24, Bible)*

"But he shall come in peacably and obtain the kingdom by flatteries." *(Daniel 11:21, Bible)*

"The reign of the ANTICHRIST is approaching. The thick vapors ... rising from the earth and obscuring the light of the sun are false maxims of irreligion and license which are confounding all sound principles and spreading everywhere such darkness as to obscure both faith and reason." *(Sister Jeanne le Royer of the Nativity, Brittany France, 18th Century)*

"The demons of the air, together with the ANTICHRIST will perform great wonders on earth and in the atmosphere, and men will become more and more perverted." *(Prophecy of La Salette, 1846)*

"The ANTICHRIST ... will appear as an angel of light (2 Corinthians 11:14), and many among you will be confused, for he will first appear to be a savior in the Middle East. But having gained power and favor he will become then power mad, drunk with power ... "

"So watch not for those who swagger and boast, and are too obviously forces of evil. For the ANTICHRIST is far too clever, and will appear first as a savior. Be not swayed by everyone who comes in robes of light ... " *(Paul Solomon, 1991)*

"(Between the years 1995 and 2000) Advent of the ANTICHRIST, who will make war against the faithful and conquer them." *(Jose Corral, in 'The End of the World Is Very Near', 1972)*

" ... ANTICHRIST ... will come as a man of peace with miraculous powers. He will come as Satan in an angel of light, but do not be deceived by his cunning." *(Jesus' message to John Leary, December 1994)*

"The child will be born with two teeth in his throat [Antichrist],
There will be a rain of stones [revolution] in Italy
Some years later there will be neither corn nor barley to satisfy men,
Who will die of hunger." *(Nostradamus, Century III Quatrain 42)*

"At that time the Prince of Iniquity who will be called ANTICHRIST will arise from the tribe of Dan. He will be the SON OF PERDITION, the head of pride, the master of error, the fullness of malice who will overturn the world and do wonders and great signs through dissimulation. He will delude many by magic art so that fire will seem to come down from heaven. The years will be shortened like months, the months like weeks, the weeks like days, the days like hours, and an hour like a moment. The unclean nations that Alexander ... shut up [Gog and Magog] will arise from the North. These are the realms whose number is like the sand of the sea. When the king of the Romans hears of this, he will call his army together and vanquish and utterly destroy them. After this he will come to Jerusalem, and having put off the diadem from his head and laid aside the whole imperial garb, he will hand over the empire of the Christians to God the Father and to Jesus Christ His Son. When the Roman Empire [Church] shall have ceased [moved to Jerusalem], then the ANTICHRIST will be openly revealed and will sit in the House of the Lord in Jerusalem. While he is reigning, two very famous men, Elijah and Enoch, will go forth to announce the coming of the Lord. Then there will be persecution, such as has not been before nor shall be thereafter. The Lord will shorten those days for the sake of the elect, and the ANTICHRIST will be slain by the power of God through Michael the Archangel on the Mount of Olives." *(Excerpt from the 'Tiburtine Sibyl', Alexander's Oracle of Baalbek, 380 A.D.)*

"He will be born in Chorazaim [Golan Heights], nourished in Bethsaida [East of the Jordan River], and reign in Capharaum [modern city of Kefar Nahum in Israel]. Chorazaim will rejoice because he was born in her, and Capharaum because he will have reigned in her. For this reason in the Gospel the Lord gave the following statement: 'Woe to you Chorazaim, woe to you Bethsaida, woe to you Capharaum - if you have risen up to heaven, you will descend to hell (Luke 10:13, 15)."

"When the SON OF PERDITION appears, he will be of the tribe of Dan, according to the prophecy of Jacob. This enemy of religion will use a diabolic art to produce many false miracles, such as causing the blind to see, the lame to walk, and the deaf to hear. Those possessed with demons will be exorcised. He will deceive many and, if he could, as our Lord said, even the faithful elect."

"Even ANTICHRIST will enter Jerusalem, where he will enthrone himself in the temple as a god (even though he will be an ordinary man of the tribe of

Dan to which Judas Iscariot also belonged)."

"In those days, the ANTICHRIST will bring about many tribulations: but God will not allow those redeemed by the divine blood to be deceived. For that reason, He will send His two servants, Enoch and Elias [Television Newsman Peter Jennings has reported that a wild haired man in Jerusalem was telling the people: 'Repent, the end is near' in 1996/1997 which was described in the Biblical Revelation 11:3, as one of two witnesses who will prophesy for 1,260 days. A man named Enoch, preaching in Israel that we are in the end time, was interviewed in March 1999 on the shortwave radio program 'Blueprint For Survival'], who will declare the prodigies of the ANTICHRIST to be false, and will denounce him as an imposter. After the death and ruin of many, he will leave the Temple in confusion; and many of his followers will forsake him to join the company of the righteous. The seducer, upon seeing himself reproached and scorned, will become enraged and will put to death those saints of God. It is then that there will appear the sign of the SON OF MAN, and he will come upon the clouds of heaven." *(The Pseudo-Methodius (680 A.D.)*

" ... The ANTICHRIST ... will center his work around the city of Jerusalem ... the Holy City will be his headquarters, but his field of labor will be the world."

"Close cooperation between the then ruling powers in the United States and the new 'spiritual' ruler will expose Americans to him in person as his visits here will be frequent and far reaching." *(Jeane Dixon, 1969)*

"The ANTICHRIST will be a phenomenon of the political order. He is not simply a religious 'heretic' whom the world at large could simply ignore. No! He will hold earthly power in his hands and use it as his instrument. All the tyrants of history are mere children to him."

"This means first of all that he will be a military figure beyond anything the world has previously seen. He will conquer the whole Earth and hold it in complete mastery with the most modern weapons. He will rule his new world Empire [The phrase 'Novus Ordo Seclorum' is printed on the back of a $1 federal reserve note] with the utmost military might and glory ... "

"War as it has been known will fade away, and the ANTICHRIST will announce himself as the 'prince of peace'."

"He will establish and lead a strange and fundamentally anti-human 'religion' of atheism and anti-religion."

"I see two definite characteristics distinguishing the ANTICHRIST: dominion over men with a rod of iron and seduction of their minds by a false ideology and propaganda. He will present himself to all mankind as the supreme ruler who stills and quells all warfare on earth, as the teacher of man's new modernized approach to life that leaves the Christian heritage behind as outmoded, and as the 'redeemer' of all men from their old fears, guilt complexes, and mistreatment of each other."

"He will be the exact opposite of Christ. He will be His adversary and at the same time appear to be his imitator."

"Despite his religiosity and appearance of humanism, however, the ANTICHRIST will in actuality be an atheist."

"But since he will set himself up as a god before all men and will demand worship of all men, he will not tolerate worship of the one true God." *(Jeane Dixon, 1969)*

"He promises you civil liberty; he promises you equality; he promises you trade and wealth; he promises you a remission of taxes, he promises you reform. This is the way in which he conceals from you the kind of work to which he is putting you ... " *(Cardinal Newman, in 'My Life and Prophecies' by Jeane Dixon, 1969)*

"The Anti-Christ Maitreya will become popular after the Holy Father leaves Rome. His followers proclaim him to be the world teacher and the Messiah of the New Age. He offers solutions to dangerous military conflicts, intractable environmental problems, and ... unequal distribution of income among nations." *(Dr. Mary Jane Even)*

"The Man of Sin will be born of an ungodly woman who, from her infancy, will have been initiated into occult sciences and the wiles of the demon ... she will conceive the SON OF PERDITION, without knowing by what father."

WHY THE END ?

"Now when he shall have attained the age of manhood, he will set himself up as a new master and teach perverse doctrine. Soon he will revolt against the saints; and he will acquire such great power than in the madness of his pride he would raise himself above the clouds; and, as in the beginning Satan said: I will be like unto the most high, and fell; so in the last days, he will fall when he will say in the person of his son, I am the savior of the world!"

"He will ally himself with the kings, the princes and the powerful ones of the Earth; he will condemn humility and will extol all the doctrines of pride. His magic art will feign the most astounding prodigies; he will disturb the atmosphere, command thunder and tempest, produce hail and horrible lightning; he will move mountains, dry up streams, reanimate the withered verdure of forests. His arts will be practiced upon all the elements, but chiefly upon man will he exhaust his infernal power. He will seem to take away health and restore it. How so? By sending some possessed soul into a dead body, to move it for a time. But these resurrections will be of short duration."

"At the sight of these things, many will be terrified and will believe in him; and some, preserving their primitive faith, will nevertheless court the favor of the Man of Sin or fear his displeasure."

"And so many will be led astray among those who, shutting the interior eye of their souls, will live habitually in exterior thing ... " *(Hildegard of Bingen, in 'Heptachronon', 1145 A.D.)*

"[ANTICHRIST] will revolutionize the world ... will fuse multitudes into one all-embracing doctrine ... a new form of 'Christianity' based on his almighty power, but leading man in a direction far removed from the teaching and the life of CHRIST, THE SON ... "

"He will ... form a small nucleus of dedicated followers when he reaches the age of nineteen. He will work quietly with them until he is twenty-nine or thirty years old, when the forcefulness and impact of his presence in the world will begin to bear his forbidden fruit ... will have the power and the propaganda machine of the United States ... advancing his cause beyond anything ever thought possible. It will be around the time of his emergence, too, that the work of the PROPHET of the ANTICHRIST ... will have reached its summit." *(Jeane*

Dixon, 1969)

"He will establish and lead a strange and fundamentally anti-human 'religion' of atheism and anti-religion ... " *(Jeane Dixon, 1969)*

"After the birth of ANTICHRIST heretics will preach their false doctrines undisturbed, resulting in Christians having doubts about their holy Catholic faith."

"The SON OF PERDITION (THE ANTICHRIST), who will reign very few of times, will come at the end day of the duration of the world, at the times corresponding to the moment just before the sun disappears from the horizon."

"It is in your good interest that you do your duty to seek the good comprehension, so that the great seducer does not entrain you in the perdition ... Arm yourself in advance and prepare for the most redoubtable of combats."

" ... The mother of the SON OF PERDITION will conceive and give birth without knowing the father. In another land, she will make men believe that her birth was some miraculous thing, seeing that she had not appointed a spouse ... and the people will regard it as a saint ... "

"The SON OF PERDITION is this very wicked beast who will put to death those who refuse to believe in him; who will associate with kings, princes, the great and the rich; who will mistake the humility and will esteem pride; who will finally subjugate the entire universe by his diabolic means."

"He will gain over many people and tell them: 'You are allowed to do all that you please; renounce the fasts; it suffices that you love me; I who am your god'."

"He will show them treasures and riches, and he will permit them to riot in all sorts of festivities, as they please ... and he will tell them: 'Those who will believe in me will receive pardon of their sins and will live with me eternally'."

"He will reject baptism and evangelism. and he will reject in derision all the precepts the Spirit has given to men of my part."

"Then he will say to his partisans: 'Strike me will a sword, and place my corpse in a proper shroud until the day of my resurrection.' They will believe him to have been really given over to death, and from his mortal wound he will make a striking semblance of resuscitation."

                   Information Pioneers Publisher

"After which he will compose himself a certain cipher, which he will say is to be a pledge of salute; he will give it to all his servitors like the sign of our faith in heaven, and he will command them to adore it. Concerning those who, for the love of my name, will refuse to render this sacrilegious adoration to the SON OF PERDITION, he will put them to death amidst the cruelest torments."

"But I will defend my two witnesses, Enoch and Elias, whom I have reserved for those times. Their mission will be to combat the man of evil and reprimand him in the sight of the faithful whom he has seduced. They will have the virtue of operating the most brilliant miracles, in all the places where the SON OF PERDITION has spread his evil doctrines. In the meanwhile, I will permit this evildoer to put them to death; but I will give them in heaven the recompense of their travails."

"Later, however, after the coming of Enoch and Elias, the ANTICHRIST will be destroyed, and the Church will sing forth with unprecedented glory, and the victims of the great error will throng to return to the fold." *(Hildegard of Bingen, in 'Scivias', 1145 A.D.)*

"Nothing good will enter into him nor be able to be in him. For he will be nourished in diverse and secret places, lest he should be known by men, and he will be imbued with all diabolical arts, and he will be hidden until he is of full age, nor will he show the perversities which will be in him, until he knows himself to be full and superabundant in all iniquities."

"He will appear to agitate the air, to make fire descend from heaven, to produce rainbows, lightning, thunder, and hail, to tumble mountains, dry up streams, to strip the verdure of trees, of forests, and to restore them again. He will also appear to be able to make men sick or well at will, to chase out demons, and at times even to resusitate the dead ... But this kind of resurrection will never endure beyond a little time, for the glory of God will not suffer it."

"Ostensibly, he will be murdered, spill his blood and die. With bewilderment and consternation, mankind will learn that he is not dead ... "

"From the beginning of his course many battles and many things contrary to the lawful dispensation will arise, and charity will be extinguished in men. In them also will arise bitterness and harshness and there will be so many heresies that heretics will preach their errors openly and certainly: and there shall be so much doubt and incertitude in the Catholic faith of Christians that men shall be in doubt of what God they invoke, and many signs shall appear in the sun and moon, and in the stars and in the waters, and in other elements and creatures, so that, as it were in a picture, future events shall be foretold in their portents."

"Then also so much sadness shall occupy men at that time, that they shall be led to die as if for nothing. But those who are perfect in the Catholic faith will await in great contrition what God wills to ordain. And these great tribulations shall proceed in this way, while the SON OF PERDITION shall open his mouth in the contray doctrine. But when he shall have brought forth the words of falsehood and his deceptions, heaven and earth shall tremble together. But after the fall of the ANTICHRIST the glory of the SON OF GOD shall be increased." *(Hildegard of Bingen in 'Vision X', 1145 A.D.)*

"Before this event the world will have apparent peace and people will think of nothing but pleasure and the bad ones will commit sins of all kinds."

"Thus the time will be reached in which ANTICHRIST will be born of ... a false virgin who will have intimate relations with the ancient serpent, the master of luxury. His father will be a bishop."

"As soon as he is born, he will have teeth and pronounce blasphemies; in short he will be born a devil. He will emit fearful cries, work miracles, and wallow in luxury and vice. He will have brothers who are also demons incarnate, and at the age of twelve, they will distinguish themselves in brilliant achievements. They will command an armed force, which will be supported by the infernal legions."

"After the SON OF PERDITION has carried out all of his evil design, he will call together all his followers and tell them that he wishes to ascend into heaven."

"In the moment of his ascension, a lightning flash will strike him, killing him."

"The mountain from which he had planned to make his ascension will at once be covered with a dense cloud from which will issue a dreadful and truly infernal odor of corruption ... At the sight of his body, the eyes of a great number of persons will open and they will be made to see their miserable error."

139   Information Pioneers Publisher

WHY THE END ?

"After the sorrowful defeat of the SON OF PERDITION ... the Church will shine with a glory without equal, and the victims of the error will be impressed to reenter the sheepfold."

"As to the day, after the fall of ANTICHRIST, when the world will end, man must not seek to know, for he can never learn it. That secret the Father has reserved for Himself." *(Hildegard of Bingen in 'Vision X', 1145 A.D.)*

"There will come a time when war will break out, more terrible than all other wars combined, which have ever visited mankind. A horrible warrior will unleash it, and his adversaries will call him ANTICHRIST. All nations of the Earth will fight each other in this war ... Woe to those who, in those days, do not fear the ANTICHRIST, for he is the father of those who are not repelled by crime. He will arouse more homicides and many people will shed tears over his evil customs." *(St Odile, 660-720 A.D.)*

" ... The coming to power of the ANTICHRIST ... He will thrive on control of the trade, food and finances, the horrible scenes in Africa will continue to get out of hand prompted by the evil one. As chaos drags on, people will call for a leader to stop the killings. This is how he will come to reign (by claiming to bring peace to the world). Once in power though, he will use his tyranny to persecute My ... elect ... It will not last but an inkling of time. For I will bring my swift justice to this evil lot and they will all be cast into the fiery abyss ... Then My era of peace and grace will be with you." *(Jesus' message to John Leary, May 1994)*

" ... During the tribulation you will see many give praise and honor to the ANTICHRIST. They will treat him as a god because of his miraculous powers." *(Jesus' message to John Leary, September 1994, in 'Prepare for the Great Tribulation and the Era of Peace', 1996)*

"The ANTICHRIST will launch a terrible persecution of people throughout the world ... This feaful tribulation will last three and a half years (the forty-two months of the Apocalypse)." *(Monk Adso, 954 A.D.)*

"The ANTICHRIST very soon annihilates the three [U.S.A., Britain, Israel]

Twenty seven years his war will last [or the effects of radioactive fallout].

The unbelievers are dead, captive, exiled;

With blood, human bodies, water and red hail [comet fragments] covering the Earth." *(Nostradamus, Century VIII Quatrain 77)*

"For two decades plus seven the great empire rules.

Famine, pestilence, blood, tears, war.

The ANTICHRIST is joyous and the multitudes

Cry out for Xerxes [Persians/Iranians]. Oppression for all in a troubled world." *(Nostradamus, Unpublished Quatrain)*

" ... All shall deny their own God and invite their fellows to praise the SON OF PERDITION, and one on another they shall fall and with swords each other destroy ... Magnifying his miracles, performing his portents, deceiver and not in truth manifesting these things, in such fashion the tyrant removeth the mountains, and simulates falsely and not truly while the multitude stands by, many nations and peoples applauding him for his illusions ... The lightnings shall be his ministers and signify his advent; the demons shall consitute his forces, and the princes of the demons shall be his disciples; to far-distant lands shall he send captains of his bands, who shall impart virtue and healing ... A great conflict ... in those times amongst men, but especially amongst the faithful, when there shall be signs and wonders wrought by the Dragon in great abundance, when he shall again manifest himself as God in fearful phantasms flying in the air, and show all the demons in the forms of angels flying in terror before the tyrant, for he crieth out loudly, changing his forms also to strike infinite dread into all men."

"Then the skies no longer rain, the earth no longer beareth fruit, the springs run out, the rivers dry up, herbs no longer sprout, grass no longer grows, trees wither from their roots and no longer put forth fruits, the fishes of the sea and the monsters therein die out, and thus they say a fetid stench emits with fearful roar, that men shall fail and perish through terror. And then in dread shall moan and groan all life alike when all shall see the pitiless distress that compasseth them by night and eke by day, and nowhere find the food wherewith to fill themselves ... For stern governors [F.E.M.A. - Federal Emergency Management Agency] of the people shall be appointed each in his place, and who so bears with him the seal of the tyrant [mark of the beast] may buy a little food."

"But before these things be, the Lord sendeth Elias, the Thesbite, and Enoch, the compassionate, that they may proclaim reverence to the race of men, and openly announce unto all the knowledge of God that they believe not nor obey the false one through fear, crying out and saying, 'A deceiver ... is he; let no one believe in him'. But few are those who shall then obey and believe in the words of these two prophets."

"Many therefore of the saints as are then found, as soon as they shall hear of the coming of the MAN OF CORRUPTION, shall most speedily flee to the deserts and lie hid in the deserts and mountains and in caves through fear, and strew earth and ashes on their heads, destitute and weeping both day and night with great humility. And this shall to them be granted by God the Holy One: And grace shall lead them unto the appointed places." *(Saint Ephraim, 4th Century, in 'Codex Barberinus XIV: The Utterances of St. Ephraim About The End Of The World, and the Consummation of the Universe, and the Tribulation of the Nations')*

"Against the faithful will he rise up in three ways ... by terror, by gifts and by wonders; to the believer in him will he give gold and silver in abundance; but those whom he shall fail to corrupt by presents he will overcome by fear, and those whom he shall fail to vanquish by fear he will seek to seduce by signs and wonders ... "

"The ruined temple also, which Solomon raised to God, he shall build and restore to its former state ... and lie that he is the son of God almighty ... Thereafter shall he send his messengers and preachers to the whole world."

"Then shall be sent into the world the two great prophets Elias and Enoch, who shall forearm the faithful with godly weapons against the attack of the ANTICHRIST, and they shall encourage and get them ready for the war ... But after they have accomplished their preaching, the ANTICHRIST shall rise up and slay them, and after three days they shall be raised up by the Lord ... MICHAEL THE ARCHANGEL shall destroy him on Mount Olivet in his pavilion and seat, in that place where the Lord ascended into heaven ... " *(Monk Adso, 954 A.D.)*

"I will commission my two witnesses to prophesy for those twelve hundred and sixty days ... If anyone tries to harm them, fire will come out of the mouths of these witnesses to devour their enemies ... These witnesses have power to close up the sky so that no rain will fall during the time of their mission."

"When they have finished giving their testimony, the wild beast that comes up from the abyss will wage war against them and conquer and kill them. Their corpses will lie in the streets of the great city, which has the symbolic name 'Sodom' ... Men from every people and race, language and nation, stare at their corpses for three and a half days but refuse to bury them ... But after the three and a half days, the breath of life which comes from God returned to them. When they stood on their feet sheer terror gripped those who saw them. The two prophets heard a loud voice from heaven say, 'come up here!' So they went up to heaven in a cloud as their enemies looked on. At that moment was a violent earthquake and a tenth of the city [Jerusalem] fell in ruins. The second woe is past, but beware! The third is coming very soon." *(Revelation 11:3-14, Bible)*

"I will send you Elijah, the prophet, before the day of the Lord comes, the great and terrible day, to turn the hearts of the fathers to their children and the hearts of the children to their fathers, lest I come and strike the land with doom." *(Malachi 3:23-24, Bible)*

"For he shall work such stupendous marvels, as to bid fire come down from heaven ... and the dead shall rise ... He shall raise the dead, not verily, but the devil shall enter some dead man's body ... and speak in him, that he may seem alive ... "

"There shall go forth the two most glorious men Enoch and Elias to announce the advent of the Lord, and them shall the ANTICHRIST slay, and after three days they shall be resusitated ... "   *(Bede the Venerable, 672-735 A.D.)*

"After the ANTICHRIST has ascended a high mountain and been destroyed by CHRIST, many erring souls will return to truth, and men will make rapid progress in the ways of holiness."   *(Hildegard of Bingen, in 'Heptachronon', 1145 A.D.)*

" ... The great empire of ANTICHRIST shall begin in the Attila [Mongolia/ China] and Xerxes [Persia/Iran] come down with an innumerable multitude of people, so that the coming of the Holy Ghost [Christ] ... driving away the abomination of ANTICHRIST who made war against the royal person of the great vicar [Pope] of Jesus Christ and against His Church and His Kingdom ... before this shall precede a solar eclipse ... "   *(Excerpt from 'The Epistle to Henry II' by Nostradamus, 1555)*

"When DAJJAL appears, his complexion will be white and his right eye will be blind, [Moslem symbol for heaven] while the left eye will shine like a bright star [Moslem symbol for hell]."   *(The Sahih of Al-Bukhari)*

"When DAJJAL appears, the women will assume the appearance of men, and the men will assume the appearance of women. When DAJJAL appears, there will be no part of the world left which he will not dominate, except the cities of Mecca and Medina [Saudi Arabia]."

"Whoever hears about DAJJAL should keep away from him ... One will come to him and he will think that he is a believer, but he will follow him on account of the doubts that he will raise in his mind."

"There will be some people accompanying DAJJAL, who will say: ... Although we know that he is an unbeliever, we still keep him company so that we may eat his food."

"His voice will be so loud that the whole world will hear him when he speaks, DAJJAL will travel the world and will request the earth to surrender its treasures, which it will willingly do."

"He will claim himself to be Allah, and whoever has a weak faith and accepts him, DAJJAL will put him into his heaven; but whoever has a strong faith in Allah and rejects DAJJAL will be put into his hellfire. However, those who go into his heaven will find that Allah has turned it into hell, and those who go into his hell will find that Allah has turned it into heaven."

"All these things DAJJAL will do and dominate the entire world in 40 days, from the largest country to the smallest island: and his first day will be in the length of one year, but the days will gradually decline into a normal day." *(Excerpt from the 'Kanz al-Ummal', Volume 7)*

"DAJJAL will remain in the earth for 40 years, a year being like a month, a month being like a week, a week being like a day, a day like the time it takes to burn a palm branch."

" ... How swift will he travel on the Earth? ... As the cloud is carried in the wind ... DAJJAL, will be jumping between the heavens and the earth. He will then give command to the sky and it will give rain to the Earth [Weather Control], and it will produce crops."

"Allah will give DAJJAL the natural power of material knowledge and the liberty to exercise in any way he wills, even to resurrect the dead."

"DAJJAL ... will cross great distances very quickly. DAJJAL will be blind in his right eye, and the left eye will shine like a star. His skin will be white. DAJJAL will have so much power that he will be able to carry heaven and hell on his shoulders."

"DAJJAL will be accompanied by beautiful women and spirits and bastard children and other kinds of people ... He will have music and singing unlike any ever heard before, and whoever hears it will follow it."

"When DAJJAL appears and he cannot bring the whole world under his power and machinations and false beliefs, the Christian nations will stand up with 80 banners or flags in an effort to make peace in the world. But they will in fact, betray the world and bring ultimate destruction to the entire human race." *(Excerpt from the 'Miskah al-Masabih')*

WHY THE END ?

"There will arise another king from Heliopolis [Egypt] and he will wage war against the king from the east and kill him. And he will grant a tax-exemption to entire countries for three years and six months, and the earth will bring forth its fruits, and there is none to eat them. And there will come the RULER OF PERDITION, he who is changed, and will smite and kill him. And he will do signs and wonders on Earth. He will turn the sun into darkness and the moon into blood. And after that the springs and rivers will dry up, and the Nile will be transformed into blood. And the survivors will dig cisterns and will search for the water of life and will not find it. And then there will appear two men who did not come to know the experience of death, Enoch and Elijah, and they will wage war upon the RULER OF PERDITION. And he will say: 'My time has come', and he will be angered and slay them. And then He who was crucified on the wood of the cross will come from the heavens, like a great and flashing star, and he will resurrect those two men ... and will wage war with the SON OF PERDITION and will slay him and all his host. Then the land of Egypt will burn twelve cubits deep ... And the SON OF GOD will come with great power and glory to judge the nine generations. And then Christ will rule, the SON OF THE LIVING GOD, with His holy angels." *(Excerpt from the 'Erythraean Sibyl', 12th Century)*

"A chief of the world, the great Henry [Kissinger] shall be,
At first, beloved, afterwards feared, dreaded,
His fame and praise shall go beyond the heavens,
And shall be contented with the title of Victor." *(Nostradamus, Century VI Quatrain 70)*

"The ANTICHRIST and his forces will cheer their victory for a moment. Then my triumph will wipe away all the evil men and evil spirits." *(Jesus' message to John Leary, May 23, 1998)*

" ... The Son of Perdition shall open his mouth in the contrary doctrine ... When he shall have brought forth the words of the falsehood and his deceptions, heaven and earth shall tremble together ... " *(Hildegard of Bingen, in 'Vision*

146   Information Pioneers Publisher

X', 1098-1179)

"There shall be signs in the sun and moon ... at this time ANTICHRIST shall have been trodden underfoot and all the world shall enjoy the faith and peace of the Most High." *(St. John Capistran, 1385-1456)*

" ... The evil ANTICHRIST will try to force everyone to worship his image ... But ... I will send a comet to destroy and defeat the ANTICHRIST and all of his armies." *(Jesus' message to John Leary, June 4, 1998)*

WHY THE END ?

Information Pioneers Publisher

WEATHER CONTROL

"And he doeth great wonders, so that he maketh fire to come down on Earth in the sight of men." *(Revelation 13:13)*

"When the great time will come ... it will be foreshadowed by striking changes in nature ... storms will have more catastrophic effects, earthquakes will destroy greater regions ... Not all of it will be the result of natural causes, but mankind will penetrate into the bowels of the Earth and will reach into the clouds, gambling with his own existence." *(Johann Friede, 1204-1257)*

"He (Dajjal) [Antichrist] will then give command to the sky and it will give rain to the Earth and it will produce crops." *(Excerpt from 'Mishkah al-Masabih')*

"Men will arise who will command storms, turning and directing them at pleasure." *(Molly Pitcher, 1731-1815)*

"And when in the egotistical nature of man attempts to CONTROL WEATHER, climate, and balances of nature ... mankind becomes rather than a guest on the planet ... " *(Paul Solomon, 1991)*

"You will see storms with a severity never seen before, because these will be enhanced by the WEATHER MACHINES [HAARP, satellites and/or turquoise-blue colored towers scattered across the U.S.A.]." *(Message to John Leary, April 13, 1998)*

"The provisions of this convention shall not hinder the use of Environmental Modification Technology for peaceful purposes ... " *(Excerpt from The United Nations 'Convention on the Prohibition of Military or any other Hostile use of Environment al Modification Techniques' - Approved December 10, 1976)*

WHY THE END ?

See the 'New York Times' May 25, 1978 article about the Weather Modification Program of the U.S. Government.

See the U.S. Code of Federal Regulations, Title 15, Chapter 9A-Weather Modification Activities or Attempts; Reporting Requirement: National Weather Modification Policy Act of 1976.

See the 'Wall Street Journal' October 2, 1992, 'Moscow Firm Offers Weather Made to Order'.

In April 1996 the Voice of Russia Radio program mentioned Weather Modification was recently produced by firing a Russian microwave plasma weapon.

See the 'Wall Street Journal' November 13, 1997, 'Malaysia To Battle Smog With Cyclones' - using new Russian technology to create cyclones.

"A method and apparatus for altering at least one selected region which normally exists above the Earth's surface. The region is excited by electron cyclotron resonance heating ... " *(Excerpt from the Abstract to U.S. Patent #4,686,605: Bernard Eastlund, August 11, 1987; by the High Frequency Active Auroral Research Project (HAARP) in Alaska, consisting of 40 acres of towers and antennas to broadcast high powered energy.)*

"Weather Modification is possible by, for example, altering upper atmosphere wind patterns by constructing one or more plumes of atmospheric particles ... " *(Excerpt from U.S. Patent #4,686,605: Bernard Eastlund, August 11, 1987, in Nexus Magazine #3-1)*

"HAARP also has a secret agenda ... even altering the local weather above an enemy's territory."
" ... HAARP's 1.7 gigawatts (1.7 billion watts) of effective radiated power in the 2.8- to 10 MHz frequency range might cause lasting damage to Earth's

upper atmosphere." *(Excerpt from 'Popular Science' Magazine, September 1995)*

"A thing existing without any senses [HAARP]
Will cause its own end to happen through artifice.
At Autun, Chalan, Langres and the two Sens
There will be great damage from hail and ice." *(Nostradamus, Century I Quatrain 22)*

A report by William Thomas, quoted in 'Contact' Newspaper (January 26, 1999), states a Boeing KC-135 and Boeing KC-10 jet aircraft have been positively identified in aerial spraying incidents. Both aircraft are used by the U.S. Air Force. It is alleged they are involved in seeding clouds to modify the weather.

Material resembling cobwebs has been collected and some people have become very ill after first contact with it. The 'USA Today' Newspaper (August 11, 1998) reported that dozens of residents of Quirindi, Australia saw 'cobwebs fall from the sky' after unidentified aircraft passed overhead.

A U.S. Air Force research study, 'Weather as a Force Multiplier' issued in August 1996 outlines how 'HAARP' and aerial cloud seeding from tankers could allow the U.S. forces to 'own the weather' by the year 2025, with their objectives being 'Storm Enhancement', 'Storm Modification' and 'Induce Drought'.

Information Pioneers Publisher

WHY THE END ?

 Information Pioneers Publisher

REBUILDING THE TEMPLE

" ... Look for the signs ... destruction of the Temple Mount and the beginning of reconstruction of a temple. And as there is a worldwide religious war, you will know that these events are upon you." *(Paul Solomon, September 16, 1991)*

" ... Great earthquake will hit Jerusalem ... " *(Jeane Dixon, 1918-1997)*

"And at that hour there was an earthquake and the tenth part of the city fell [Jerusalem], and in the earthquake there were slain of men seven thousand ... " *(Revelation 11:13, Bible)*

" ... As there is the taking of that Mount and the destruction of that Temple now placed, then look for the beginning of that war of wars. For as there is the destruction of ... the Mount, and the attempts to rebuild the Temple of Solomon, so in that time will there be set in conflict man against man, for religious purpose, for religious causes." *(Paul Solomon, September 20, 1973)*

" ... That Son of Perdition and adversary who exalts himself ... he who seats himself in God's Temple [the sign that the battle of Armageddon is near] and even declares himself to be God ... the lawless one will be revealed, and the Lord Jesus will destroy him with the breath of his mouth and annihilate him by manifesting his own presence. The lawless one will appear as part of the workings of Satan, accompanied by all the power and signs and wonders at the disposal of falsehood - by every seduction the wicked can devise for those destined to ruin because they have not opened their hearts to the truth in order to be saved." *(II Thessalonians 2:3-10, Bible)*

"The ruined temple also, which Solomon raised to God, he shall build and restore to its former state ... and lie that he is the son of God almighty." *(Monk Adso, 954 A.D.)*

WHY THE END ?

Preparations are underway to reconstruct the Temple through the work of the Temple Institute which has reconstructed many of the implements that will be required when Temple sacrifices are restored. There is a requirement in the Bible: Numbers 19:1-10 that priests purify their bodies with the cremated ashes of an unblemished red heifer before they enter the Temple. The July 20, 1998 issue of 'The New Yorker' Magazine reported cattle rancher Clyde Lott and Rabbi Chaim Richman are searching to find a special red heifer in order to build the third Temple in Jerusalem.

See the article in 'Time' magazine (October 16, 1989) 'Time for a New Temple?: Traditionalist Jews hope to rebuild their sacred edifice, but a mosque and centuries of enmity stand in the way'.

" ... After an earthquake hits the Holy Land ... the Temple of the Dome of the Rock ... the Moslem mosque ... will be destroyed. As a result a new Jewish Temple will be built [Temple of Solomon]. And because it's being built on the site of their sacred mosque, Moslems ... disguised as Jews will desecrate the temple by committing ritual suicide within it ... this will be a signal for ... the war cry that will lead up to the battle of Armageddon." *(Excerpt from 'Conversations With Nostradamus', Volume Two, by Dolores Cannon, 1990)*

"The five foreigners having entered the temple;
Their blood will desecrate the land.
The example made of the Toulousians will be very hard,
Made by the man who comes to wipe out their laws." *(Nostradamus, Century III Quatrain 45)*

"Most of the church houses ... anticipate a momentary 'liftoff' to some nebulous being in the clouds the minute ... temple going in Jerusalem and the temple is desecrated." *(Hatonn, February 6, 1991)*

" ... The prophets have referred to ... an earthquake on the Holy Mount ... see it as a nuclear detonation affecting the Holy Mount which will cause Israel to seem justified in reclaiming ... the rebuilding of the Temple."

" ... Look for the time when world speculation turns to the possibility that a nuclear device has come into the the hands of Syria ... and the denial of it, and the tension mounts, know that here is upon you that devastation that begins a major war among nations." *(Paul Solomon, April 3, 1988)*

" ... Jerusalem shall be trodden down by nations until the times of nations are fulfilled." *(Luke 21:24, Bible)*

"The great city will be thoroughly desolated
Of the inhabitants a single one will not remain:
Wall, sex, temple and virgin violated,
By iron, fire, pestilence, canon people will die." *(Nostradamus, Century III Quatrain 84)*

" ... The buildings of the temple ... not one stone will be left on another ... all be torn down ... " *(Matthew 24:1-2, Bible)*

"And when ye shall see Jerusalem encompassed with armies, then know that the desolation therof is nigh." *(Luke 21:20, Bible)*

"And the people of a leader who will come shall destroy the sanctuary. Then the end shall come as a torrent ... On the temple ... shall be the horrible abomination." *(Daniel 9:26-27, Bible)*

"When you see the Abominable and destructive presence standing where it should not be ... those in Judea must flee to the mountains. If a man is on the roof terrace, he must not come down or enter his house to get anything out of it. If a man is in the field, he must not turn back to pick up his cloak. It will go badly with pregnant and nursing women in those days ... Those times will be more distressful than any between God's work of creation and now, and for all time to come." *(Mark 13:14-19 and Matthew 24:15-20, Bible)*

                       Information Pioneers Publisher

WHY THE END ?

"With a roll of thunder, the clouds parted and I beheld Jerusalem laid low by a frighful tempest; its walls had fallen as from blows of a battering ram, and blood ran through the streets; the enemy had taken possession of the city."

"The abomination of desolation ruled the city."

"And it was here that I beheld the Patriarch emerge from the temple that had been invaded by the sons of Baal. He fled, carrying with him the Ark of the Covenant, and fleds towards the sea where the sun sets."

"Afterward, I beheld upon the horizon a brilliant CONFLAGRATION. Then my vision clouded over and I neither saw nor heard anything more. Then the Spirit said to me: 'This is the beginning of the last days of Earth'." *(Prophecy of Premol, 17th Century)*

"When the people will see the horror in Jerusalem and the lands there about, of which the prophets have already spoken, then the end will come."

"When this happens, whoever is at that time in the land of Judea, should flee to the mountains he who is on the roof, should not come down from it to get anything from, out of his house. He who is in the field should not come back in order to get his coat or any other of his possessions."

"There will follow great grief as has never been before since the beginning of the world until now, and also never will be again. And, if these days were not shortened, no man would remain alive; but the days will be shortened for the sake of the spirit and wisdom, and for the sake of the people who serve the truth and the laws."

"There shall be ... heavy projectiles ... and they shall strike the cities throughout the lands. Fire will come out of these projectiles and burn the world so that hardly anything will survive ... And, if at that time the Celestial Sons would not appear in order to bring it to a standstill ... not one person would survive upon the face of the Earth."

"Since the human race will, at that time, number at least ten times five hundred million people, two parts thereof will be destroyed and killed. When, at that point, someone will say to the people, 'Behold, here is Immanuel!' They shall not believe it, because many false Immanuels and false prophets will rise up and do great signs and wonders, so that if it were possible, also even the wise and knowing would be misled."

"Soon after the grief of that time, sun and moon will no longer radiate, and the stars will fall from heaven and the powers of the heavens will become shaky. The structure of the heavens will be disturbed because of the senselessly erupted power of men who will be living in greed, power and addiction."

"There will then appear a sign in the sky ... the Celestial Sons coming in the clouds of the sky, and ... will judge harshly against senselessness ... God ... will send forth His Guardian Angels ... and will gather his followers from the four winds, from one end of the Earth unto the other end." *(Excerpt from 'And They Called His Name Immanuel', a Phoenix Journal, 1989)*

WHY THE END ?

Information Pioneers Publisher

WORLD WAR III

"After the Great War there will be no peace. The people will rise and all will fight against each other ... The World War [WWII] will not make people better but much worse ... Tell your children that their children will live to see the time when the Earth will be cleared. God will do away with people because there will be no charity among men. Religious faith will decline; priests will not be respected; people will be intent only on eating and drinking ... great wealth will not endure long, for the red caps will come. People will hide in the forests and many will go into exile. After this civil conflict and general clearing, people will love each other as much as previously they hated one another."

"When women walk around in pants, and men have become effeminate, so that one will no longer be able to tell men from women, then the time is near."

"People will build houses everywhere, high houses, low houses, one after another. When everyone builds, when everywhere buildings rise, everything will be cleared away."

"There will be a holy sign in the heavens, that a very severe Master will come and take off the skin of the people. He will not rule very long, then when all that has happened as I have said, then comes the great clearing away."

"The Bavarian land will be devastated, and the land of Bohemia (Czechoslovakia) will be cleaned out as by a broom. Over all these places and over the Bohemian mountain will come the Reds [Russians] ... not the French, but the Reds."

"It will happen overnight. While many people sit together in a guest house, outside the soldiers will draw near over the bridge. The mountain will be black with its people, and all will flee, each man will run through the forest. He who has two loafs of bread and loses somebody, he should let them lie and move on, so that he will come through with one loaf."

"However, when you see the horror of the devastation, of which the Prophet Daniel has spoken [' ... On the temple ... shall be the horrible abomination.', Daniel 9:27], then flee as in Judea, to the mountain, and who is on the road, and who is in the field, do not turn around to fetch your garment."

"The people will be sick and nobody can help them. Those who will make it must have an iron head."

"Then afterward a good time will come, that which is 'loved by Jesus Christ', and holy men will do wonders. Once people have their faith again, a long period of peace will follow."

"Then there will be a shortened summer; winter and summer will not be distinguishable." *(Mathias Lang, 1753-1820)*

"The scourge being past, the world shall be made smaller,
Peace for a long time, lands inhabited,
Everyone shall go by air, land and sea.
And then the WARS shall begin anew." *(Nostradamus, Century I Quatrain 63)*

"There will be a series of WARS until the LAST WAR, which will then be fought by the ten Kings of Antichrist, all of whom will have one and the same plan and will be the only rulers of the world. Before this comes to pass, there will be a kind of false peace in the world. People will think of nothing but amusement. The wicked will give themselves over to all kinds of sin." *(Prophecy of La Salette, September 19, 1846)*

"When wild flowers lose their fragrance, when grace leaves man, when rivers lose their health ... then the GREATEST ALL-OUT WAR will come."

"The greatest and the angriest will strike against the mightiest and the most furious!"

"When this horrible WAR starts woe to those armies that fly over skies, better off will be those who fight on ground and water ... burning people will fall from the sky ... "

"Those who will run and hide in the mountains with three crosses will find shelter and will be saved to live afterwards in abundance, happiness and love, because there will be no more WARS." *(Mitar Tarabic, 1829-1899)*

"There will come a time when WAR will break out, more terrible than all other wars combined, which have ever visited mankind. A horrible warrior will unleash it, and his adversaries will call him Antichrist. All nations of the Earth will fight each other in this war. The fighters will rise up to the heavens to take the stars and throw them on the cities, to set ablaze the buildings and to cause immense devastations. Oceans will lie between the great warriors, and the monsters of the sea, terrified by everthing that happens on or under the sea, will flee to the deep. Battles of the past will only be skirmishes compared to the battles that will take place, since blood will flow in all directions. The Earth will shake from the violent fighting. Famine and pestilence will join the war. The nations will then cry, 'Peace, peace', but there will be no peace. Thrice will the sun rise over the heads of the combatants, without having been seen by them. But afterwards there will be peace, and all who have broken peace will have lost there lives. On a single day more men will have been killed than the catacombs of Rome have ever held ... and people will ascend the highest mountains to praise God, and nobody will want to make war anymore. Strange signs will appear in the skies: both horns of the moon [crescent symbol - Islam] will join the cross [Christianity]. Happy will be those who will have survived the war, since the pleasures of life will begin again, and the sun will have a new brilliance." *(St. Odile, 7th Century)*

"All around me I see a terrible, bloody WAR, which approaches from Midnight, the North, and Evening, the East. I heard that Lucifer ... would be let go for a time, fifty or sixty years before the year 2000. I saw the Earth covered in darkness, everything was withered and barren, everything made the impression of pining away. It seems that even the waters of the springs were exhausted. I saw how the labor of darkness multiplied among the people, I saw countries and people in the greatest distress, and fighting each other violently. In the center of the battleground was a giant abyss, into which the warring factions seemed to fall." *(Anna Emmerich, 1820)*

"The lady showed me a WAR. It will come much later. It is a newer, strange WAR. The lady showed me the globe. She pointed to the east and said,

WHY THE END ?

'From there it shall come. Europe must watch out. Warn the people of Europe.' And then she said to me: 'Watch out and listen to me. The East against the West. Europe must watch out. Unlucky England. New unluck comes over the Earth ... There will come a great conflict, America, Russia, Asia.' The Lady held out her hand to cover the area of the Ukraine, and I saw a great fire in the upper left in Russia. It appeared like an explosion which came out of the sea. The Lady said: 'And then there shall be nothing' ... I saw only the dried out Earth and horizon that remained." *('The Mother of All People' message to a Dutch Maiden, 1940's)*

" ... If people ... do not return to God with truly Christian living, another terrible WAR will come from the East to the West. Russia with her secret armies will battle America ... will overrun Europe. The River Rhine will be overflowing with corpses and blood. Italy will also be harassed by a great revolution, and the Pope will suffer terribly." *(Blessed Virgin Mary to Sister Elena Aiello, August 22, 1960)*

"A TERRIBLE WAR will ensue. The enemy will come from the east like a flood. In the evening they will call 'Peace, Peace', but the next day they will be before our doors. There will be an early and beautiful spring in the year in which the war will start. The cows will walk through opulent grass in the meadows in April. Wheat can be harvested, but oats not anymore. The conflict, in which one half the world will oppose the other half, will not be of long duration. God will scare the warring factions by producing a terrible natural catastrophe." *(Anonymous, published in 'Voix Prophetiques' by Abbe Curique, 1872)*

"A WAR will come, before which all previous wars will fade. Streams of fire will come from clouds, where there are no clouds. And in the middle will be the great water. Big eagles will fly in the skies and moles will be the models for soldiers under the Earth ... Great armies with iron horses and dragons will be seen, and everything will be different than it has ever been. Battles will rage on and in the air, and whole cities on this side and across the great water will be destroyed. All capital cities on both sides of the water will be buried under rubbish and ashes, and it will be a great groaning and moaning. The horrors of war will be also on and over the water, and the enemy will be smitten ... with many casualties ... and then everything will be over ... And the whole world will jubilate ... Blessed who survives these times, because they will be succeeded by times of great peace." *(Book of Pilgrimage from the Marienthal Monastery, 13th Century)*

"Woe to the inhabitants of Earth! Sanguinary WARS will break out, a killing rain will pour down and even the birds will fall from the sky. Thunder and lightning will destroy cities. All universe will be seized by terror. But God will let himself be reconciled with mankind ... Thereupon water and fire will purify the Earth and the period of true peace will begin." *(Melanie Calvat of La Salette, 1846)*

"The huge WAR will erupt in the second half of the TWENTIETH CENTURY. Fire and smoke will fall from the sky. The waters of the ocean will become mist, and the foam will rise to tremendous heights and everyone will drown."

"Millions and millions of men will die from hour to hour. Whoever remains alive will envy the dead. Everywhere one turns one's glance there will be anguish and misery, ruins in every country. The time draws nearer, the abyss widens without hope. The good will perish with the bad, the great with the small, the Princes of the Church with the faithful, the rulers with their people. There will be deaths everywhere because of the errors committed by the crazed and the followers of Satan, who will then and only then rule the world."

"At last, those who survive will at every chance newly proclaim God and His glory and they will serve Him as when the world was not so perverted." *(The Third Prophecy of Fatima, Portugal, 1917, published in the German 'Neus Europa', October 15, 1963, and in the French paper 'Le Monde et la Vie', September 1964)*

" ... The THIRD WORLD WAR, the great WAR of destruction to mankind. A WAR that has never been met with a sequel upon mankind! A WAR of

 Information Pioneers Publisher

destruction so great that countries shall disappear in a fraction of a SECOND!
So great will be the power of 6 that he shall start this WAR!"

"While your leaders throughout your world are crying for peace ... they
prepare for WAR." *(Blessed Virgin Mary to Veronica Lueken, July 14, 1979)*

"The terrible WAR that is being prepared in the west
The ensuing year will come the pestilence
So very horrible that young, old, nor beast
Blood, fire, Mercury, Mars, Jupiter in France." *(Nostradamus, Century
IX Quatrain 55)*

"By the end of this century, a critical quantum leap is possible. Either
man will die in a THIRD WORLD WAR or man will take a jump and will
become a new man." *(Acharya Rajneesh, 1977)*

"Before the turn of the Century, WAR breaks out in Turkey and spreads
throughout the Middle East. Soon, other nations are drawn in - creating a THIRD
WORLD WAR scenario."

"Libya to take Egypt first, then Saudi Arabia which has Mecca." *(Excerpt
From 'Reality Also Has A Drumbeat', a Phoenix Journal, 1992)*

*Native American Hopi Prophecy states that WORLD WAR III will be
started by the people who first received the light - China, Palestine, India and
Africa. The United States will be destroyed by a gourd of ashes which will fall
to the ground, boiling the rivers and burning the Earth, where no grass will
grow for many years, and causing a disease that no medicine can cure.*

" ... The first phase of WORLD WAR III ... occurs mainly in Europe.
The war ends with the Anti-Christ's leadership being acclaimed as he plays the
role of mediator." *(Dr. Mary Jane Even)*

"WORLD WAR III, starvation and Earth Changes will take place ...
approximately in 2000 ... as a domino effect ... close to one another." *(Hopi*

'Grand Father' on Art Bell Radio Show, June 15, 1998)

" ... The two alliances in the next WAR. The Western Alliance (United States, Canada, Europe and European Russia) fighting against the Eastern Axis (China, Asia, 2/3 of the former Soviet Union, the Persians, Arabs and all of Islam)." *(Excerpt From 'To All My Children', a Phoenix Journal, 1993)*
[i.e. The Beast vs. The Dragon/China]

"The rule will be left to two.
They will hold it for a short time.
Three years and seven months having passed,
They will go to WAR." *(Nostradamus, Century IV Quatrain 95)*

" ... Russia, The United States, Czechoslovakia and China ... will be involved in the THIRD WORLD WAR." *(Our Lady to Patricia Talbot in 'The Coming Chastisement' by Brother Craig Driscoll, 1995)*

"It was my impression that from the start of the THIRD WORLD WAR this was all a continuous panorama, with different stages of development appearing simultaneously. First, world conflagration, then the break-down of national governments, followed by starvation, disease, and natural disasters." *(D. Modin, 1947 in 'Prophecy: 1973-2000')*

" ... Between the nations will come a THIRD UNIVERSAL CONFLAGRATION, which will determine everything. There will be entirely new weapons. In one day more men will die than in all previous wars combined. Battles will be fought with artificial guns. Gigantic catastrophes will occur. With open eyes will the nations of the Earth enter into these catastrophes. They will not be aware of what is happening, and those who will know and tell, will be silenced. Everything will become different than before, and in many places the Earth will be a great cemetery. The THIRD GREAT, GREAT WAR will be the end for many nations." *(Stormberger, 18th Century)*

WHY THE END ?

"There will be TERRIBLE WAR. On one side will be the peoples of the West, on the other those of the East. They will arrive with a multitude of soldiers. The WAR will be fought for a long time with indecisive results until they reach the Rhine. There they will fight for three days until the waters of the Rhine will be all red. Then the affair will be completely decided at the Battle of the Birch Tree, where white, blue, and grey soldiers will fight with such might and rage that those multitudes will be completely rubbed out. Then there will be peace and calm everywhere." *(Monk of Werl, 1701)*

"At the Birch Tree the armies of the West will fight a terrible battle against the armies of the East, and after many bloody sacrifices be victorious. The soldiers of the East will retreat ... The armies of the East will be completely annihilated and only a few will escape to return home with the news of defeat. After these days of mishap and misery, happiness and peace will return to Germany, even though in the first year women will have to march behind the plow." *(Peter Schlinkert)*

" ... The unaffected East against the West will resort to heavy weapons ... A WAR will follow after a winter which really will be no winter, when there will be a soulless snow that will fall. The flowers will bloom very early in this year, and the cows will be up to their knees in grass by April. The first soldiers that come will wear cherry blossoms on their helmets. The rye will be brought in before the battle but the wheat won't. The soldiers are animals and will eat the wheat in the fields."

"In the nearby lower Germany, the battle will be decided. There will be battles like the world has never seen before. This terrible battle will begin by the Birch Forest near Bodberg. For three days they will fight: covered with wounds, they will fight until they stand in blood." *(Birch Tree Prophecy in 'The Proceedings of the Heavenly Renewal from the Unknown Who Became Illuminated', Cologne, 1701)*

"A small people will arise and bring WAR into the world ... Poison will fall as rain upon the fields, which will bring great hunger into Germany ... a great king will rise and win victory for the just cause. The survivors of the adversary armies will flee as far as the Birch Tree: there the last battle will be decided for the good cause. Those who have been hiding in the mountains will return to plant the fields. Those brothers who have escaped the holocaust will return from abroad with their children and they will live again in peace at home. It will be a good and happy time." *(Spielbahn, 1772)*

"In the year when the WAR begins, it was possible to bring the corn in already, but not the wheat. Before this war there will be a time of general disloyalty: men will take evil for goodness and honor, deceit for politeness ... There will be a general collapse of the fiber of society. This war will begin in the East. The war will break out very quickly. In the evening, one will want to say 'Peace, Peace', but there is no peace, and in the morning the enemy will be at the door and all will resound with the din of war. It will last but a few days, and those who can hide for a few days will be safe. Also, the pullout will be quite fast. One throws wheels and carriages into the water or the fleeing enemy will take everything with them. The people of over half the world will stand against each other. God will scare the two enemies with all his might. Only a few Russians will be able to return home to be able to take care of their situation there. The land will lose a lot of population so that women will have to work in the fields and seven girls will brawl for a man. The priesthood will be so rare that one will have to walk seven hours to hear the mass ... The Roman Chair will stand empty for some time ... This will not however be a war of religion, but all who believe in Jesus Christ will have a common cause ... A principal sign of the times in which the WAR will break out will be the general indifference in matters of religion and the general corruption of mores in many places. At that time they will give believers the name of fools, and the faithless will pretend to be men of light." *(Wessel Dietrich Eilert, 1764-1833)*

"The beginning of a terrible time of blood will come when there will be a fierce battle near Cologne. It will be impossible to prevent this horrible devastation: gruesome WAR and destruction cannot be turned away. People will walk in blood up to their ankles. At last a foreign king will arise and gain

WHY THE END ?

victory for the just side. The remaining enemy will retreat to the little Birch Tree, and there the last battle will be fought for the righteous cause. The foreigners have brought black death [biological weapons] with them: whatever is spared by the sword, will be eaten by the pestilence. The land will be deserted and ownerless." *(Bernard Rembold, 1689-1793)*

"The least of the signs of the last hour will be a fire which will gather mankind together from the East and the West." *(The Sahih of Al-Bukhari)*

"Fire come from the sky will strike the West
And then the south will rush upon the East.
Worms will die of hunger without even finding a root to feed upon.
This will be the THIRD WORLD WAR,
Which will light the warlike fires of the reds,
Who will rule, and at the end there will be famine." *(Nostradamus, Sixain 27)*

"The THIRD GREAT WAR comes, when three high-ranking men will be killed. A totally black [evil] column of people will come from the East ... The second great push will come over Saxony westward ... the third army column from the northwest will go westward over Berlin."
"Then the movement moves to the north and cuts off the third army."
"Then it rains a yellow dust [biological weapon] in a line. The Golden City of Prague will be destroyed ... It continues in a straight line to the sea by the bay."
"The tanks drive, but those who sit inside are covered with death. There where it falls, nothing will live. No trees, no flowers, no animals, no grass. Everything will whither and turn black. The houses will stand."
"What it is, I don't know and cannot say. It is a long line. He who crosses it dies. The soldiers of the East cannot cross to the West, and the soldiers of the West cannot cross to the East. The wind blows the deadly cloud to the East. Suddenly the eastern armies collapse. They throw away everything they carry with them and try to escape to the north. But none of them will return."

"But by the Rhine things will be finalized. From the three army movements not one soldier will be able to return home. There will be so many dead ... thousands of bodies black, the rotting flesh falls from the bones."

"Then comes a single aircraft from the East. It throws a 'neutralizer' in the great water by England. Then the water lifts in one single piece as high as a tower and falls back down. It makes an earthquake and a giant wave and everything will be overflooded. Almost all of England and the European coast will sink except for a few mountain peaks."

"Simultaneously, a new land will arise which existed earlier [Atlantis]. Three great cities will sink. One through water [London]. The second will sink [New York], and the third just falls apart [Rome]. The city with the steel tower [Paris] will be set on fire by its inhabitants and will be leveled ... "

"Also in Italy it will be very bad. All priests except six will be murdered. The Pope will flee."

"Simultaneously, there will stand up a large man, and at that point the WAR stops. The whole thing does not take very long."

"In Russia a new revolution will breakout, and a civil war. The dead bodies will be so numerous that they will have difficulty removing them from the streets. The Russian people will begin to believe in Christ and the Cross will be honored again."

"The leaders will kill themselves, and in the blood the blame will be washed away. I see a red mass mixed with yellow faces. I see a total uprising and a horrible massacre and plunder. Then they will sing the Easter song and burn candles before pictures of Mary. Through the power of prayer of Christianity, this monster of Hell will die, and even the young will begin to believe again in the Virgin Mary and God."

"It will become dark on one day during the WAR. Then a huge thunderstorm will appear with bolts of lightning and thunder and an earthquake will move the Earth. Do not go out of the house. No lights will burn except for candle lights [three days darkness]. The stream of people stops. Whoever inhales the dust will develop cramps and die. Do not open the windows. Hang the windows with black paper on the glass. All open water will become poisonous, and all open food which has not been canned. Also all foods in glass will not make it."

"Outside the dust moves. Many people will die. After seventy-two hours everything will be over. But I will say to you again, do not go outside, do not look out of the window. Let the candles burn, keep water, and pray. Overnight more people will die than in the combined two world wars."

"Thereafter the Pope will return and the first great 'Te Deum' will be sung in the Dome in Cologne."

"During this time the climate will change. It will become warmer, and the southern fruits and grapes will grow very well in Bavaria. There will come a long, happy time, and those who live to experience it will be very, very happy ... "

"The year 1999 will bring destruction, followed by peace. A darkness of seventy-two hours will precede peace. The time of the year may be autumn, for there will be snow on the mountains, but not yet in the lowlands. The sign of the Cross will appear in the heavens. The WAR will end as quickly as it began, and a natural phenomenon will end it. The last battle will be near Cologne, and it will be won by the West ... "

"The THIRD WORLD WAR will come, but I cannot predict the year. It will be preceded by SIGNS in the skies, which will be seen by millions of people. War will begin on a rainy night, shortly before harvest time, when the ears are full. WAR will begin after the assassination of an eminent politician in Czechoslovakia or in Yugoslavia. An invasion from the East will follow."

"Nothing has changed. Indeed, events have come even closer and I can see them even better. I see two men who will kill the 'third high-ranking' person. They have been paid to do so. One of the murderers is a small black man, the other is a somewhat taller white man. It could possibly happen in the Balkans, but I'm not sure about it. Prior to the war there will be a fruitful year with good vegetable crops and plentiful fruits. After the murder of the "third", WAR will erupt without warning during the night. I see dust and I see three numbers, two eights and a nine. I do not know what the numbers mean, nor do I know the date and the time." *(Alois Irlmaier, 19th Century)*

" ... The enigmatic date of 1999. Why do I call that date enigmatic? Because it appears that at that point in time, the Occident will no longer exist.

Powerful and sudden upheavals are shaping up." *(Hades, French Astrologer)*

"Got about sixteen years even - maybe ... WAR? ... Big one over world ... It come from Africa ... but the Watchers will stop it ... soon after stuff start, they gonna take control."

"Big bombs gonna go across sky. One, maybe two more even come here. It enough to stop power. It upset Earth Mother. She gonna shake ... They gonna stop that. No more bombs then come ... " *(No-Eyes in 'Spirit Song' by Mary Summer Rain, 1987)*

"The entire world astonished by the blow of steel [missles].
Strangely given by the crocodile [Africa],
To the very great one [U.S.A.], relative of the leech [Israel].
And shortly after there will be another blow
By foul play committed against the wolf [Germany],
And of such deeds one will not see the results." *(Nostradamus, Sixain 45)*

"The purveyor will put all to rout,
Leech and wolf, he will not heed my word
When Mars will be in the sign of Aries [War in March/April],
Joined to Saturn, and Saturn to the moon,
Then your greater misfortune will take place,
The Sun then in exaltation." *(Nostradamus, Sixain 46)*

On March 29, 1975, Veronica Lueken had a vision of a map of Jerusalem, Egypt, Arabia, French Morocco and Africa ... "The start of the GREAT WORLD WAR ... " *(Blessed Virgin Mary to Veronica Lueken)*

"Revolution in Rome, Italy, Africa and Western Europe." *(Veronica Leuken)*

WHY THE END ?

"From Fez [Morocco in NW. Africa] the invaders will penetrate further into Europe,
Whose cities will be ablaze, whose inhabitants will be murdered.
The great leader of Asia [China] will come by land and sea with a great army,
In blues and greys they will pursue those of the cross [The Church] to death." *(Nostradamus, Century VI Quatrain 80)*

"Nuclear strikes in October 1999." *(Dimitre Duduman, 1996)*

" ... It will begin to involve all nations of the region and beyond to virtually every nation in the world. And the WAR ... will be fought between this time and the year 2000 ... " *(Paul Solomon, January 21, 1991)*

"Fire the color of gold, from heaven to Earth shall be seen,
Stricken of the high born, a marvelous event.
Great murder of mankind, great loss of infants,
Some dead looking, the proud one [Antichrist] shall escape." *(Nostradamus, Century II Quatrain 92)*

"I see right before my eyes ... a rainfall of blood and fire which seems to come from Heaven. I see an endless sea and atomic bombs exploding. But I do not succeed in understanding the mysterious value of such visions, and I cannot grasp their exact meaning." *(Mother Elena Leonardi, January 31, 1970 in 'Prophecies! The Chastisement and Purification' by Albert J. Herbert, 1986)*

"A great peace movement will follow world disarmament talks, but while peace seems to be on everyone's mind in the West, sudden destruction and war will occur in 1999." *(Jeane Dixon, 1918-1997)*

" ... The nature of the battle of ARMAGEDDON ... beginning ... in the Middle East ... will involve nations in what might be called WORLD WAR III, or the GREAT WAR of ARMAGEDDON, and so shall it be a WAR to end all

WARS." *(Paul Solomon, 1991)*

"ARMAGEDDON will occur when Russia, Libya, Ethiopia, and Iran invade Israel." *(Louis Hamon 'Cheiro', 1926)*

"Battle of Armagh-Edom to occur in 1999 in New Jerusalem." *(Excerpt From 'The Dark Side of the Force' by D.E.G., 1995)*

" ... All the sky was blood red ... Then I remembered my father telling me that before the great WAR the sky turned blood red."
" ... When America burns ... China, Japan and other nations to go against the Russians ... and push them all the way to the gates of Paris. Over there they will make a treaty, and appoint the Russians as their leaders. They will then unite against Israel ... That's when the Messiah will come ... At that time the battle of ARMAGEDDON will be fought." *(Dumitru Duduman in 'Dreams and Visions from God', 1996)*

"Without the brotherhood of the world, there will again come ARMAGEDDON ... " *(Edgar Cayce, 1926)*

"Armageddon will be the great conclusion of the changes ... " *(Excerpt from 'Daybreak - The Dawning Ember' by Mary Summer Rain, 1991)*

"Scenes from World War III came to life before me ... I saw a world filled with fighting and chaos ... this final WAR, an ARMAGEDDON if you will, was caused by fear ... a fear so great that humans willl give up all freedoms in the name of safety." *(Dannion Brinkley)*

"The gods will make it appear to mankind
That they are the authors of a great WAR.
Before the sky was seen to be free of weapons and rockets,
The greatest damage will be inflicted on the left." *(Nostradamus, Century I Quatrain 91)*

173   Information Pioneers Publisher

WHY THE END ?

"When a fish pond that was a meadow shall be mowed,
Sagittarius being in the ascendent [Nov 23-Dec 21, 1999],
Plague, famine, death by the MILITARY hand,
The CENTURY approaches renewal."   *(Nostradamus, Century I Quatrain 16)*

"A winter will come, darkness for three days, lightning, thunder and cleft in the Earth ... A poisonous breath will fill the night with dust. Black pestilence, the worst human battle ... "   *(Prophecy of Passau, 19th Century)*

"At night they will think they have seen the sun [nuke explosion]
When pig half-man [masked jet pilot] is seen:
Noise, shouts, battle, in heaven fighting is seen:
And brute beasts will be heard to speak."   *(Nostradamus, Century I Quatrain 64)*

"At sunrise a great fire will be seen.
Noise and light extending toward the North
Within the world death and cries are heard,
Death awaiting them through weapons, fire and famine." *(Nostradamus, Century II Quatrain 91)*

"After the rather long milky rain [nuclear fallout],
Several places in Rheims [forest] will be touched by lightning
Oh what a bloody battle is approaching them,
Fathers and sons kings will not dare approach." *(Nostradamus, Century III Quatrain 18)*

"The year that Saturn and Mars are equally fiery [in Leo, June-July 2006]
The air hot, dry, long trajectory
From secret fire, the great heat burns the place to ashes
Little rain, hot, arid WARS, incursions."   *(Nostradamus, Century IV Quatrain 67)*

"The great eastern city of Achem [Mecca backwards] shall be encompassed and assaulted on all sides by a great power of armed men ... Their sea forces shall be weakened by the western men, and to that kingdom shall happen great desolation, and the great cities shall be depopulated, and those that shall come in shall be comprehended within the vengeance of the wrath of God ... The sacred place shall be converted into a stable for cattle ... and put to profane uses." *(Nostradamus in 'The Epistle to Henry II', 1555)*

"Egypt will be desolated, Arabia burned with fire, the land of Ausonia [Italy] burned, and the sea provinces pacified." *(Pseudo-Methodius, 680 A.D.)*

"A fleet shall suffer a shipwreck near the Adriatic sea,
The Earth quakes, a motion of air comes upon the land;
Egypt trembles for fear of the Mohammedan increase,
The Herald [Commander-in-Chief] surrendering shall be commissioned to cry." *(Nostradamus, Century II Quatrain 86)*

" ... Two mighty ones will face each other [Beast & Dragon]. The wrangle between these two will begin in the second half of the twentieth century. It will overthrow mountains and silt up rivers. A great change shall come to pass, such as no mortal man will have expected; heaven and hell will confront each other in this struggle, old states shall perish and light and darkness will be pitted against each other with swords, but it will be swords of a different fashion. With these swords [lasers] it will be possible to cut the skies and to split the Earth. A great lament will come over all mankind and only a small batch will survive the storm, the pestilence and the horror. And neither of the two adversaries will conquer nor be vanquished. Both mighty ones will lie on the ground, and a new mankind will come into existence. God possesses the key to everything. Blessed is he who will then still be able to praise him, having obeyed all his commandments. And the great monarch of the world will create new laws for the new mankind and will cause a new age to begin, in which there will be only one flock and one shepard, and peace will be of long, long duration, for the glory of God in heaven and on Earth." *(Barthalomew Holzhauser in*

WHY THE END ?

'Visiones', 1646)

"A leader with a blue helmet [United Nations troops wear blue helmets] will enter Foix [southwest France],

He will prevail less than a change of Saturns appearance [less than 4 years],

A leader with a white helmet [Muslim], an Arab Turk, his heart will fail him,

With the Sun, Mars and Mercury near Aquarius [Age]." *(Nostradamus, Century IX Quatrain 73)*

"A forerunner of Antichrist will marshall an army drawn from all nations, united under his banner [United Nations]. He will lead them in a bloody WAR against those still faithful to the living God. He will shed much blood in eradicating the cult of the living God and by taking His place. Then there will be seen many types of punishment on Earth besides the disease and hunger which will be universal. WARS will follow WARS and the final one will be led by one of the ten kings of Antichrist who will have only one will and will be the only ones to rule in the world."

"Before this event the world will have apparent peace and people will think of nothing but pleasure and the bad ones will commit sins of all kinds." *(Melanie Calvat, 1831-1940)*

"They went out to assemble all the kings of the Earth for battle on the Great Day of God the Almighty ... The devils then assembled the kings in a place called in Hebrew 'ARMAGEDDON'." *[Mountain of Megiddo - 55 miles north of Jerusalem on the plain Esdraelon between the coast and rift valley of Jordan]* *(Revelation 16:14-16, Bible)*

"Before the consummation ... the whole place will shake ... with great thundering ... then the rulers will be sad ... then the age will begin, and they will be disturbed. Their kings will ... be intoxicated with the fiery sword, and they will ... wage WAR against one another, so that ... the Earth is intoxicated with bloodshed ... And the seas will be disturbed by those wars. Then the sun will become dark ... and the moon will cause its light to cease ... The stars of the sky will cancel their circuits ... And a great clap of thunder will come out ... of a great force that is above all the forces of chaos ... They will be obliterated because of their wickedness ... " *(Excerpt from 'On the Origin of the World', translated by Hans Gerhard Bethge, 4th Century)*

"Mars and the Sceptre [Jupiter], being conjoined together [June 21,2002],
Under Cancer shall be a calamitous WAR,
A little while after a new King shall be anointed,
Who, for a long time, shall pacify the Earth." *(Nostradamus, Century VI Quatrain 24)*

" ... WAR, turmoil and strife, ARMAGEDDON   WARS and rumors of WARS ... they will be stopped by the forces in the heavens." *(Edgar Cayce, 1877-1945)*

"She [No-eyes] was telling me that missles would be exchanged, but only a few. The missles would target areas of major power, communication and arsenal areas ... The Earth Watchers ... would use their highly advanced technology to stop the exchanges. (These Earth Watchers are intelligent beings who are concerned about the welfare of the Earth, in respect to possible adverse chain reactions out into the universe) ... Mankind was not going to be allowed to annhihilate himself or ... his world. (They would use a force field that was yet incomprehensible to us)." *(Mary Summer Rain)*

"After they have killed a great number they will raise a cry of victory, but suddenly the good will receive help from above." *(The Nun of Belez, 19th Century)*

"The SIGN OF THE CROSS will appear in the heavens. The WAR will end as quickly as it began ... " *(Alois Irlmaier, 19th Century)*

"Many people will want to come to terms
With the great lords who will want to bring WAR upon them:
They will not want to hear anything of it from them,
Alas! If God does not send peace to the Earth [Ball of Redemption]."
(Nostradamus, Century VIII Quatrain 4)

" ... Watch unto Syria for therein lies the solution of world peace or the THIRD WAR of your world. It will be the destruction of three-quarters of the world. A world aflame followed by the Great Comet Ball of Redemption as it is sometimes called." *(Excerpt From 'Skeletons In The Closet', a Phoenix Journal, 1990)*

"Watch for the major revolution in Africa, Western Europe and especially upheaval and revolution in Italy which touches the Vatican. Then watch for the fleeing of the Pope into safety outside of Rome. Then very soon will come THE WARNING followed closely by a Great Miracle - in Spain, but which shall touch the world; at this time it is probable that it will be in the area of Garabandal."

"After these things will come the GREAT 'CASTIGATION' (discipline) It will come forth in two major portions. First will be a WORLD WAR of horrendous attack and counter attack which will be incredible for at least a period of three days, and then a comet, a FIERY COMET will come for a period of at least another three days." *(Excerpt from 'Phoenix Journal Express', Volumes 1 & 2, 1990)*

"The third climate comprehended under Aries [World War III],
In the year 2025, the 27th of October.
The King of Persia shall be taken by those of Egypt;
Battle, death, loss, a great shame to the Christians." *(Nostradamus, Century III Quatrain 77)*

"In the year 2025, Red China will have reached an economic and political stability sufficient to forge ahead and become the great conqueror." (Jeane Dixon, 1969)

======================*===========*===========*

WHY THE END ?

Information Pioneers Publisher

GOG & MAGOG

"And Christian one [Catholics] fights Christian two [Protestants in Ireland]
And nations sigh, yet nothing do
And yellow men [China/Magog] great power gain
From mighty bear [Russia/Gog] with whom they've lain.
These mighty tyrants will fail to do
They fail to split the world in two.
But from their acts a danger bred
An ague [plague], leaving many dead.
And physics find no remedy
For this is worse than leprosy
Oh many signs for all to see
The truth of this prophecy." *(Mother Shipton, 1488-1561)*

"Satan will be released from his prison. He will go out and seduce the nations in all four corners of the Earth, and muster for war the troops of Gog [Russia] and Magog [China] ... and surrounded the beloved city where God's people were encamped [The United States of America, one nation under God], but fire came down from heaven and devoured them. The devil who led them astray was hurled into the pool of burning sulphur, where the beast and false prophet had also been thrown." *(Revelation 20:7-10, Bible)*

"And the word of the Lord came unto me, saying, Son of Man, set thy face against GOG, the Land of MAGOG, the chief prince of Meshech [area between Black Sea and Caspian Sea] and Tubal [Area under Black Sea in Turkey; Yeltsin's birthplace] ... "

"And say, thus saith the Lord God; Behold, I am against thee, O GOG, the chief prince of Meshech and Tubal ... "

"And thou shalt say, I will go up to the land of unwalled villages ... all of them dwelling without walls, and having neither bars nor gates [U.S.A.]."

"And thou shalt come from thy place out of the NORTH parts ... all of them riding upon horses, a great company, and a mighty army."

"And thou shalt come up against my people of Israel, as a cloud to cover the land; it shall be in the latter days ... And it shall come to pass at the same time when GOG shall come against the land of Israel ... mountains shall be thrown down and the steep places shall fall, and every wall shall fall to the ground ... " *(Ezekiel 38:1-23, Bible)*

"As a griffon shall come the King of Europe,
Accompanied by those of the NORTH [Russia],
Of reds and whites shall conduct a great troop,
And then, shall go against the King of Babylon [U.S.A.]." *(Nostradamus, Century X Quatrain 86)*

"And the land of GOG and MAGOG is of the land Edom ... And they will come to fight and they will wage war against jerUSAlem and Messiah ben David [Enoch?] and Elijah and all the people in it." *(Eliziezer Ashkenazi in 'Sefer Ta'am Z'qenim')*

" It shall seem, from the kingdoms spoiled by the EASTERN men, that God has loosed Satan from his infernal prison, to cause to be born the great DOG and DOHAN [Gog and Magog], who shall make so great and abominable a breach in the Churches ... " *(Nostradamus in 'The Epistle to Henry II', 1555)*

"Before the time comes for their release from behind the barrier, Allah will send Jesus from heaven to slay Dajjal, and Jesus will still be on this Earth when the time comes for YAJUJ and MAJUJ to be set free. Then Allah will tell Jesus to take the believing servants of Allah with Him and shelter them in the mountains. Then Allah will then break the barrier and let YAJUJ and MAJUJ free, and they will surge forth and devour everything upon the Earth. All vegetation, animals, the waters of the whole world and even human beings will be devoured by them, and not a single drop of water will be left in the Gulf of Tiberius. Their voice will be so loud that the whole world will shake and tremble at the power of it. After they have devoured everything they will still not be satisfied, and they will rush through the sky and begin to shoot arrows into the heavens in order to try and kill Allah. And Allah in turn will fulfill their wish and command the angels to put blood on the arrows and return them to the Earth."

"When they see the arrows return to Earth covered in blood, they will believe that they have killed Allah. Then they will say: 'We have killed Allah [God], now let us try to dominate the moon and sky'."

"At that time Allah will send down some kind of disease upon them which will eat all the flesh from their bodies ... The smell from their bodies when they die from this disease will spread all over the world. Then it is that Jesus, with all other Muslims who have hidden in the mountains, will pray to Allah to save them from the disease and death. Then a great cloud will cover the sky and Allah will send down rain for 40 days. At first the rain will be red, the color of blood. It will then turn green and will wash away the smell of the bodies. The rain will finally become clear and purify everything." *(Excerpt from the 'Mishkah al-Masabih')*

"And when YAJUJ [Gog/Russia] and MAJUJ [Magog/China] are let loose, they shall sally forth from every elevated place." *(Quran 21:96)*

"A powerful wind will rise in the NORTH carrying heavy fog and the densest dust by divine command and ... they will be stricken with fear. After that so few men left ... " *(Hildegard of Bingen, 1145 A.D.)*

"Then the 'Gates of the NORTH' will be opened and the strength of those nations which Alexander shut up there will go forth. The whole Earth will be terrified at the sight of them; men will be afraid and flee in terror to hide themselves in mountains and caves and graves. They will die of fright and very many will be wasted with fear. There will be no one to bury the bodies. The tribes which will go forth from the NORTH will eat the flesh of men and will drink the blood of beasts like water ... and even women's abortions. They will slay the young and take them away from their mothers and eat them. They will corrupt the Earth and contaminate it. No one will be able to stand against them." *(The Pseudo-Methodius, 680 A.D.)*

WHY THE END ?

"And at the time of the end shall the king of the south push at him and the king of the NORTH shall come against him like a whirlwind ... " *(Daniel 11:40)*

"Russia will march upon all the nations of Europe, particularly Italy, and will raise her flag over the Dome of St. Peter's. Italy will be severely tried by a great revolution, and Rome will be purified in blood for its many sins, especially those of impurity. The flock is about to be dispersed and the Pope will suffer greatly." *(Blessed Virgin Mary to Sister Elena Aiello, 1961)*

"Italians will fight terribly against Russians ... I see the whole field full of burned ships with scorched wings, and people still alive in flames, and those who are burnt even more have shrunk down to the size of children!" *(Mitar Tarabic, 1829-1899)*

" ... If people ... do not return to God ... another terrible WAR will come from the East to the West. Russia with her secret armies will battle America; will overrun Europe. The River Rhine will be overflowing with corpses and blood. Italy will also be harassed by a great revolution, and the Pope will suffer terribly." *(Mother Mary to Sister Elena, August 22, 1960)*

"Mortal sequence in death of the house seven [G-7]
Hail, tempest, pestilent evil furies:
King of the East, all of the West in flight,
He will subjugate his former conquerors." *(Nostradamus, Presage 40)*

"Against the REDS, sects shall gather themselves,
Fire, water, iron, rope, by peace it shall be destroyed
Those that shall conspire, shall be put to death,
Except one, who above all shall ruin the world." *(Nostradamus, Century IX Quatrain 51)*

"I see yellow [China] warriors and red warriors [Russia] advancing against the rest of the world ... Europe will be completely covered with a yellow fog [biological weapon/poison gas] that will kill the cattle in the fields. Those nations which began the war ... will perish by terrible fire." *(Francesca De Billiante Of Savoy, 20th Century)*

"Then the sixth angel blew his trumpet, and I heard a voice coming from the horns of the altar of gold in God's presence. It said to the sixth angel. 'Release the four angels that are tied up on the banks of the great river Euphrates!' ... This was precisely the hour, the day, the month, and year for which they had prepared to kill a third of mankind. Their cavalry troops ... two hundred million in number [China has 250+ million troops] ... The horses' heads were like heads of lions, and out of their mouths came fire and sulphur and smoke. By these three plagues - the smoke and sulphur and fire which shot out of their mouths - a third of mankind was slain." *(Revelation 9:1-18, Bible)*

"And the sixth angel poured out his vial upon the great river Euphrates; and the water thereof was dried up [Dam valves closed], that the way of the kings of the EAST [China invasion] might be prepared ... And he gathered them together into a place called in Hebrew tongue Armageddon." *(Revelation 16:12-16, Bible)*

" ... The Euphrates River ... There is now capability of totally closing off the lake from the river bed and the ability to cross that river is at hand now. And ... you will have opened the very route presented for the Asian masses of troops to move across that area and the price shall be dearly extracted from those who had planned to take the world. When the dam is closed, it is over for that area to the East of that River if you be against God and the peoples of that area. Israel will be pushed all the way into Turkey and will go down before the mighty hordes." *(Excerpt from 'Rise of the Antichrist', Volume 2, a Phoenix Journal, 1998)*

WHY THE END ?

"And we said thereafter to the children of Israel, dwell securely in your land, but when the second of the warnings comes to pass we shall bring you a crowd, gathered out of various nations." *(Quran 17:104)*

"It is the claim of great prophets and seers that it will be the CHINESE who will march across the world to the North and push Israel into Turkey after crossing the 'dry' Euphrates remember?" *(Hatonn, January 23, 1997)*

"When the EASTERN WAR appears, then know the end is near." *(Joanna Southcott, 1750-1814)*

"I have projected my quest for information into the year 2000 and see CHINESE and Mongol troops invading the Middle East. I see devastating battles raging uncontrollably east of the Jordan River. It is a war of EAST against WEST; it will be an almost futile fight against an overwhelming foe ... and great losses will be suffered by the Orientals."
"The biggest danger the world faces in the future is Red CHINA. When peace negotiations have seemingly concluded in the first quarter of the twenty-first century, Red CHINA will show her teeth." *(Jeane Dixon, 1969)*

" ... The 800 year Oriental Cycle due to strike now in the present time and culminate in WORLD WAR III or ARMAGEDDON." *(Excerpt From 'To All My Children', a Phoenix Journal, 1993)*

"The fiery eyed DRAGON [China] when he cometh on the waves ... with full belly, and shall oppress the children of thee ... Famine also pending and fratricidal strife, then is nigh the end of the world and the last days ... " *(Excerpt from the 'Sibylline Fragment', 2nd Century B.C.)*

"A prince from the EAST with a great army will move throughout Europe." *(Rudolfo Gilthier, 1675)*

"Nothing compares previously to anything like this. Out of the EAST comes a DRAGON [China], who looks gross. Out of his 9 tongues and 99 eyes there will shoot deadly lightning and out of his open mouth there will blow a poisonous breath ... Thousands of people will lie to rest with horribly twisted faces, and will freeze in spite of the warmth. The end is at hand ... Yellow dust clouds and poisonous dusts will take the breath of man and animal. In the city there is fire everywhere. The Earth moves, deep crevices open and draw into them the dead and the living ... Everything sinks into the black depths. From Vysehrad comes a fireball, blunders fly through the air and everywhere there is screaming, and a fire ocean. Everything that was the result of men, lies in disarray and ashes. Life is wiped out ... " *(The Seeress of Prague, 17th Century)*

"CHINA may run out of oil in the next twenty years and ... will need food when the next famine develops. The food is in Southeast Asia, and the oil is in Arabia." *(Excerpt From 'To All My Children', a Phoenix Journal, 1993)*

"Pluto [China's planetary ruler] in the sign of Scorpio 1984-1999 ... only after 1984 will China bc in full possession of her power." *(Hades, French Astrologer)*

" ... As soon as the CHINESE develop adequate logistics and lines of communication, they will be a most formidable threat to all contiguous areas." *(Herman Kahn, Analyst for Center for International Studies)*

"From the ASIAN land he shall come, mounted on the Trojan chariot [C.O.S.CO./China Ocean Shipping Co. set up in Long Beach Naval yard] ... then he shall encounter the great black beast of blood [U.N.] ... " *(Excerpt from the 'Sibylline Fragment', 2nd Century B.C.)*

"The west coast will be invaded by ASIANS, but they will be beaten back ... " *(Alois Irlmaier, 19th Century)*

WHY THE END ?

" ... The great eagle [U.S.A.] with a leader will come again from the rock island. A final battle will be delivered. The wild horde [Mongols/China] will be defeated and made to pay ... They ... will not return ... to their homeland." *(St. Hilarion, 291-371 A.D.)*

"The year 1999 and seventh month,
From the sky will come a great king of terror
To raise again the great king of Angoulmois [Mongols/China],
Before and after, Mars will reign at will."   *(Nostradamus, Century X Quatrain 72)*

"The three great powers [USA, Russia, China]
Will hatch plots and the Bourbon will be far away.
One of the three [China] will conspire against the two others and,
At the end of October, her work will be seen."   *(Nostradamus, Presage 44)*

"Near Sorbin, to invade Hungary,
The herald of Buda [China], shall give notice,
The chief EASTERNER, Sallon of Sclavonia,
Shall convert them to the Asiatic law." *(Nostradamus, Century X Quatrain 62)*

"The EASTERNER [China] will leave his seat,
To pass the Apennine mountains to see Gaul:
He will transpierce the sky, the waters, and the snow,
And everyone will be struck by his rod."   *(Nostradamus, Century II Quatrain 39)*

 "The abomination from the EAST [China] makes his purpose
The papacy falters. A strange conflict between
The devout and the pagans [Holy War]. A flock seemingly
Foresaken, yet divine plans [Help from above] for intercession arise."

188   Information Pioneers Publisher

(Nostradamus, Unpublished Quatrain)

"Libra will see the Hesperias ['Lands of the West'] govern
Holding the monarchy of heaven and Earth:
No one will see the forces of Asia [China] Perish,
Only seven hold the hierarchy in order." *(Nostradamus, Century IV Quatrain 50)*

"The leaders of Aquilon [U.S.A. & Russia], two in number, will be victorious over the Orientals, and so great a noise and tumult of warfare will they produce, that all the Orient will shake with their terror because of these two brothers, who are not yet brothers." *(Nostradamus in 'The Epistle to Henry II', 1555)*

" ... The last grear war occurs around 2015 and its, the U.S.A. against CHINA." *(Sean David Morton on Art Bell Radio Show, November 1, 1998)*

=====================*===========*===========*

WHY THE END ?

 Information Pioneers Publisher

THE WARNING & THE THREE DAYS DARKNESS

"When the people lack a proper sense of awe, then some awful visitation will descend upon them." *(Chinese Tao)*

"Yes, the WARNING is coming soon. This will be a frightening experience, for some may die from fright alone. It will be a supernatural awakening to show people their sins ... It will be a review of your life experiences in a twinkling of time." *(Message given to John Leary, 1993)*

"Prepare for my WARNING. It will come when you least expect it. Be watchful and have your soul ready by frequent Confession. Those in mortal sin will experience great grief at the time of the WARNING." *(Jesus' message to John Leary, June 1994)*

"My WARNING will announce the beginnings of these evil times. Be watchful and prepared. Ask for My help and I will protect you during these times." *(Jesus' message to John Leary, May 1994) [Leary received this message upon seeing a football, therefore, it could occur during football season September-December, due more likely in October according to Nostradamus in 'The Epistle to Henry II']*

"My WARNING for all of you is coming soon. This will be a time when every soul will see their lives as I do (in full detail). It will be a brief review of your life. No one will doubt that it is from a supernatural origin. Certain men may reject it but they cannot deny it will happen. From this point on, events will quicken as the evil tribulation will gradually unfold. Pray and repent for this will try men's souls to the limit. Ask for My help and I will protect your souls from the demons. This will last but a short time and then My glory will be bestowed on the Earth." *(Jesus' message to John Leary, January 1994)*

" ... Soon you will witness a display of supernatural mercy in My WARNING to mankind. This will be a grace of understanding each will receive to understand how the sins of their lives so offend me ... Each person will be outside of time and will be able to view their life ... They will see all the good things and bad things they have done. Most of all you will recognize which things utilized your time on Earth the best. You will see how effective your prayers were and what value came to all your actions. In this way you will realize that praying and doing good works with love are the best use of your time." *(Jesus' message to John Leary, April 1994)*

" ... This is the WARNING ... You will see all the events of your life both good and bad ... but even more fearful for some, you will see the current status of your soul at the time (whether you are headed for heaven or to hell). You will know if you have rejected Me, that this is your last chance to choose Me or not. After this event your soul's destiny will lie completely with your freewill, but you will have also a brief view of your destination at the time." *(Jesus' message to John Leary, August 1994)*

"The WARNING which must be sent upon man must be effective. And in the mercy of the Father, a great spectacle will then be placed in the sky for all to see. However, the agents of hell will try to disprove the hand of the Father in this Miracle." *(Blessed Virgin Mary to Veronica Lueken, December 24, 1973)*

"The WARNING is meant to help us see what we are doing - how much evil we are doing - how much pain we are causing God. Everyone will experience it wherever they may be - regardless of their condition or knowledge of God - it will take place all over the world." *(Mari Loli of Garabandal, Spain, September 29, 1978 in 'Signs, Wonders and Response' by Albert J. Herbert, 1993)*

"Man will feel that the very powers of the elements have shaken the very foundations of his being. So great will be the impact of this WARNING from the Father that none will doubt that it had come from the Father ... It will be a major awakening to many. The rumbling and the shaking of the elements will set fright into many hearts ... Hearts will shudder with fear and men will drop from fright ... Many signs of an angry God will appear before you ... " *(Message from Blessed Virgin Mary to Veronica Lueken, April 21, 1973)*

"For the WARNING is coming upon mankind. There will be a tremendous explosion and the sky shall roll back like a SCROLL. This force will go to the very core of every man and he will then understand his offenses to his God. The WARNING will be of short duration, however; and then many will continue on the road to perdition, so hard have their hearts become."

"At the end of the WARNING there will be a great MIRACLE, but scientists will later rationalize it. The MIRACLE you seek ... will be a great WARNING to mankind." *(Message from Blessed Virgin Mary to Veronica Lueken, June 12, 1976)*

"It will seem as though it were already the end of the world. And in this cataclysm everything will be separated from the sky; which will turn white as snow." *(Jacinta Marto of Fatima, 1920)*

"The day of the Lord will come like a thief, and on that day the heavens will vanish with a roar ... " *(2 Peter 3:10, Bible)*

"The sky disappeared like a SCROLL that is rolled up ... " *(Revelation 6:12-17, Bible)*

" ... The Eternal Father will send a WARNING to mankind, a great WARNING of such magnitude that very few will doubt that it comes from the Eternal Father and is not man-made." *(Message from Blessed Virgin Mary to Veronica Lueken, July 25, 1978)*

" ... There is to come upon you a great WARNING, of such magnitude that every man, woman and child will feel the burning fires within." *(Blessed Virgin Mary to Veronica Lueken (September 28, 1974)*

"All who remain in the light of grace will have no fear. They will pass through this great period of WARNINGS without suffering." *(Blessed Virgin*

Mary to Veronica Lueken, April 5, 1975)

"The Father chooses to send upon you first a great manifestation, a WARNING. And should you not listen to the voice within you, He will have no recourse but to go forth with the plan for full cleansing." *(Blessed Virgin Mary to Veronica Lueken, May 10, 1973)*

"I have told you the WARNING happens first, followed by the Pope's exile and the mark of the beast being demanded of everyone." *(Jesus' message to John Leary, May 10, 1998)*

"I give you one indication that the time is ripe. When you see, when you hear, when you feel the revolution in Rome, when you see the Holy Father fleeing, seeking a refuge in another land, know that the time is ripe." *(Jesus' message to Veronica Lueken, September 14, 1976)*

" ... Suddenly the revolution will terminate with a great MIRACLE and astonish the world. The few evil ones who remain will be converted. The things that will happen will be as an image of the end of the world." *(Maria Terreaux in 'Prophecies! The Chastisement and Purification' by Albert J. Herbert, 1986)*

"A MIRACLE similar to that at Fatima, a great wonder to convince many ... will last for about a quarter of an hour and will be visible from Garabandal, Spain, and the surrounding mountains. Our Holy Father [Pope] will see it no matter where he is at the time. This MIRACLE will take place on a date which will be announced eight days before. Afterwards, God will leave a sign in memory of it." *(Excerpt from the Internet website: www.webcom.com/enddays/ darkness.html)*

" ... It will be visible all over the world; it will be the direct work of God, and will take place before the MIRACLE ... I can reveal the date only eight days before it happens. What I can say is that it will coincide with the feast-day of a holy martyr; that it will occur at 8:30 p.m. on a Thursday; that it will be visible to all the people who are in the village of Garabandal or the surrounding mountains; the sick who see it will be cured and the unbelievers will believe. It will be the greatest MIRACLE that Jesus has ever performed in the world. There will be no doubt that it will be for the benefit of humanity. A trace of the MIRACLE will remain at Pini forever. It will be able to be filmed and to appear on television."

"I have seen the CHASTISEMENT ... I can assure you that it is worse than being enveloped in fire, worse than having fire above and beneath you. I do not know how much time will elapse between the MIRACLE and the CHASTISEMENT." *(Conchita Gonzalez, January 1, 1965)*

"According to Conchita, the MIRACLE, lasting fifteen minutes will take place sometime between the 8th and 16th of March, April or May, on a Thursday evening at 8:30 p.m." *(Albert J. Herbert in 'Signs, Wonders and Response', 1993)*

"Believe what you see in Garabandal, and turn back from your ways that have been created by Satan. Return to the Father; do penance and atonement, for your CHASTISEMENT will soon follow upon the great spectacle." *(Blessed Virgin Mary to Veronica Lueken, December 24, 1973)*

"The WARNING promised to mankind will not be long in coming ... given to you as a merciful act of the Father to awaken mankind before it is too late and the great CHASTISEMENT will be sent upon you." *(Blessed Virgin Mary to Veronica Lueken, July 25, 1974)*

"Should this GREAT MIRACLE be cast aside and rationalized by atheistic, scientific men, I assure you ... the CHASTISEMENT will come upon you with great force." *(Blessed Virgin Mary to Veronica Lueken, July 15, 1974)*

"When God decides to take action ... it will be a mere turning off of your capability to produce power ... When that happens all electronic and electric supply will go offline - ALL POWER. Not even your automobiles will run. Will you be WARNED? Yes, you were." *(Hatonn, March 14, 1995)*

"And the fifth angel poured out his vial upon the seat of the beast, and his kingdom was full of DARKNESS." *(Daniel 7:25, Bible)*

" ... DARKNESS shall cover the Earth ... " *(Isaiah 60:2-3, Bible)*

" ... For near is the day ... a day of clouds, doomsday for the nations shall it be." *(Ezekiel 30:2-3, Bible)*

"And I will cover the heavens ... and ... make the stars thereof DARK. I will cover the sun with a cloud and the moon shall not give her light." *(Ezekiel 32:7-8, Bible)*

" ... We have stumbled at noonday as in DARKNESS ... " *(Isaiah 59:10, Bible)*

" ... The sun to go down at noon and ... will DARKEN the Earth in the clear day." *(Amos 8:8-9, Bible)*

" ... The day of the Lord comes, cruel, with wrath and burning anger; to lay waste the land, destroy the sinners with it! The stars and the constellations of the heavens send forth no light; the sun is DARK when it rises, and the light of the moon does not shine. Thus will I punish the world for its evil and the wicked for their guilt. I will put an end to the pride of the arrogant, the insolence of tyrants I will humble." *(Isaiah 13:9-11, Bible)*

"That day is a day of wrath, a day of tribulation and distress, a day of calamity and misery, a day of DARKNESS and obscurity ... " *(Zephaniah 1:15, Bible)*

"Before the great DARKNESS comes, the deep night of atheism will descend upon the Earth and will envelop everything." *(Blessed Mary to Father Stefano Gobbi of Italy, January 5, 1974 in 'The Three Days Darkness' by Albert J. Herbert, 1996)*

"I will let you have a foretaste of the eternal DARKNESS soon for THREE DAYS. Many, if not most of the people will perish during that time of DARKNESS, but those who possess the eternal light ... will remain illuminated within." *(Leslie Garay, August 24, 1994 in 'The Visionaries - U.S.A. - Today' by Albert J. Herbert, 1993)*

" ... The three phases of cleansing. The first is the THREE DAYS OF DARKNESS; the second is the Seven Year Famine; and the third is the Battle of Armageddon, at which time the Children of God will not be on the Earth, but will have been evacuated." *(Excerpt from 'God, Too, Has A Plan 2000!', a Phoenix Journal, 1992)*

" ... The first sifting is through THREE DAYS OF DARKNESS!" *(L.G.A., October 29, 1984 in 'The Three Days Darkness' by Albert J. Herbert, 1996)*

"The THREE DAYS OF DARKNESS, as has been foretold through My messengers of far and near past, will be the days of Satan's final harvest for his stench-laden kingdom! Every one of my people have to prepare for those crucial days, lest they too will be lost forever." *(Leslie Garay, Harvard Scientist, December 3, 1992 in 'The Visionaries - U.S.A. - Today!' by Albert J. Herbert, 1993)*

"Man has only one means now to avert the planned CHASTISEMENT and WARNING. The WARNING and the CHASTISEMENT will follow soon upon each other if man continues on his present course. He must now humble himself before the world ... and make atonement for the many offenses against his God. Only in this manner will I ... be able to hold back the destruction which is fast heading towards the Earth." *(Blessed Virgin Mary to Veronica*

WHY THE END ?

Lueken, September 28, 1973)

"Beware of the sunrise ... beware of the flash, pull down the blinds, stay in the house, don't go outside or you won't return." *(Veronica Lueken)*

"It's as though everything has exploded in the sky - the flash ... very hot ... very warm ... it feels like a burning of everything. Now the sky is very white ... colors ... blues, purples ... It's like a huge explosion ... and then a warning: 'Your WARNING before CHASTISEMENT!' Flash, fire and the voice within you! 'The FINAL WARNING before CHASTISEMENT'." *(Veronica Lueken, April 21, 1976)*

"As the day follows night, so shall this WARNING follow soon. Beware of the sunrise! Do not look up to the sky - at that time of the FLASH! Beware of the sunrise! Do not look up to the sky at the FLASH [will burn eyes]. Close your windows, draw your shades. Remain inside. Do not venture outside your door, or you will not return. Pray! Prostrate yourself upon your floor. Pray with arms outstretched and beg for mercy of God the Father. Do not seek or receive your animals into your homes, for the animals of those who have remained of well spirit will be taken care of."

" ... How many will try to go back and restore their homes when it is too late. Keep blessed candles, water, blankets, food within your homes. The candles of those who have remained in the state of grace shall not be extinguished, but the candles in the homes of those who have given themselves to Satan shall not burn."

"I say to you, as night follows day a great DARKNESS shall descend upon mankind. When the WARNING is sent upon man, there will be no doubt in the minds of man that it descends from the heavens. However, those who have already committed themselves to Satan will see and yet not believe." *(Blessed Virgin Mary to Veronica Lueken, September 28, 1973)*

"I have come to save the souls going on the wrong road, that they may be converted ... A GREAT CASTIGATION is near." *(Our Lady to Miguel Angel*

Poblete, Penablanca, Chile, June 12, 1983 in 'Signs, Wonders and Response' by Albert J. Herbert, 1993)

"An unusual CHASTISEMENT of the human race will take place towards the end of the world." *(Blessed Mary of Agreda, Spain, 17th Century)*

"A great CHASTISEMENT will come over all mankind, not today or tomorrow, but in the second half of the twentieth century. What I have already announced at La Salette ... I repeat to you now. Humanity has not developed as God desired. Mankind has been sacrilegious and has trampled underfoot, the wondrous Blessings of God. No longer does order reign anywhere. Even in the highest places Satan reigns and directs the course of things. Satan will even succeed in infiltrating into the highest positions of the Church ... If mankind will not oppose these evils ... If the chief rulers of the world and of the Church will not actively oppose these evils ... Then will God punish mankind even more severely and heavily than He did at the time of the great deluge." *(The Third Prophecy of Fatima, Portugal, 1917)*

"These are the warnings, these are signs to look for. And when you see these things happening, know that the CHASTISEMENT is coming ... Russia ... as soon as she steps foot into Italy the DARKNESS will fall upon this Earth."
" ... Something is pushing the Holy Father out of the Vatican ... right after that the Vatican is overtaken ... This is the final thing to happen that angers God so much that he would cause DARKNESS to fall and the CHASTISEMENT to come ... " *(S.F., American Mother, March 26, 1983 in 'The Three Days Darkness' by Albert J. Herbert, 1996)*

"The Anti-Christ Maitreya will become popular after the Holy Father leaves Rome ... He shows himself on TV throughout the world, saying that he is going to do something fearful to mankind. This happens immediately before the Great WARNING. Being a great deceiver, he tries to take credit for the Great WARNING as if he was its author. He will say that he will make a great event take place to prove that he is the master."

Information Pioneers Publisher

WHY THE END ?

"The sun has several implosions [solar flares] causing a great flash. These implosions are the sign that the Blessed Virgin Mary is coming ... to cover the Earth ... with a thick white cloud which holds everyone in place. The Earth stops rotating and all machines stop working."

"The Virgin Mary will cover the Earth with a white cloud like snow. All the Earth will stop working for three days. A comet [wormwood in Revelation 8:11] will penetrate this white cloud blanket and hit the Earth. People will see their own sins in a flash as in a personal judgement before God ... " *(Dr. Mary Jane Even from the Internet website: www.webcom.com)*

"Watch for the major revolution in Africa, Western Europe and especially upheaval and revolution in Italy which touches the Vatican [then to the Mideast]. Then watch for the fleeing of the Pope into safety outside Rome [will occur in secrecy, but will leak out]. Then very soon will come THE WARNING [the world will be held hostage - God will take over] (Voice: 'YOUR WARNING BEFORE THE GREAT CHASTISEMENT'), entire beam network detonated - will encapsulate planet for three days [during Three Days of Darkness - candles will burn for those in a state of grace] followed closely by a Great MIRACLE - in Spain, but which shall touch the world; at this time it is probable that it will be in the area of Garabandal."

"After these things will come the GREAT CASTIGATION (Discipline) It will come forth in two major portions. First will be a WORLD WAR [enemy will respond with nuclear weapons (a plot to hold God's people hostage)] of horrendous attack and counter attack ... for at least a period of three days, and then ... a fiery comet [The Ball of Redemption/Wormwood/Herculobus] will come at least another three days." *(Excerpt From 'Phoenix Express', Volumes I & II, 1990)*

"There will come a great revolution in Africa ... a great impact upon the U.S. for many very strategic metals are received from Africa ... "

"This will be followed - overlapping - by great and widespread revolution in western Europe ... There will also be a major revolution in Rome/Italy. These things will be so devastating - stretching from the Middle East and all the way across into the west until it will seem as though it were already the end of the world."

"At Garabandal, Spain the word was handed down of how it would be in those places and sent forth as a WARNING to all nations and peoples; the WARNING was to allow mankind to make a correction of the conscience of the world. The WARNING would be like a revelation of your errors, and it would be seen and experienced by 'believers' and 'non-believers' and people of all religions ... "

"Dying will be preferable to a mere five minutes of what is awaiting you. It will be as fire. It will burn your flesh as you recognize a flame burning your skin, but you will feel it with your bodies and within your very souls. All nations, everyone will experience it (not one will be exempt). It will be as though everything has exploded in the sky -- there will be a great and blinding flash! ... It is a blast of burning heat like the opening of a blast-furnace door in a smeltering plant -- it feels like intense burning which surrounds the whole being from which the consciousness cannot escape. First the entire sky is milky white and the only light is reflected from the whiteness and then the colors which seem to flash and swirl from the deepest tones of blues, purples and crimson -- but the golden glow of life itself is not present."

"Then from out of the heavens somewhere seems to come a VOICE -- A GREAT VOICE. It is not carried on the winds but rather it is broadcast to every living being and heard from within that none shall be missed. It will tell you that this is 'YOUR WARNING BEFORE CHASTISEMENT'. There will be the great flash, the seeming fire, and the voice within -- this will be the final WARNING before the great tribulation of CHASTISEMENT."

"Many will make soul transition in the midst of the 'WARNING'. All who remain in the light of Grace will have no fear, they will pass through the great WARNING without what you will call physical suffering to any great extent. But many will die in this great 'WARNING' and there shall be much death to the physical perception."

"You of Earth have been given two reprieves -- the third shall not be given as such. It is a final WARNING that will come and you will know that the ending play will not be reversed. What you do, however, will make a difference in magnificence as to what shall be your experience."

"As a signal ... when the Pope of the Vatican flees Rome and seeks refuge in another land -- KNOW THAT THE TIME IS RIPE! It will take place in secrecy but the word shall be leaked out that he has fled."

"The sky shall roll back like a consuming SCROLL. This force shall go within the very core of the human being. He will understand his offenses to his God. However, this warning will be of short duration and man shall continue upon his road to perdition for his probability of massive change has not come about ... Mankind's hearts are hardened so greatly that it is not likely that he will change, on the whole."

"There shall be a great settling in of a deadly quiet upon mankind following a massive darkness of spirit and a darkness of atmosphere. The very sounds of Mother Earth shall be heard as the wail of a birthing mother."

"As day follows night, shall this WARNING follow soon now ... As this comes into thy consciousness, move into thy places of safety, beware most specifically of the sunrise -- do not look into the sunrise or unto the sky or into the flash! Close your windows and you who have prepared, move within your cave-like bunkers and seal your windows. REMAIN INSIDE!! DO NOT VENTURE OUTSIDE YOUR DOOR -- DO NOT GO OUT ONCE CLOSED WITHIN FOR IF YOU HAVE PLANNED AND PREPARED THOSE ONES OF YOUR OWN WILL BE IN SHELTER ELSEWHERE AND YOUR HERDS AND FLOCKS WILL HAVE BEEN PLACED IN PROTECTION AS THE WARNING BEGINS. DO NOT GO OUTSIDE -- STAY WITHIN -- FOR IF YOU LEAVE IN THE MIDST FOR ANY REASON, YE SHALL NOT RETURN."

"In the midst of the blazing blast, prostrate yourselves as flat against the foundation of the floor or Earth and stretch out your extremities while protecting your eyes between your arms for the light will penetrate unto the darkest corners and the energy waves will impact the body while passing through most of the housing material. Some of the beams will most readily be directed through the Earth itself but you can shield yourselves. During the WARNING, do not struggle to bring your animals within your actual dwelling bunkers for this WARNING shall be as a warning to the human and the animals of those who remain of well spirit will be taken care of quite nicely. The WARNING might well come without pre-warning and if so, go within your houses, do not look up to the sky and shield your eyes from the flash! Close your windows! Draw your blinds! AND REMAIN INSIDE! DO NOT VENTURE OUTSIDE YOUR DOOR, OR YOU WILL NOT RETURN! GET FLAT ON THE FLOOR ON THE LOWEST LEVEL OF YOUR DWELLING AND WITHIN THE DARKEST PORTION, AND FLATTEN YOURSELF AGAINST THE FLOOR IN THE FLATTEST MANNER POSSIBLE."

"I FURTHER SUGGEST THAT WHILE YOU ARE PROSTRATE UPON THE FLOOR THAT YOU CONTINUALLY PRAY AND PETITION MERCY OF YOUR GOD, THE FATHER, FOR WE SHALL BE ALLOWED TO SHIELD THOSE OF YOU WHO ASK IN GOD's NAME FOR PROTECTION."

"Keep candles which are of quality in that you ask blessings upon your choices and actually mentally or verbally, sanctify them, have water set aside for thy needs -- within your dwelling place where it can be pulled forth for use without going without your dwelling. Have blankets, quilts or coverings for you will need them for protection first from the heat, and then from the frigid chill. And, of course, you will need food to survive for a period of some several days."

"As a sign unto you, the candles of those who have remained in this state of Grace shall not be extinguished, but the candles in the homes of those who have given themselves unto Satan shall not burn!!"

"This 'WARNING' will bring many back unto the Lighted Path for they shall be turned back from their road that leads into the void."

"The WARNING which will be sent upon many must be effective. And in the mercy of the Father, a great spectacle will then be placed in the sky for all to see. However, the agents of Hell will try to ... disprove the hand of the Father in this Miracle."

"On 'WARNING DAY' (W-Day), the Conspiracy will have pushed to the brink of holding the entire world hostage. God shall take over at that point and the entire beam network above your outer stratum shall be detonated. This will produce an intermeshing network of beam reactions which shall basically encapsulate the planet for some projected period of at least three days. What will strike you as humans, from that great distance, will be something quite like microwaves which will create the sensation of intense heat from all directions and inside to outside. There shall be resulting atmospheric upheaval and total confusion but you who are prepared and remain inside with your light shields will survive nicely. This is the WARNING that things will get nasty indeed from that time forward."

"The 'enemy' will regroup (for he also knows this is coming) and he will respond with war of an Earth scale but with Earth based beam systems and nuclear weaponry. The reason they will do this is again in an attempt to hold God's people hostage and/or annihilate you." *(Excerpt from 'Skeletons In The Closet', a Phoenix Journal, 1990)*

"Night becomes day, a great fright everywhere [Flash]
A WARNING fulfilled and a woman [Mother Mary of Fatima] seeks vengeance.
Great rumblings in Sicily, Dijon [in France], Rome. Dread.
Blood flows in the cities while a false god cringes [Antichrist]."
(Nostradamus, Unpublished Quatrain)

"The divine fire and the fire of hell will arrive and last during the DAYS OF DARKNESS indicated by all the saints. My luminous cross will appear in the sky. It will be the sign that the final events are close, and will remind all of My terrible passion, so that they will have time to reflect, for I shall not punish the world WITHOUT PREVIOUS ANNOUNCEMENT. All will have time to comprehend the significance of that cross in the sky, and everyone shall see it. All will know, even those who reject it ... "

"As soon as you perceive the disturbed signs of the very cold night: Go inside, shut and lock all doors and windows, pull down the shades, keep the doors and windows well covered, go and stay away from doors and windows. Do not look out, do not go outside for any reason, and do not talk to anyone outside ... Anyone who looks out or goes out will die immediately! The wrath of God is holy and He does not want us to see it."

"All will be black, and the only thing which will give light will be blessed wax candles; even these will not burn in the house of the godless scoffers. Once lit, nothing will put them out in the houses of the believers ... Be sure to keep a supply of blessed wax candles in your homes - also - Holy Water to be sprinkled freely around the house, especially at doors and windows. Bless yourself and others with it ... Keep on hand a sufficient supply of food, water and blankets ... do not count on any utilities."

"Take care of your animals by leaving enough food and water outside for them to last these days. God will preserve the property of the elect, including their animals. It is assumed that house pets be kept inside."

"Pray with outstretched arms, or prostrate on the floor, pleading for many souls to be saved." *(Anonymous European Holy Person, 1965, Excerpt from the Internet website: www.webcom.com/enddays/darkness.html)*

"The DAYS OF DARKNESS will come. Those who pray will be saved." *(Mother Mary to Casimierz Domanski, of Ohlau, Poland, March 4, 1986 in 'The Three Days Darkness' by Albert J. Herbert, 1996)*

"This catastrophe shall come upon the Earth like a flash of lightning at which moment the light of the morning sun shall be replaced by black DARKNESS. No one shall leave the house or lookout of a window from that moment on. The wicked shall behold my divine heart. There shall be great confusion because of this utter DARKNESS in which the entire Earth shall be enveloped and many, many shall die from fear and despair."

"Those who shall fight for my cause shall receive grace from my divine heart ... However, many shall burn in the open fields like withered grass. The godless shall be annihilated, so that afterwards the just shall be able to start afresh."

"On the day, as soon as complete DARKNESS has set in, no one shall leave the house or look out of the window. The DARKNESS shall last a day and a night, followed by another day and a night. But on the night following, the stars will shine again, and on the morning the sun will rise again, and it will be springtime!"

WHY THE END ?

"In the DAYS OF DARKNESS, my elect shall not sleep ... They shall pray incessantly ... Hell will believe itself to be in possession of the entire Earth, but I shall reclaim it." *(Padre Pio, February 7, 1950 in 'The Three Days Darkness' by Albert J. Herbert, 1996)*

"In the east ... a large sun as red as blood against the sky a great DARKNESS rose slowly like mist. It was black as night. It rose higher and higher into the atmosphere ... When the DARKNESS reached the sun it began to cover it, up to halfway slowly and then faster and faster, and the last bit quite quickly."

" ... The deep DARKNESS came down quickly to the Earth and completely enveloped it. The DARKNESS was so profound that one could see nothing ... as though the end of the world had come ... "

"But after the DARKNESS the Earth remained a waste. The beautiful warm sun rose to shine upon the Earth and all living things upon it, but only here and there was any human being still alive." *(Julka of Yugoslavia in 'The Three Days Darkness' by Albert J. Herbert, 1996)*

"There will come a brief DARKNESS over the land when all souls will be laid bare before me. You will see how your lives would be judged before Me, but you will be given a short time to change your lives." *(Jesus' Message to John Leary, April 7, 1998)*

"There will come a sign, which everyone in the world, in an interior way, will experience ... and they will know this is from God, and they will see themselves as they really are in the sight of God." *(The Blessed Virgin Mary to Christina Gallagher, March 30, 1988)*

"A little more about the great distress ... A strong warm wind will come from the south ... It will seize upon the whole globe and cause dreadful storms. After this about ten claps of thunder at once will strike the Earth with such force that it will shudder throughout. This is a sign that the great tribulation and the black DARKNESS are beginning. These will last THREE DAYS AND THREE

NIGHTS."

" ... People should go into their houses, close them up well, darken the windows, bless themselves and the house with holy water, and light blessed candles. Outside such dreadful things will be happening, that those who ventured to look will die. All the devils will be let loose on Earth, so that they can destroy their prey themselves."

"The guardian angels will watch over the people who are spared. The buildings which ought to be preserved will be raised and protected by God's power in the moment of the most dreadful horror ... there will be not many priests left." *(Julka of Yugoslavia in 'The Three Days Darkness' by Albert J. Herbert, 1996)*

"The demons will howl upon the Earth and call many, in order to destroy them. They will imitate the voices of relations and acquaintances, who have not reached a safer place. Once the horror commences, do not open your door to anyone at all!"

"In many places several people will gather together from fear. From this same group, some will perish, others remain alive. For this day and moment, and for that DARKNESS, many will have prepared the blessed candles, but they will not burn, if the people have not lived in accordance with my commandments; others will even be unable to light them for fear. But for those who believe, although they have but a stub of the blessed candle, it will burn for these THREE DAYS AND NIGHTS without going out. Some people will fall into a deep sleep ... so as not to see what is happening on the Earth. All the buildings on Earth will collapse, and only here and there will a simple, modest little house remain, in which the light of the candle will glimmer. In many places, the heaps of corpses will be so great, that no one will be able to make a passage through, on account of these bodies, there will not be anyone to bury them." *(Message from Christ in 'The Three Days Darkness' by Albert J. Herbert, 1996)*

" ... The DARKNESS settles in with a weight that shall be unbearable for many people ... so black that a man shall not be able to see his hand before his face ... not only shall there be physical dangers, but all the hordes of demons that have been held in check shall be released ... they shall sweep upon mankind as an unholy swarm of locusts and shall seek to devour all whom they encounter." *(Brother B, May 19, 1983 in 'The Three Days Darkness' by Albert J. Herbert, 1996)*

" ... Great dense clouds seemed to be rolling into place in front of the sun. These clouds were so black that they shut off all light totally ... and in addition we could feel it. Very heavy and oppressive! ... There was a lot of noise during this time of DARKNESS ... After an uncertain length of time the noise seemed to die down and upon looking out the window ... it was growing lighter outside." *(Brother B, December 20, 1983 in 'The Three Days Darkness' by Albert J. Herbert, 1996)*

"An intense DARKNESS will come over the Earth, for a duration of THREE DAYS AND THREE NIGHTS. Nothing will be visible and the air will be pestilential. Artificial light will be impossible. The faithful should remain in their homes, pray the rosary and beg God's mercy. All the enemies of the church, open and unknown, will perish over the whole Earth in this universal DARKNESS with the exception of some who will be converted." *(Amparo Cuevas, stigmatist of Spain, December 18, 1981 in 'The Three Days Darkness' by Albert J. Herbert, 1996)*

"A great DARKNESS will come upon the world. The heavens will shake. The only light will come through the Son of God and Man." *(Jesus' message to Christina Gallagher in 'The Coming Chastisement' by Brother Craig Driscoll, 1995)*

"The anger of God is at hand and the world will be struck by great calamity ... The world will be convulsed in a new and terrible war! Deadly armies will destroy nations, peoples, and all the things they love. In this profane struggle, much that has been made by the hand of man will be destroyed. The dictators of the Earth - truly infernal monsters - will raze the churches with their sacred food. Clouds bright with fire will suddenly appear across the sky and a storm of fire will beat down on all the world. This terrible scourge, never before seen in human history, will last for SEVENTY-TWO HOURS. The recusant will be reduced to powder, and many will be lost in the obstinacy of their sins. Then the power of light will be seen above the power of darkness." *(Sister Elena Aiello, 1959)*

"The confusion will be so general that men will not be able to think aright, as if God had withheld His Providence from mankind, and that, during the worst crisis, the best that can be done would be to remain where God has placed us, and persevere in fervent prayers ... At that time there will be such a terrible crisis that people will believe that the end of the world has come ... The very elements will be convulsed. It will be like a little general Judgement." *(Father Nectou, 18th Century)*

"Do not be afraid about the THREE DAYS OF DARKNESS that will come upon the Earth. Those who live my messages and an interior life of prayer will be advised by an interior voice a week or three days before it happens." *(Our Lady to Brother L. at Medjugorje, August 15, 1987 in 'Signs, Wonders and Response' by Albert J. Herbert, 1996)*

"The lacerated coastlines meant inundated areas which will take place before the THREE DAY DARKNESS." *(Anonymous Scientist, August 26, 1986 in 'The Three Days Darkness' by Albert J. Herbert, 1986)*

"After the THREE DAYS OF CHASTISEMENT are over, there will be no ungodly persons left, the godless will be annihilated. Seventy-five percent of humanity will be destroyed, more men than women. Everyone left on Earth will believe in God with all their hearts. The devastation will be astonishingly great, but the Earth will be purified ... When all seems lost, then in a twinkling, all will be saved, the sun will shine again and it will be as springtime, all fair and beautiful. The Holy Angels will descend from heaven and spread the spirit of peace over the Earth and the just will be able to start life anew."

WHY THE END ?

"Some nations will disappear entirely, and the face of the Earth will be changed. There will be no more big business, huge factories and assembly lines which will sap men's souls and moralities. People will return to the land."

"Our Holy Church will rise again, and religious communities will flower. A feeling of immeasurable gratitude will possess the hearts of those who survive this ordeal ... Then will follow the era of peace as promised by the Blessed Virgin at Fatima." *(Excerpt from the Internet website: www.webcom.com)*

"When the moment of the last crisis has come, there will be nothing to do but to stay where God has placed us, lock ourselves indoors and pray until the wrath of Divine Justice has passed." *(Father Nectou, 18th Century)*

"It will become dark on one day during the war. Then a huge thunderstorm will appear with bolts of lightning and thunder and an earthquake will move the Earth. Do not go out of the house. No lights will burn except for candle lights. The stream of people stops. Whoever inhales the dust will develop cramps and die. Do not open the windows. Hang the windows with black paper on the glass. All open water will become poisonous, and all open food which has not been canned. Also all foods in glass will not make it."

"Outside the dust moves. Many people will die. After SEVENTY-TWO HOURS everything will be over. But I will say to you again, do not go outside, do not look out of the window. Let the candles burn, keep watch, and pray. Overnight more people will die than in the combined two world wars."

"Thereafter the Pope will return and the first great 'Te Deum' will be sung in the Dome in Cologne [Germany]."

"The year 1999 will bring destruction, followed by peace. A DARKNESS of SEVENTY-TWO HOURS will precede peace. The time of the year may be autumn, for there will be snow on the mountains, but not yet in the lowlands. The sign of the cross will appear in the heavens. The war will end as quickly as it began, and a natural phenomenon will end it." *(Alois Irlmaier, 19th Century)*

"A solar flare will hit Earth in ... 1999 ... will cause a seering (purging) of the planet and we will lose many trees ... it is the ascension process of the planet

... will cause THREE DAYS OF DARKNESS ... a Judgement." *(Victoria Angelis on the Mike Jarmus Radio Show, 1997)*

"There will be a time when there will be DARKNESS or so much burning light as to afflict everyone and specifically the ones who take no care to ... protect selves. They will be burned, blinded and there will be no electric power and indeed, the result will be a very dark kingdom ... There will be nothing to relieve the pain and suffering and no one to attend the afflicted." *(Excerpt from 'Rise of the AntiChrist', Volume 2, a Phoenix Journal, 1998)*

"In this CHASTISEMENT ... billions will be lost. Many lives will be lost." *(Blessed Virgin Mary to Veronica Lueken, October 6, 1973)*

"You ... bring upon yourself a punishment far greater than ever has been seen upon Earth and never shall be seen again, for when you go through this CHASTISEMENT, there will be few creatures left upon the Earth." *(Blessed Virgin Mary to Veronica Lueken, April 13, 1974)*

"During a DARKNESS LASTING THREE DAYS, the people given to evil ways will perish so that only one fourth of humanity will survive. The clergy, too, will be greatly reduced in number, as most of them will die in the defense of the faith or of their country." *(Sister Marie de Jesus Crucifice of Pau, France, 1878)*

"There shall be a THREE DAYS DARKNESS, during which the atmosphere will be infected by innumerable devils, who shall cause the deaths of large multitudes of unbelievers and wicked men. Supernatural prodigies shall appear in the heavens. There is to be a short but furious war, during which the enemies of religion and of mankind shall be universally destroyed. A general pacification of the world, and the universal triumph of the Church are to follow." *(Sister Palma Maria d'Oria, 19th Century)*

WHY THE END ?

" ... The sun will be darkened and faith alone will give light." *(Melanie Mathieu of La Salette in 'The Three Days Darkness' by Albert J. Herbert, 1996)*

"The DARKNESS that is coming is going to be happening during the daytime when people are going to be confused at the hour in which it takes place ... so thick and so immense that you could reach out and almost touch this darkness that was there."

" ... Thunder ... something that no one has ever heard ... fire would come down from the sky ... people were hiding behind things such as trees and houses ... but the one thing I heard ... God saying that there was no place for them to hide ... "

"And there was nothing but desolation. The bodies that were hit were still lying in the same places they were hiding in. There was nothing that was left." *(S.F., American Mother, 1983 in 'The Three Days Darkness' by Albert J. Herbert, 1996)*

"There will come THREE DAYS OF CONTINUED DARKNESS."

"The blessed candles of wax alone will give light during the horrid darkness. One candle will last for three days. But in the houses of the godless they will not give light. During those THREE DAYS the demons will appear in abominable and horrible forms; they will make the air resound with shocking blasphemies."

"The Lightning will penetrate the homes, but will not extinguish the light of the blessed candles! Neither wind nor storm nor earthquakes will extinguish it. Red clouds like blood will pass in the sky, the crash of thunder will make the Earth tremble; lightning will flash through the streets at an unusual time of the year; the Earth will tremble to its foundations; the ocean will cast its foaming waves over the land; the Earth will be changed into an immense cemetery; the corpses of the wicked and the just will cover the face of the Earth."

"The famine that will follow will be great. All vegetation will be destroyed as well as three fourths of the human race. The crisis will come all of a sudden and the CHASTISEMENT will be worldwide." *(Marie Julie Jehanney of La Fraudais, France, 1891)*

"And on the fifth day, at the sixth hour, there shall be great DARKNESS over the world until evening, and the stars shall be turned away from their ministry. In that day all nations shall hate the world and despise the life of this world. These are the signs of the fifth day." *(The Apocalypse of Thomas)*

"The death of the impentinent persecutors of the Church will take place during the THREE DAYS OF DARKNESS. He who outlives the DARKNESS and the fear of these days will think that he is alone on Earth because the whole world will be covered with corpses." *(St. Gaspari del Bufalo, 19th Century)*

"There shall come upon the whole Earth an intense DARKNESS lasting THREE DAYS AND NIGHTS. Nothing will be visible and the air will be laden with pestilence, which will claim mainly but not only the enemies of religion. During these THREE DAYS, artificial light will be impossible. Only sacred candles can be lighted and will afford light. During this alarm, the faithful should stay in their houses and recite the rosary and give misericords to God. He who out of curiosity opens his window to look out or leave his house will fall dead on the spot."

"On this terrible occasion so many of these wicked men, enemies of His Church, and of their God, shall be killed by this divine scourge, that their corpses around Rome will be as numerous as the fishes, which a recent inundation of the Tiber had carried into the city. All the enemies of the Church, secret as well as known, will perish over the whole Earth during that universal DARKNESS, with the exception of some few, whom God will soon after convert. The air will be infested by demons, who will appear under all sorts of hideous forms."

"After the THREE DAYS DARKNESS, Saints Peter and Paul, having come down from heaven, will preach throughout the world and designate a new Pope." *(Anna Maria Taigi, 1769-1857)*

"By this time mankind will be stricken with terror. Birds will be like reptiles and will not use their wings. Animals of the ground, in fear and alarm, will raise such a clamor that it will make human hearts tremble. Men will flee into their abodes in order not to see the weird occurrence. Finally, complete

WHY THE END ?

DARKNESS will set in and last for THREE DAYS AND THREE NIGHTS."

"During this time, men, deprived of the power of light, will fall into a slumber-like sleep from which many will not awaken, especially those who have no spark of spiritual life. When the sun will again rise and emerge, Earth will be covered with a blanket of ashes like snow in winter, except that the ashes will have the color of sulfur. Damp fog will ascend from the ground, illuminated by igneous gases."

"Of mankind there will be more dead than there have been casualties in all wars. In the abodes of the children of light, the Book of Revelations will be read, and in the palaces of the Church they will await the arrival of the great COMET. On the seventh day after the return of light, Earth will have absorbed the ashes and formed such a fertility as has not been experienced ever before ... The survivors will proclaim ... peace and will institute the millennium, announced by the MESSIAH in the light of true brotherly and sisterly love for the glory of the Creator and for the blessedness of all mankind." *(Johann Friede, 1204-1257)*

"I have decided to show my power by THREE DAYS AND THREE NIGHTS OF DARKNESS. Note very clearly these things which are very necessary for the souls ... mankind's sins increase day after day. If there is not a strong measure, the gentle lambs will be caught by the wolves." *(God to Theresa, S. Vietnam, 1977 in 'Signs, Wonders and Response' by Albert J. Herbert, 1996)*

"The celestial bodies that are always visible to the eye,
Shall be DARKENED for these reasons,
The body with the forehead, sense and head invisible [lack of self-control],
Diminishing the sacred prayers [lack of spirituality]." *(Nostradamus, Century IV Quatrain 25)*

"A doomsday for the nations is a mild expression of My divine wrath which is about to be poured out upon the Earth for its purification." *(Message to L.G.A., March 17, 1986)*

"I will let you have a foretaste of the eternal DARKNESS soon for THREE DAYS. Many, if not most of the people will perish during that time of DARKNESS. But those who possess the eternal light ... will remain illuminated within." *(L.G.A., October 13, 1986)*

"Suddenly Allah will DARKEN the whole world with smoke; the night will last 72 hours or longer. The sun will rise in the west, instead of the east, and it will travel only one-third of its course before setting again. On the next day, the sun and moon will resume their normal course."

"This will be the last opportunity to repent to ALLAH, for then he will close the door of mercy. The Earth will quake and Mt.Safa near Mecca will split open ... Then ALLAH will hold the DAY OF JUDGEMENT." *(The Quran)*

"I will plunge the Earth into DARKNESS for THREE DAYS AND NIGHTS and ... when the sun rises after those days and nights, the purified Earth shall shine ... my remnant ... will experience it." *(Message to L.G.A., February 23, 1986 in 'The Three Days Darkness' by Albert J. Herbert, 1996)*

"The passing of the old world will see this planet in DARKNESS for THREE DAYS AND THREE NIGHTS, accompanied by a violent shaking." *(C.H. Kramer, 1946)*

"Bahanna's intrusion into the Hopi way of life ... Our prophecy foretells that the third event will be the decisive one."

"This third event will depend on the Red symbol which will take command, setting the four forces of nature (Meha) in motion for the benefit of the sun. When he sets these forces in motion the whole world will shake and turn red and turn against the people who are hindering the Hopi way of life. To all these people Purification Day will come ... He will come unmercifully. His people will cover the Earth like red ants. We must not go outside to watch. We must stay in our houses. He will come and gather the wicked people who are hindering the red people who were here first." *(Native American Hopi Prophecy)*

<u>WHY THE END ?</u>

"The DAYS OF DARKNESS about which I have told you many times are approaching." *(Mother Mary to Casimierz Domanski, November 1, 1985 in 'The Three Days Darkness' by Albert J. Herbert, 1996)*

"There are signs ... which show a leading up, through even a climactic period of increasing trials and tribulations and disasters of all types, to the peak finale of the THREE DAYS DARKNESS. These signs are both natural and human if you choose to do it that way -- but also are spiritual and supernatural in observation according to your level of knowledge." *(Hatonn, June 18, 1992)*

"The THREE DAYS OF DARKNESS between April and July 1999." *(Victoria Angelis on the Mike Jarmus Radio Show, 1998)*

"THREE DAYS OF DARKNESS ... from 3rd to 9th month of 1999 ... " *(Brian Kirkwood in 'Survival Guide to Earth Changes', 1994)*

=====================*===========*===========*

THE PHOTON BELT

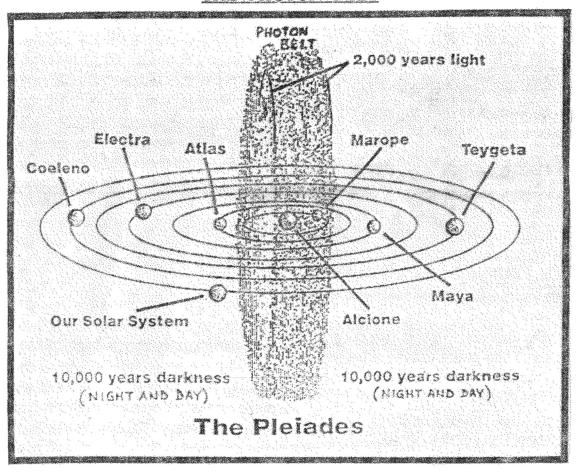

The Pleiades

THE PHOTON BELT

"You are in the Photon Belt - you just can't see the rays. However, it will intensify tremendously and you are going to have the unlucky experience of probably having the Radiation Belt around your planet ignited. This is going to be a very bright day for about three full days ... I still recommend that you have the darkest ... goggles." *(Hatonn, October 19, 1995)*

"It is a fact that ... Jesus Christ was birthed in late summer of 8 B.C. ... MSNBC made a statement [on December 24, 1997] ... 'Christ born about 7 B.C.'. So let us compromise ... at 7-1/2 years before what is now called ... the Common Era."

"Now turn your attention to the prophecies of this time ... where the projections are a period of 7-1/2 years ... plus the 3 -1/2 years of tribulation and transition into this end expected ... you have to realize that your counting, as in year 2000, does not leave you time for 'getting ready' for it has already transpired ... When you come to year 2000 in your counting - you will be into year 2011 and that is when the explosion of photons are due to recycle upon you." *(Hatonn, December 25, 1997)*

"Photon belt will mark the end of your present civilization as you know it and negative hierarchical government control ... " *(Excerpt from 'You Are Becoming A Galactic Human' by Virginia Essene and Sheldon Nidle, 1994)*

"It takes our sun 24,000 years to complete an orbit of 10,000 years of 'darkness' (day/night) then 2,000 years of light then 10,000 darkness, etc. ... Nostradamus in his quatrain about the end of the world as you know it in 1999, 'And it will rain no more, but in 40 years, it will be normal'; ... signs: strange colors in the sky ... a perception of less light even though it be mid-summer ... animals in early hibernation ... warm winters ... tinnitus."

"If sun enters first, there will be immediate darkness. This is going to last about 120 hours and then it will move into continuous light because you will be refocusing magnetically and this pulls you more into the orbiting system of

WHY THE END ?

Pleiades where you're going to have at least two suns ... at any given time for a long period of time you will be experiencing a form of light or sunlight throughout your 24 hours. You won't be having darkness because of the balance of the rays from either direction."

"The interaction between the solar radiation and the Photon Belt will make the sky look as if it is full of falling stars and all the molecules will become excited and atomic structures will change and all things will become luminescent. You will all glow in the dark ... Then there will be constant light."

"You are literally being moved in the galaxy ... where you will ... get light from two suns ... It is a place created for the inhabitants who make the transition and this will probably take place during the period of the null zone when everyone is responding to the correct vibration frequency so that it is easier to get you off your planet and replaced onto the new and more beautifully created place ['I go to prepare a place for you', John 14:2, Bible] where you will have more balance and harmony to continue."

"The ones on a higher level of understanding and knowing will probably go at least to the 5th dimension but you will set up a society in truth in that dimension ... without the evil counterpart to pull you down."

" ... Refer to the Revelation ... it says 'There will be no sun, moon or stars' ... there's not going to be any electricity. The batteries will simply not work ... have your own generator run by a separate fuel system than ... your big electric grid because many things are going to be happening at the same time as this shock hits."

"Everything will be jolted tremendously and therefore, you are going to have earthquakes and other geographic types of incidences occurring which will also probably interrupt your flow of lifeline necessities."

"Don't worry about new planets in your solar system ... you are being shifted ... moving on into a higher level of solar orbiting." *(Hatonn, April 25, 1992)*

"The nebula of the greater Bear [Golden Nebula/Photon Belt] will arrive in the vicinity of Earth ... and will fill the space of five hundred suns at the horizon. It will more and more cover up the light of the sun until the days will be like nights at full moon. The illumination will not come from the moon, but from Orion, which constellation, by the light of Jupiter, will send forth its rays on the Greater Bear and will dissolve its nebula with the force of light ... Finally, complete darkness will set in and last for three days and three nights." *(Johann Friede, 1204-1257)*

"Near Rion [Orion] and towards Blanche-laine [Milky Way]
Aries, Taurus, Cancer, Leo, Virgo,
Mars, Jupiter, the Sun shall burn a great plain [Photon Belt entrance with the appearance of the sky on fire]
Woods and cities, letters hidden in a wax candle [no electricity - can only read by candlelight]." *(Nostradamus, Century VI Quatrain 35)*

"Day 1: Enter Photon Belt 'null zone' - alters body of all living things/ electric devices do not work/total darkness.
Day 2: Atmosphere compressed/bloating feeling/sun cools down/climate cools.
Day 3-4: Atmosphere dimly lit like dawn/photon energy devices operable/ stars reappear in sky.
Day 5-6: Every living thing invigorated/incredible psychic abilities/elder brothers and sister-counselors and guides will appear." *(Excerpt from 'You Are Becoming A Galactic Human' by Virginia Essene and Sheldon Nidle, 1994)*

A toroid shaped photon (light) band/zone was discovered in 1961 by astronomers using satellite instrumentation, described as an electromagnetic cloud-like mass or 'Golden Nebula', now called a Monasic Ring or the 'Photon Belt'. This belt of light is composed of ultra-high energy light particle/frequency/ waves called photons. A photon is the result of the collision/merging of an anti-electron (positron) and electron.

Our solar system orbits around the central sun, Alcione, which is 500 light years away and located in the Photon Belt continuously. It takes our solar system 24,000 years to make one complete cycle around Alcione. Our solar system will soon enter the photon belt for 2,000 years [The Golden Age].

     Information Pioneers Publisher

WHY THE END ?

This belt of light expands and contracts thus giving two possible scenarios. Since Earth revolves around the Sun it will be alternately ahead of the Sun and at times behind, so either could enter the Photon Belt first. If Earth enters first, it could compress and ignite the Van Allen radiation belt that is above Earth for 3-4 days (120 hours) which will appear as the sky on fire (a blinding flash), but it is a cold light (no heat). This would be followed by darkness. It takes 5-6 days to complete the entrance into this 'null zone' including approximately three days of total darkness due to the compression of solar and stellar light which will blot out the sun and stars. This is described in the Book of Revelations: when the sun and moon and stars will fail to give their light. The result will be an energy vacuum - cancellation of the electromagnetic field of Earth and the electric utilities will not work.

As we have been feeling the fringes of these photons since 1962, the magnetic field of the Earth has been decreasing - now near zero - causing the strange migration patterns of animals and insects and strange human behaviors. As the solar system moves closer into it, all molecules become more and more excited and many people will not know how to deal with it - they will run around like crazy. As we approach the null zone, the increased pressure on the Earth's atmosphere will cause increased pressure of the surface leading to increased seismic and volcanic activity and weather changes. The opening of the ozone hole signaled the approaching Photon Belt. The Photon Belt is also affecting the sun - resulting in massive solar flares.

The Photon Belt contains high levels of gamma rays and other particles similar to X-rays which are killing the frogs and causing the quick sunburns people are experiencing from the invisible penetrating rays and not because of ozone depletion as the news media constantly claims. The rays will cause carcinomas and blindness since most people have a deteriorating body from malnutrition (mineral deficiency) and low frequency development (negative attitudes). Warm ocean waters signal its approach along with the melting of the polar ice caps with increased volcanic activity under them. By year 2011 we will be in the peak of it. Before we are completely into the Photon Belt, the Earth will cleanse itself of the contamination that humanity has heaped upon it. The purpose of the Photon Belt is to raise the consciousness of star systems,

                                       Information Pioneers Publisher

and its inhabitants.

Signs of entering this period will be strange lighting and colors; with less light even in mid-summer (a gradual darkening). Animals will hibernate early. When we enter, all molecules will become excited, it will feel like a jolt or shock from a light socket and you will become luminescent or semi-etheric. This means the physical body will be able to rejuvenate itself and be virtually ageless.

"Now I am going to tell you a mystery. Not all of us shall fall asleep, but all of us are to be changed - in an instant, in the twinkling of an eye, at the sound of the last trumpet. The trumpet will sound and the dead will be raised incorruptible, and we shall be changed." *(1 Corinthians 15:51-52, Bible)*

" ... Those present ... in that time will be changed in a moment, in the twinkling of an eye. Not that you would drop the physical body here, but suddenly you will understand that physical body and the light body, and transmute that deep, denser material into light ... So will you then be more alive than ever has been before." *(Paul Solomon, June 15, 1973)*

During the entrance into the 'null zone', you will need food and water for at least a week (store food that needs little or no cooking, such as dehydrated or freeze dried foods) and an alternative source to cook food such as propane/ butane, gel alcohol, kerosene or candles as electricity will not be available. You must stay indoors during this time, or face the intense X-ray like photons. Various people suggest covering windows with foil or emergency blankets to prevent the photons from entering which can cause blindness. Portable Generators will not work as electricity will be cancelled out by the photon/null zone, but they will be back on line quicker than the electric grid which will probably be disrupted and jolted due to earthquakes and other Earth Changes. You should have a wind-up clock or watch, kept wound, and a log to mark off when day and night have passed.

After complete entrance into the Photon Belt, gradually the day/night cycle will end. This is because the Alcione system has other suns which will shine on Earth, resulting in daylight 24 hours a day. Space travel will be easy through this band of photons as it will be used to power ships at the speed of light. The altered atmosphere will result in no rain for 40 years.

"For forty years the rainbow will not appear.
For forty years it will be seen every day:
The parched Earth will wax more dry,
And great floods will accompany its appearance." *(Nostradamus, Century II Quatrain 17)*

"The night shall be no more. They will need no light from lamps or the sun ... " *(Revelation 22:5, Bible)*

"Your entire solar system is now coming into the Great Initiation ... heading directly for the Super-Sun [Alcione] which governs your galaxy ... " *(Sanat Kumara in 'The Wisdom of the Rays', Volume 1, 1997)*

"After the turning of the Earth, there will be two suns. This will become a binary sun system ... The atmosphere will change in components. The solar system will be different. A new sun will be added ... " *(Excerpt from 'Mary's Message to the World' by Annie Kirkwood, 1991)*

"The hidden sun eclipsed by Mercury
Will be placed only second in the heavens.
Hermes will be made the food of Vulcan,
The Sun will be seen pure, shining and golden." *(Nostradamus, Century IV Quatrain 29)*

Earth's previous passage into the Photon Belt:

"And there was a thick darkness in all the land of Egypt for three days. They saw not one another, neither rose from his place for three days." *(Exodus 10:22, Bible)*

"A threefold day and threefold night concluded a world age." *(Excerpt from the 'Anugita', Ancient Iranian document.)*

Earth's previous all light cycle:

"There shall be one continuous day ... not day and night, for in the evening time there shall be light." *(Zechariah 14:7, Bible)*

" ... And night shines as the day." *(Psalm 139:12, Bible)*

The rotation of Earth will diminish and with reduced solar radiation the climate will cool - resulting in a the growth of ice caps down to the 40th degree latitude, beginning an ice age.

=====================*===========*==========*

WHY THE END ?

FALSE SECOND COMING

" ... There were FALSE prophets among the people, even as there shall be among you lying teachers who shall bring in sects of perdition and deny the Lord ... bringing upon themselves swift destruction." *(2 Peter 2:1, Bible)*

"There will come two, then, who appear as saviors. This, then, will be the difficulty, to distinguish who is the world savior." *(Paul Solomon, September 16, 1991)*

" ... Believe not every spirit ... because many FALSE prophets are gone out into this world." *(1 John 4:1, Bible)*

"Beware of FALSE prophets who come to you in sheep's clothing, but inwardly they are ravening wolves." *(Matthew 7:15, Bible)*

"Wherefore, by their fruit ye shall know them." *(Matthew 7:20, Bible)*

"Many will come in my name saying, 'I am he; and The time is at hand'; Do not follow them. Neither must you be perturbed when you hear of wars and insurrections. These things are bound to happen first, but the end does not follow immediately." *(Luke 21:8-9, Bible)*

"And then if any man shall say to you, lo, here is Christ, or, lo, he is there, believe him not. For FALSE Christs and FALSE prophets shall show signs and wonders, to scducc if it were possible even the elect." *(Mark 13:21-27 & Matthew 24:23-26, Bible)*

"They will tell you he is to be found in this place or that. Do not go running about excitedly." *(Luke 17:22-23, Bible)*

"Many FALSE prophets will rise up and do great wonders, so that if it were possible also even the wise and knowing would be misled ... Therefore when they shall say 'He is in the desert' man shall not go out and 'Behold he is in the chamber', they shall not believe ... " *(Excerpt from 'Butterflies, Mind Control-The Razor's Edge', a Phoenix Journal, 1994)*

"Be on your guard. Let no one mislead you. Any number will come attempting to impersonate me. I am he, they will proclaim, and will lead many astray." *(Mark 13:5-6, Bible)*

"Many will come attempting to impersonate me. 'I am the Messiah!' They will claim and they will deceive many. You will hear of wars and rumors of wars. Do not be alarmed. Such things are bound to happen, but that is not yet the end ... Many will falter then, betraying and hating one another. FALSE prophets will arise in great numbers to mislead many." *(Matthew 24:5-6, Bible)*

"But do not trust any and every spirit ... test the spirits, to see whether they are from God, for there are many prophets FALSELY inspired." *(John 4:1-2, Bible)*

"Project Blue Beam ... deals with the gigantic space show: three-dimensional optical holograms and sounds, laser projections of multiple images in different parts of the world, each area receiving a different image, according to its predetermined national religious faith. This new 'god' image will talk in all languages ... ELF (Extra Low Frequency), VLF (Very Low Frequency) and LF (Low Frequency) waves will reach the people of the Earth through the insides of their brains, making each person believe God is speaking to him from within his own soul. Such rays, from satellite, are fed from the memory of computers ... These rays will then interlace and interweave with the natural thinking processes to form what we call 'artificial talk'." *(Serge Monast in the 'USA Patriot' magazine, January 1995)*

"If you see larger than life image in the sky or panoramic scene depicting Christ's return together with a huge wide blue beam that people are being herded into (in fields and parking lots) run in the other direction." *(Hatonn)*

"And deceiveth them that dwell on the Earth by the means of these miracles which he had power to do in the sight of the beast." *(Revelation 13:14, Bible)*

"Voices will be heard in the air, and men will strike their heads against the wall." *(Melanie Calvat, 1831-1940)*

" ... Prophecies of end days ... many FALSE Immanuels and FALSE Prophets will rise up ... Soon after the grief of that time, the sun and moon will no longer radiate, and the stars will fall from heaven and the powers of the heavens will become shaky. There will then appear a sign in the sky. And then all the generations on Earth will cry and will see the Celestial Sons coming in the clouds of the sky ... " *(Excerpt from 'And They Called His Name Immanuel', A Phoenix Journal, 1989)*

"My Son shall return the way he left, as He ascended into the Heavens. He will come down, return, descend from the Heavens with the armies of Heaven behind Him. Accept none who will pass themselves off to you as the Christ, the living God! Reject those creatures of hell in human form. Reject them though they may come to you with great powers of Satan." *(Blessed Virgin Mary to Veronica Lueken, July 14, 1979)*

WHY THE END ?

 Information Pioneers Publisher

THE ECLIPSE

"When the ECLIPSE of the sun then will be
The divine omen will be seen in the plain daylight
Quite otherwise will one interpret it
High price unguarded, none will have provided for it." *(Nostradamus, Century III Quatrain 34)*

" ... The coming of the holy ghost [Christ] ... driving away the abomination of Antichrist ... And before this shall proceed a solar ECLIPSE, the most dark and obscure that was since the creation of the world ... " *(Nostradamus, 'The Epistle to Henry II', 1555)*

Eclipses In Year 1999 (4):
•*January 31 (penumbral lunar) - Africa, Asia, Australia.*
•*February 16 (annular solar, 39 seconds) - Indian Ocean, Australia.*
•*July 28 (partial lunar, 40%) - Asia, Australia, Americas.*
•*August 11 (total solar, 2 minutes 23 seconds) - Europe, Mid East, India.*

Eclipses In Year 2000 (6):
•*January 21 (total lunar, 1 hour, 18 minutes) - Americas, Africa, Europe.*
•*February 5 (partial solar, 58%) - Antarctica.*
•*July 1 (partial solar, 47%) - extreme South Pacific, Patagonia.*
•*July 16 (total lunar, 1 hour 47 minutes) - Asia, Australia, Pacific Ocean.*
•*July 31 (partial solar, 60%) - Siberia, North Pole, Alaska, N. Canada, Greenland.*
•*December 25 (partial solar, 72%) - North America.*

Eclipses In Year 2001 (5):
•*January 9 (total lunar, 1 hour 2 minutes) - Africa, Europe, Asia.*
•*June 21 (total solar, 4 minutes 56 seconds) - S. Atlantic, Southern Africa, Madagascar.*
•*July 5 (partial lunar, 50%) - E. Africa, Asia, Australia.*

231

•*December 14 (annular solar, 3 minutes 53 seconds) - Pacific Ocean, Costa Rica.*
•*December 30 (penumbral lunar) - Asia, Australia, Americas.*

Eclipses In Year 2002 (5):
•*May 26 (penumbral lunar) - Asia, Australia, Americas.*
•*June 10 (annular solar, 22 seconds) - Pacific Ocean.*
•*June 24 (penumbral lunar) - Africa, Asia, Europe.*
•*November 20 (penumbral lunar) - Americas, Europe, Africa, Asia.*
•*December 4 (total solar, 2 minutes 3 seconds) - Southern Africa, Indian Ocean, Australia.*

Eclipses In Year 2003 (4):
•*May 16 (total lunar, 52 minutes) - Americas, East & West Africa.*
•*May 31 (annular solar, 3 minutes 34 seconds) - Iceland, Greenland.*
•*November 9 (total lunar, 23 minutes) - Americas, Africa, Europe.*
•*November 23 (total solar, 1 minute 57 seconds) - Antarctica.*

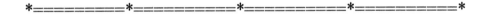

WHY THE END ?

THE SECOND COMING

"What will be the sign of your COMING and the end of the world? In reply Jesus said to them: ... Let no one mislead you. Many will come attempting to impersonate me ... and they will deceive many. You will hear of wars and rumors of wars. Do not be alarmed. Such things are bound to happen, but that is not yet the end. Nation will rise against nation, one kingdom against another. There will be famine and pestilence and earthquakes in many places. These are the early stages of the birth pangs ... False prophets will rise in great numbers to mislead many. Because of the increase in evil, the love of most will grow cold. The man who holds out to the end, however, is the one who will see salvation. This good news of the kingdom will be proclaimed throughout the world as a witness to all the nations. Only after that will the end come." *(Matthew 24:3-14, Bible)*

"But in those days, after that tribulation, the sun shall be darkened and the moon shall not give her light and the stars of heaven shall fall and the powers that are in heaven shall be shaken. And then shall they see the SON OF MAN coming in the clouds with great power and glory. Learn a lesson from the fig tree. Once the sap of its branches runs high and it begins to sprout leaves, you know that summer is near. In the same way, when you see these things happening, you will know that HE is near, even at the door." *(Mark 13:24-29, Bible)*

"You will behold CHRIST IN THE AIR -- NOT ON THE AIR as some prominent TV evangelists have suggested. Owning a television set is not a prerequisite to viewing this coming 'in power and great glory' ... every part of the world shall see the COMING and know of its presence - even unto the darkest corner of Africa or the tribes of the Amazon - to the native in the regions of the poles. They have not television and yet THEY WILL SEE AND KNOW!" *(Excerpt from 'I And My Father Are One', a Phoenix Journal, 1991)*

" ... HE IS COMING with the clouds and every eye will see Him." *(Revelation 1:7, Bible)*

WHY THE END ?

"He that hath ears to hear, let him hear that music of the COMING OF THE LORD ... and art thou ready to give account of what thou hast done with thine opportunity in the Earth ... for there must come an answering." *(Edgar Cayce, 1877-1945)*

"I heard the most beautiful music ... things are going to happen up in the air that have never been experienced or seen by people before - war, turmoil and strife, Armageddon - war and rumors of wars; that they will be stopped by the forces of the heavens." *(Edgar Cayce, 1877-1945)*

"The Day of the Great 'Telling' that has been prophesied ... becomes imminent when your affairs become more chaotic ... There shall shortly come ... a bow stretched across the heavens such as Earth-man has never seen in all his memory, for the translation of a planet comes but once from third to fourth translation ... The bow across the sky shall be magnificent in color and will emanate musical sounds that shall come to the ear of all men ... it shall first appear as a great violet radiance over the entire world ... "
"Some day ... You shall look upon a great purple plain ahead, a golden light that draws you to it by its heat and warmth ... It shall be on Earth as it is in Heaven ... The great master teacher will close of the circle and again come forth upon this place of Earth." *(Archangel Michael, September 26, 1989)*

"The sign of the SON OF MAN will appear before the great Chastisement." *(Blessed Virgin Mary to Veronica Lueken, April 14, 1974)*

" ... The name of the city of my God, the new Jerusalem which he will send down from heaven, and my own name is new [Sananda]." *(Revelation 3:12, Bible)*

"He shall bear a new name ... it is Sananda." *(Excerpt from 'Space-Gate', a Phoenix Journal, 1989)*

"As the lightning of the east flashes to the west, so will the COMING of the SON OF MAN be." *(Matthew 24:27, Bible)*

" ... The glory of God ... come from the east ... " *(Ezekiel 43:2, Bible)*

" ... In the SECOND COMING - He will come again and receive His own, who have prepared themselves through that belief in him and acting in that manner ... " *(Edgar Cayce, 1877-1945)*

"As for the exact day or hour, no one knows it, neither the angels in heaven nor the SON, but the FATHER only. The COMING OF THE SON OF MAN will repeat what happened in Noah's time. In the days before the flood people were eating and drinking, marrying and being married, right up to the day Noah entered the ark. So will it be at the COMING OF THE SON OF MAN. Two men will be out in the field; one will be taken and one will be left. Two women will be grinding meal; one will be taken and one will be left. Stay awake ... You cannot know the day your Lord is coming ... The SON OF MAN is COMING at a time you least expect." *(Matthew 24:36-44, Bible)*

" ... The sun shall be turned into darkness, and the moon into blood, before the terrible day of the LORD come." *(Joel 2:20-31, Bible)*

"The sun and the moon shall be darkened, and the stars shall withdraw their shining. The LORD also shall roar out of Zion ... and the heavens and the Earth shall shake, but the LORD will be the hope of his people ... " *(Joel 3:9-21, Bible)*

"There shall be signs of the sun and moon when there shall be created a man stronger than any prince and he shall renew the face of the Church. At this time Antichrist shall have been trodden down underfoot and all the world shall enjoy the faith and peace of the most high." *(St. John Capistran, 1385-1456 A.D.)*

WHY THE END ?

"The lion Monarch shall be made famous unto all and shall subvert kingdoms, peoples, and nations. Then God shall send a KING FROM THE SUN, who shall cause all the people of the Earth to cease from disastrous war. He will take away the intolerable yoke of slavery which is placed upon our necks, and he will do away with impious laws and violent chains. When he shall come there shall be fire and darkness in the midst of the black night." *(Excerpt from the 'Sibylline Fragment', 2nd Century B.C.)*

"The seducer ... will put to death those saints of God. It is then that there will appear the sign of the SON OF MAN, and HE will come upon the clouds of heaven." *(The Pseudo-Methodius, 680 A.D.)*

"In the end like lightning flashing from heaven shall come GOD OUR KING ... in the clouds with glory unimaginable. And behold His Glory shall run the serried Hosts of Angels and Archangels, all breathing flames, and a river full of fire, with a frightful crash ... "

"How may we then endure ... when we shall see the fiery river coming out in fury like the wild seething ocean, and the hills and valleys consuming, and all the world and the work therein; then ... with that fire the rivers shall fall, the springs shall vanish, the sea dry up, the air be agitated, the stars shall fall out from the sky; the sun shall be consumed, the moon shall pass away, the heavens rolled up like a scroll ... " *(Saint Ephraim, 4th Century)*

"A great change will come to pass, such as no mortal man will have expected. Heaven and hell will confront each other in this struggle ... light and darkness will be pitted against each other with swords ... of a different fashion. With these swords it will be possible to cut up the skies and to split the Earth. A great lament will come over all mankind and only a small batch will survive the tempest, the pestilence and the horror." *(Pastor Bartholomaeus, 1613-1658)*

"And then HE who was crucified on the wood of the cross will come from the heavens, like a great flashing star, and he will resurrect those two men. And HE who was hung on the cross will wage war with the Son of Perdition and will slay him and all his host. Then the land of Egypt will burn twelve cubits deep ... And then the SON OF GOD will come with great power and glory to judge the nine generations. And then CHRIST will rule, the SON OF THE LIVING GOD, with his Holy Angels." *(Excerpt from the 'Erythraean Sibyl', 12th Century)*

" ... Allah will send JESUS from heaven to slay Dajjal, and JESUS will still be on this Earth when the time comes for Yajuj and Majuj to be set free. Then Allah will tell JESUS to take the believing servants of Allah with Him and shelter them in the mountains." *(Excerpt from the 'Mishkah al-Masabih')*

"There shall come a silence upon the lands and then shall the trumpet sound and all shall know that it is the time of the coming of the FATHER and the SON and the MOTHER, in perfection." *(Hatonn, December 12, 1995)*

"The beast [U.N.] ... even though it is an eighth king, is really one of the seven and is on its way to ruin. The ten horns you saw represent ten kings [E.E.U.] ... they will possess royal authority along with the beast, but only for an hour. Then they will come to agreement and bestow their power and authority on the beast. They will fight against the Lamb but the Lamb will conquer them, for He is the LORD OF LORDS and the KING OF KINGS; victorious, too, will be His followers - the ones who were called: the chosen and the faithful." *(Revelation 17:11-14, Bible)*

"A new LEADER FROM THE HEAVENS brings the people
Together as one, all factions die and are reborn
Exalted clergy bends to a higher rule. Angels are
Seen in joy. The Red Man [communism] dissolves in a bottomless pit." *(Nostradamus, Unpublished Quatrain)*

"In the Millennium, two, the KING'S SON, before the turn,
Is seen by all amid thunderclaps.
Angry, the rubble of war and pestilence, the sins,

WHY THE END ?

The fish [Church] returns to power after a long sleep."   *(Nostradamus, Unpublished Quatrain)*

"Lord 'Jesus' quickly coming with his lofty reign,
First setting behind the few, at the time of Iran:
The male with the inside influence, the ghastly red,
The young fearing the Barbarian terror."   *(Nostradamus, Century IX Quatrain 5)*

"I will work wonders in the heavens above and signs on the Earth below: blood, fire, and a cloud of smoke. The sun shall be turned to darkness and the moon to blood before the COMING of that great and glorious DAY OF THE LORD. Then shall everyone be saved who calls on the name of the Lord." *(Acts of the Apostles 2:18-21, Bible)*

"There will be SIGNS in the sun, the moon, and the stars. On the Earth, nations will be in anguish, distraught at the roaring of the sea and the waves. Men will die of fright in anticipation of what is coming upon the Earth. The powers in the heavens will be shaken. After that, men will see the SON OF MAN coming on a cloud with great power and glory. When these things begin to happen, stand erect and hold your heads high, for your deliverance is near at hand."
" ... The sun will be darkened and the Earth shall be broken up in diverse places and then shall be proclaimed ... that HIS star [ship] has appeared ... He becomes manifested before men."   *(Edgar Cayce, 1877-1945)*

"The king of the world will appear to all men when comes the time of the war of good against evil."   *(Excerpt from 'The Hollow Earth' by Raymond Bernard, 1969)*

" ... The LORD himself will come down from heaven at the word of command, at the sound of the Archangels voice and God's trumpet ... "   *(I Thessalonians 4:16-17, Bible)*

" ... Christ the first fruits and then, at his COMING, all those who belong to him. After that will come the end ... " *(I Corinthians 15:23-24, Bible)*

" ... The sons of men be warned that the DAY OF THE LORD is near at hand ... In the SECOND COMING - He will come again and receive his own, who have prepared themselves through that belief in Him and acting in that manner ... and the time draws near ... " *(Edgar Cayce, 1877-1945)*

"CHRIST ... will appear a SECOND TIME not to take away sin but to bring salvation to those who eagerly await him." *(Hebrews 9:28, Bible)*

"If anyone in this faithless and corrupt age is ashamed of me and my doctrine, the SON OF MAN will be ashamed of him when he comes with the Holy Angels in his Father's glory." *(Mark 8:38, Bible)*

"The SON OF MAN will come with his Father's glory accompanied by his Angels. When he does, he will repay each man according to his conduct." *(Matthew 16:27, Bible)*

" ... You will see the SON OF MAN sitting on the right hand of the mighty one and coming on the clouds of heaven." *(Matthew 26:64, Bible)*

"Immediately after the TRIBULATION of those days, the sun will be darkened, the moon will not shed her light, the stars will fall from the sky [star ships], and the HOSTS OF HEAVEN will be shaken loose. Then the sign of the SON OF MAN will appear in the sky, and all the clans of the Earth will strike their breasts as they see the SON OF MAN coming on the clouds of heaven with power and great glory. He will dispatch his ANGELS with a mighty trumpet blast, and they will assemble his chosen from the four winds, from one end of the heavens to the other. From the fig tree learn a lesson. When its branch grows tender and sprouts leaves, you realize that summer is near. Likewise, when you see all these things happening you will know that HE is near, standing at your door." *(Matthew 24:29-33, Bible)*

WHY THE END ?

"There will be signs in the sun, the moon, and the stars. On the Earth, nations will be in anguish, distraught at the roaring of the sea and the waves. Men will die of fright in anticipation of what is coming upon the Earth. The powers in the heavens will be shaken. After that, men will see the SON OF MAN coming on a cloud with great power and glory." *(Luke 21:25-27, Bible)*

" ... Jesus who has been taken up from you into heaven shall come in the same way as you have seen him going up to heaven." *(Acts 1:10-11, Bible)*

"You shall see heaven opened and the angels of God ascending and descending upon the SON OF MAN." *(John 1:47-51, Bible)*

"See! Like storm clouds he advances like a hurricane his chariots ... " *(Jeremiah 4:13, Bible)*

"See, the storm of the Lord! His wrath breaks forth in a whirling storm that bursts upon the heads of the wicked. The anger of the Lord shall not abate until he has done and fulfilled what he has determined in his heart. When the time comes - you shall fully understand." *(Jeremiah 23:19-20, Bible)*

"For the day of the LORD is coming ... a day of darkness and of gloom, a day of clouds and of somberness, like dawn spreading over the mountains ... Before them a flame devours, and after them a flame enkindles ... As with the rumble of chariots [spaceships] they leap on the mountaintops ... Before them the Earth trembles, the heavens shake; the sun and the moon are darkened, and the stars withhold their brightness. The Lord raises his voice at the head of his army ... For great is the DAY OF THE LORD ... " *(Joel 2:1-11, Bible)*

"Notice the fig tree ... when they are budding ... know for yourselves that summer is near. Likewise when you see all the things happening of which I speak, know that the reign of God is near ... Be on guard lest your spirits become bloated with indulgence and drunkenness and worldly cares. The great day will close in on you like a trap. The day I speak of will come upon all who dwell on

　　　　　242

the face of the Earth. So be on the watch. Pray constantly for the strength to escape whatever is in prospect, and to stand secure before the SON OF MAN." *(Luke 21:29-35, Bible)*

"The SON OF MAN in his day will be like the lightning that flashes from one end of the sky to the other ... As it was in the days of Noah, so will it be in the days of the SON OF MAN. They ate and drank, they took husbands and wives, right up to the day Noah entered the ark - and when the flood came, it destroyed them all. It was much the same in the days of Lot: they ate and drank, they bought and sold, they built and planted. But on the day Lot left Sodom, fire and brimstone rained down from heaven and destroyed them all. It will be like that on the day the SON OF MAN is revealed. On that day, if a man is on the rooftop and his belongings are in the house, he should not go down to get them; neither should the man in the field return home." *(Luke 17:24-31, Bible)*

"When the SON OF MAN comes in his glory, escorted by all the Angels of heaven, He will sit upon his royal throne, and all the nations will be assembled before him. Then he will separate them into two groups." *(Matthew 25:31-32, Bible)*

"Great shall be your trials. Greater still your rejoicing, having preserved in the time of darkness [three days], you shall witness My Glorious Return." *(Message to Cyndi Cain, November 2, 1992) in 'The Visionaries - U.S.A. - Today!' by Albert J. Herbert, 1993)*

"Not one stone will remain upon the other without being broken ... When will this happen and what will be the sign? See to it that no one leads you astray. For Many will come in my name and say 'I am Immanuel'. And they will lead great numbers of ones astray. People will hear about wars and war cries. They shall see and not be startled. This is what must happen, but that is not yet the end. Because people will rise against one another and one kingdom against another and there will be times of great need and earthquakes and great floods all about the lands. This is the beginning of great calamities, and great cataclysms. Soon the people with the knowledge will be surrendered to grief and many will be killed. They will be hated for the sake of truth in their teaching and for their wisdom."

"Many kinds of cults will rise up against one another, and much blood will flow and many hearts and spirits will be broken. Many will succumb as a result of these conflicts and will betray one another, and will hate one another because they remained small in spirit. Love will become cold and deadened in many, many people. Hatred will rule over all the world and evil will reign for a long period of time. But he who persists in the truth will survive. This lesson will be preached throughout the entire world ... And then the end will come. When the word of truth has gone forth throughout the total of the lands ... "

"When the people will see the horror of destruction in Jerusalem and the lands thereabout of which the prophets have already spoken, then the end will come. When this happens, whoever is at that time in the land of Judea, should flee to the mountains. He who is on the roof, should not come down ... He who is in the field should not come back in order to get his coat or any other of his possessions. Woe to women who are pregnant ... for they will suffer much grief and death. There will follow great grief as has never been before since the beginning of the world until now, and also will never be again ... "

"And if these days were not shortened, no man would remain alive. But the days will be shortened for the sake of the spirit and wisdom and for the sake of the people who serve truth and the laws ... There shall be machines made from metal for use in the air, on the waters and on land, to kill one another in great masses ... with heavy projectiles ... fire will come out of these projectiles and burn the world; so that hardly anything will survive and that which does survive will not long be spared. They will put the cornerstones of life itself into the projectiles [scalar waves] in order to kindle the deadly fires. And, if at that time the Celestial Sons would not appear in order to bring it to a standstill ... No one person would survive upon the face of the Earth."

"Since the human race, at that time, number at least ten times five hundred million people, two parts thereof will be destroyed and killed. When at that point, someone will say to the people, 'Behold here is Immanuel'. They shall not believe, because many false Immanuels and false prophets will rise up and do great signs and wonders, so that if it were possible, also even the wise and knowing would be misled."

"Therefore, when they shall say. 'He is in the desert', man shall not go out, and 'behold he is in a chamber', they shall not believe. Since I will most certainly return at that point in time, I will let them recognize me. This is how the law is written and thus shall it be. For, as lightning starts with the rise and radiates until its setting, thus will be my coming among the heavenly hosts with whom I shall have my renewed life at that time ... "

"Soon after the grief of that time, sun and moon will no longer radiate, and the stars will fall from heaven and the powers of the heavens will become, shaky. The structure of the heavens will be disturbed because of the senselessly erupted power of men whom will be living in greed, power and in addiction."

"There will appear a sign in the sky. And then all the generations on Earth will cry and will see the Celestial Sons coming in the clouds of the sky ... And will judge harshly against senselessness. Since God is the ruler over the three human races He, therefore will Judge through his representatives. He will send forth his guardian angels with loud trumpets and will gather his followers from the four winds, from one end of the Earth unto the other end." *(Excerpt from 'And They Called His Name Immanuel', a Phoenix Journal, 1989)*

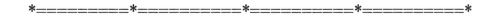

                                       Information Pioneers Publisher

WHY THE END ?

JUDGEMENT DAY

"The kingdom of God is near. It will begin with something that will come so suddenly as to be unexpected." *(Marta Robin of France, 1981 in 'The Three Days Darkness' by Albert J. Herbert, 1996)*

" ... God will pass JUDGEMENT on the secrets of men through Christ Jesus." *(Romans 2:16, Bible)*

"The LAST JUDGEMENT will follow the Abomination. Signs will precede. There will be four kinds of unusual color in the elements and a change in the heavenly bodies. There will be a celestial sign in that the air will appear at times yellow, at times pitch-black, now green, now clear red. Apollo will be split, now in ten, now in four, now in two parts; the moon will run together with the sun. Those dwelling on the Earth will be struck with fear when they see all the stars bloody ... there will be collision of kingdoms, seizure of thrones, earthquakes and famines. Out of desire for food, mothers will abase their sons and daughters in debauchery ... All these things are indications of the Abomination for whom there is no rule." *(Excerpt from 'The Erythraean Sibyl', 12th Century)*

"The LAST JUDGEMENT will be imminent; the signs will precede it. The sun will be frequently eclipsed and stretching out in vast fashion will destroy. The Euphrates will be dried to mere trickle; Aetna will be laid open on two sides ... After this the sea will sink to the depths ... Then the heavens will be opened in four parts, there will be thunder, and the inhabitants of the Earth will hear the threats of JUDGEMENT. Ineffable things will blare forth on the trumpet."

"Then all the kings and princes will appear ... No discrimination of wealthy or poor will take place there, but only the weighing of merits. Then crimes will be made evident, fear and trembling and horror of the abyss set out for punishment will strike all so that there will be weeping and gnashing of teeth. They will stretch out their hands in prayer, but the lamb will be inflexible; he will be fearful in punishing. In his sight will be lightning and thunder, merit along with

WHY THE END ?

sins ... He will JUDGE the good and the evil to lift the former on high and allow hell to swallow the latter to the fate of the demons." *(Excerpt from 'The Erythraean Sibyl', 12th Century)*

" ... JUDGEMENT DAY. Whether that day is actually a thing as scientifically explainable as the entering of your solar system into a Photon Belt, or the shifting of man's vibratory frequency to a higher one, or the final confrontation between Good and Evil (or all of the above) - a day of decision and atonement is coming ... " *(Korton, January 10, 1998)*

" ... The DAY OF THE LORD comes cruel, with wrath and burning anger; to lay waste the land and destroy the sinners within it! The stars and constellations of the heavens send forth no light; the sun is dark when it rises: and then light of the moon does not shine. Thus I will punish the world for its evil and the wicked for its guilt ... For this I will make the heavens tremble and the Earth shall be shaken from its place, at the wrath of the Lord of Hosts on the day of his burning anger." *(Isaiah 13:9-13, Bible)*

"We shall all have to appear before the JUDGEMENT OF GOD." *(Romans 14:10, Bible)*

"A GREAT CHASTISEMENT [punishment] will come over all mankind; not today or tomorrow, but in the second half of the twentieth century." *(The Third Prophecy of Fatima, Portugal, 1917)*

"For the wrath of God is revealed from heaven against all ungodliness and unrighteousness of men, who suppress the truth in unrighteousness." *(Romans 1:18, Bible)*

"Liars, imposters, those that are covetous, and all those that have only a form of Godliness, but deny the power of God, I will JUDGE them, and then I will JUDGE the whole world. I will shake it from it's foundations." *(Message to Dumitru Duduman in 'Dreams and Visions from God', 1996)*

"Then one of the seven angels ... said, ' ... I will show you the Judgement in store for the great harlot who sits by the waters of the deep ... I saw a woman [Vatican] seated on a scarlet beast ... on her forehead was written 'Babylon the great, mother of harlots and all the worlds Abominations' ... The seven heads are seven hills on which the woman sits enthroned [Rome/Vatican sits on seven hills] ... They are also seven kings, five have already fallen, one lives now, and the last has not yet come; but when he does he will only remain a short while. The beast which existed once but now exists no longer, even though it is an eighth king, is really one of the seven and is on its way to ruin. The ten horns you saw represent ten kings [Ten members of European Union] who have not yet been crowned; they will possess royal authority with the beast, but only for an hour. Then they will come to agreement and bestow their power and authority on the beast. They will fight against the Lamb but the Lamb will conquer them, for he is the lord of lords and king of kings; victorious, too, will be his followers ... The woman you saw is the great city [Rome] which has sovereignty over the kings of the earth." *(Revelation 17:1-18, Bible)*

" ... A king ... shall stand up against the Prince of Princes but he shall be broken without hand." *(Daniel 8:23-25, Bible)*

"The law of the sun [creator], and of Venus [love] in strife,
Appropriating the spirit of prophecy [the end times],
Neither one nor the other will be understood,
The law of the great Messiah will hold through the sun [One Light]."
(Nostradamus, Century V Quatrain 53)

"The JUDGEMENT will come suddenly and be of short duration. Then comes the triumph of the Church and the reign of brotherly love. Happy indeed they who live to see those blessed days." *(Father Maria Clausi, 1849)*

"Mankind is approaching hard times, because as soon as the measure of its sins will be full, it will be called to account by the superior power above us. You may call this event as you wish: 'JUDGEMENT DAY', 'Final Settlement', or 'Doomsday'. It will come, most likely very soon. Whoever will survive this settlement will see an entirely new Earthly existence manifested." *(Mahatma Ghandhi)*

" ... The DAY OF JUDGEMENT is coming, the time when the wheat must be sorted from the chaff if this planetary system is to move upward on the evolutionary spiral." *(Ramala Prophecy, 20th Century)*

"Man forgot the principle thing! He did not take into account ... that before the thousand-year reign of peace everything has to become new in the JUDGEMENT ... everything that is old has first to become new ... a change, a transformation of the old! ... Hence the millennium! ... Thus does man stand before his God!" *(Dr. Richard Steinpach, the Grail Message Prophet)*

"Meishu Sama ... declared that the event considered as the biblical 'LAST JUDGEMENT' a great cataclysmic action will take place in the spiritual realm followed by a similar counter-event in the physical world ... It was revealed to him that humanity is standing at the threshold of a great transitional period, a turning point from the old age of darkness to the New Age of light ... He was told that only as people become attuned to this higher vibration will they change their attitudes and be better able to pass through the coming period of flux." *(Excerpt from 'Beyond Prophecies and Predictions' by Moira Timms, 1994)*

"My JUDGEMENT will only be as harsh as your relationship with Me is." *(Christ to Veronica Garcia, September 27, 1992 in 'The Discernment of Visionaries and Apparitions Today' by Albert J. Herbert, 1994)*

"The Earth will tremble and will suffer. It will be terrible, a minor JUDGEMENT. For those who are not in a state of grace it will be frightful." *(Our Lord at Heede, Germany, 1937 in 'Prophecies! The Chastisement and Purification' by Albert J. Herbert, 1986)*

"But woe unto them that falsify this my word and commandment, and draw away them that hearken to the commandment of life; for together with them they shall come into everlasting JUDGEMENT." *(The Epistle of the Apostles)*

"The nations have raged in anger, but then came your day of wrath and the moment to JUDGE the dead: The time to reward your servants the prophets and the holy ones who revere you, the great and the small alike; the time to destroy those who lay the Earth to waste." *(Revelation 11:18, Bible)*

"The Earth and the sky fled from his presence until they could no longer be seen, I saw the [spiritually] dead, the great and the lowly, standing before the throne. Lastly, among the scrolls, the book of the living was opened. The dead were JUDGED according to their conduct as recorded on the scrolls ... Each person was JUDGED according to his conduct." *(Revelation 20:12-13, Bible)*

" ... When the just JUDGEMENT OF GOD will be revealed, when he will repay everyman for what he has done: eternal life to those who strive for glory, honor, and immortality by patiently doing right; wrath and fury to those who selfishly disobey the truth and obey wickedness. Yes, affliction and anguish will come upon everyman who has done evil ... But there will be glory, honor, peace for everyone who has done good ... " *(Romans 2:5-10, Bible)*

"The end has come upon the four corners of the land! Now the end has come upon you; I will unleash my anger against you and JUDGE you according to your conduct and lay upon you the consequences of your abominations shall be in your midst ... Disaster upon disaster! See it coming! ... Because of his sins, no one shall preserve his life. They shall sound the trumpet, yet no one shall go to war, for my wrath is upon the throng."

"Even those who escape and flee to the mountains ... I will put them all to death ... Their silver and gold cannot save them on the day of the Lord's wrath." *(Ezekiel 7:1-19, Bible)*

WHY THE END ?

"The kings of the Earth rise up, and the princes conspire together against the Lord and against his anointed ... HE who is throned in heaven laughs; the Lord derides them. Then in anger he speaks to them; he terrifies them in his wrath." *(Psalms 2:2-5, Bible)*

"Behold the eyes of the Lord God are upon the sinful kingdom, and ... will destroy it from the face of the Earth." *(Amos 9:8, Bible)*

"The year 2000 will not pass before the JUDGEMENT comes, as I have seen it in the divine light." *(Sister Nativity of Brittany, France, 18th Century)*

"The time draws near when I shall come to JUDGE those who live on the Earth, the time when I shall inquire into the wickedness of wrongdoers, the time when Zion's humiliation will be over, the time when a seal will be set on the age about to pass away."
"Whoever is left after that I have foretold, he shall be preserved, and shall see the deliverance that I bring and the end of this world is mine. They shall all see the men who were taken up into heaven without ever knowing death. Then shall men on Earth feel a change of heart and come to a better mind. Wickedness shall be blotted out and deceit destroyed, but fidelity shall flourish, corruption be overcome, and truth, so long unfruitful, be brought to light." *(II Esdras 6:18-28, Apocrypha)*

"For the LORD OF HOSTS will have His day against all that is proud and arrogant, all that is high, and it will be brought low ... And the LORD alone will be exalted, on that day. The idols will perish forever. Men will go into caves in the rocks and into the holes in the Earth; from the terror of the LORD and the splendor of his majesty, when he arises to overawe the Earth. On that day men will throw to the moles and the bats the idols of silver and gold they made for worship." *(Isaiah 2:12-20, Bible)*

"No more will treacherous gold and silver be nor Earthly wealth, nor toilsome servitude, but one fast friendship and one mode of life will be with the glad people, and all things will common be, and equal light of life. And wickedness from Earth in the vast sea shall sink away. And then the harvest-time of mortals is near. Strong necessity is laid upon these things to be fulfilled." *(Excerpt from the 'Sibylline Fragment', 2nd Century B.C.)*

"Behold, the Lord comes with ten thousand of his saints to execute JUDGEMENT to all ... " *(Jude 14, Bible)*

" ... Great Spirit ... give truth to peoples ... give peoples free will ... give people long, long rope ... He give all peoples many chances ... He give many years' time to peoples. He gonna stop one day. One day he gonna come. He gonna make it stop. He gonna draw final line. He gonna put believers on one side and no believers on other. He gonna let people's vibrations shake and break Earth Mother. Believers be already ready - they be in safe groups. Others be confused - they no ready. They caught full of shame with pants down. They sorry they no listen. He sorry too - but it already too late, time over - it all settled then." *(No-Eyes in 'Spirit Song' by Mary Summer Rain, 1987)*

" ... Great Spirit ... gonna get rid of evil all over! ... Great Spirit gonna come after many big changes on Earth Mother, after big changes all places ... " *(No-Eyes in 'Spirit Song' by Mary Summer Rain, 1987)*

"For He has set a day when He will JUDGE the world with justice." *(Acts 17:31, Bible)*

" ... The day of the Lord is coming like a thief in the night. Just when people are saying 'Peace and security', ruin will fall on them ... " *(1 Thessalonians 5:3, Bible)*

" ... All who have not believed the truth but have delighted in evildoing will be condemned." *(2 Thessalonians 2:11-12, Bible)*

Information Pioneers Publisher

" ... Be on guard against the wrath of the great God, when to all men shall come the height of famine, and, being overpowered, they meet dire JUDGEMENT. King shall seize upon king and wrest his land away, and nations waste and plunder nations, and lord plunder tribes, and leaders flee to another land, and Earth itself be changed ... Then from the sunrise God will send a king who will make the Earth cease from evil war, killing some, others binding with strong oaths ... And then will God speak with a mighty voice to all rude people of an empty mind; and JUDGEMENTS from the mighty God shall come upon them, and they all shall be destroyed by an immortal hand. And fiery swords shall fall from heaven on Earth, and mighty lights shall come down flaming in the midst of men. And Mother Earth shall be tossed in those days by an immortal hand, and fish of the sea." *(Excerpt from the 'Sibylline Fragment', 2nd Century B.C.)*

"Sun and moon are darkened, and the stars withold their brightness. The Lord roars from Zion, and from Jerusalem raises his voice; the heavens and the Earth quake, but the Lord is a refuge to his people." *(Joel 4:15-16, Bible)*

"When the Son of Man comes in his glory, escorted by all the angels of heaven, he will sit upon his royal throne, and all the nations will be assembled before him. Then he will separate them into groups ... The sheep he will place on his right hand, the goats on his left. The King will say to those on his right ... You have my Father's blessing. Inherit the kingdom prepared for you from the creation of the world ... Then He will say to those on his left: Out of my sight, you condemned, into that everlasting fire prepared for the devil and his angels!" *(Matthew 25:31-41, Bible)*

"God will punish them in an unprecedented manner. Woe to the inhabitants of the Earth! God will send His CHASTISEMENT and no one will be able to save himself from all the evils gathered together." *(Prophecy of La Salette, 1846)*

" ... The day of the Lord; a day of clouds, doomsday for the nations shall it be." *(Ezekiel 30:2, Bible)*

" ... This is the day of the Lord God of Hosts, a day of vengeance, vengeance on his foes!" *(Jeremiah 46:10, Bible)*

"The Lord's foes shall be shattered. The most high in heaven thunders; the Lord JUDGES the ends of the Earth, now may He give strength to His King, and exalt the horn of His anointed." *(I Samuel 2:10, Bible)*

"And there shall be just riches for men, for the government of the great God shall be a just JUDGEMENT." *(Excerpt from 'The Greek Sibyllae', 380 A.D.)*

" ... The heavens and the Earth are reserved by God's word ... for the day of JUDGEMENT, the day when godless men will be destroyed." *(2 Peter 3:7, Bible)*

"The word that I have spoken ... shall JUDGE him in the last day." *(John 12:48, Bible)*

"When your JUDGEMENT dawns on the Earth, the world's inhabitants learn justice." *(Isaiah 26:9, Bible)*

"Therefore in JUDGEMENT the wicked shall not stand, nor shall sinners, in the assembly of the just." *(Psalms 1:5, Bible)*

" ... All things ... concerning the day of the Lord will be fulfilled in a twenty-four hour day." *(Zephaniah 2:2, Bible)*

"The end has come upon the four corners of the land! Now the end is upon you; I will unleash my anger against you and JUDGE you according to your conduct and lay upon you the consequences of all your abominations."

WHY THE END ?

(Ezekiel 7:2-3, Bible)

"But the JUDGEMENT shall sit, and they shall sit, and they shall take away his dominion, to consume and destroy it until the end." *(Daniel 7:25, Bible)*

"When all shall appear lost, all will be saved. It is then that the Prince shall reign, whom people did not esteem before, but whom they shall seek. The triumph of religion will be so great that no one has ever seen the equal." *(Sister Marianne of the Ursulines in Blois in 'Prophecies! The Chastisement and Purification' by Albert J. Herbert, 1986)*

"In days to come, the mountain of the Lord's house shall be established as the highest mountain ... He shall JUDGE between the nations, and impose terms on many peoples. They shall beat their swords into plowshares and their spears into pruning hooks: One nation shall not raise the sword against another, nor shall they train for war again." *(Isaiah 2:2-4, Bible)*

"And the seventh angel poured out his vial into the air; and there came a great voice out of the temple of heaven, from the throne, saying, it is done. And there were voices, and thunders, and lightnings; and there was a great earthquake, such as was not since men were upon the Earth, so mighty an earthquake, and so great. And the great city [Jerusalem] was divided into three parts. And the cities of the nations fell ... And every island fled away, and the mountains were not found. And there fell upon men a great hail out of heaven ... about the weight of a talent [10 lbs.]." *(Revelation 16:17-21, Bible)*

"I will assemble all the nations and bring them down to the Valley of Jehosophat [means Judgement of Yahweh], and I will enter into JUDGEMENT with them there ... " *(Joel 4:2, Bible)*

"Let the nations bestir themselves and come up to the Valley of Jehosophat; for there will I sit in JUDGEMENT upon all the neighboring nations ... For near is the Day of the Lord in the valley of decision. Sun and moon are darkened and the stars withold their brightness. The Lord roars from Zion, and from Jerusalem raises his voice; the heavens and the Earth quake but the Lord is a refuge to his people." *(Joel 4:11-16, Bible)*

"And it will be toward the climax of that battle that the Mount of Olives will be split into two parts creating a valley ... " *(Paul Solomon, August 14, 1984)*

"Lo, a day shall come for the Lord when the spoils shall be divided in your midst. And I will gather all the nations against Jerusalem for battle ... Then the Lord shall go forth and fight against those nations, fighting as on a day of battle. That day his feet shall rest on the Mount of Olives, which is opposite Jerusalem in the East. The Mount of Olives shall be cleft in two from east to west by a very deep valley, and half of it shall move to the north and half of it to the south. And the valley of the Lord's mountain shall be filled up when the valley of those two mountains reaches its edge; it shall be filled up by ... the earthquake. Then the Lord God shall come and all his holy ones with him."

"On that day there shall no longer be cold or frost. There shall be one continuous day ... not day and night, for in the evening time there shall be light."

"The Lord shall become king over the whole Earth; on that day the Lord shall be the only one, and his name the only one."

"And this shall be the plague with which the Lord shall strike all the nations that have fought against Jerusalem; their flesh shall rot while they stand upon their feet, and their eyes rot in their sockets, and their tongues shall rot in their mouths."

"On that day there shall be among them a great tumult from the Lord; every man shall seize the hand of his neighbor, and the hand of each shall be raised against that of his neighbor." *(Zechariah 14:1-13, Bible)*

"Lands will split and swallow the myriads of people at Armageddon ... from the Dead Sea to the Red Sea." *(Excerpt From 'As The Blossom Opens', a Phoenix Journal, 1993)*

"The sun being in the 20th of Taurus, the Earth shall so quake,
That it shall fill and ruin the great theatre [battlefield],
The air, the heaven and the Earth shall be so obscured and troubled.
That unbelievers shall call upon God, and his saints."   *(Nostradamus, Century IX Quatrain 83)*

"When the calm ends, the Earth will so quake,
The Great Theater, filled, will lie in ruins;
Air, sky, Earth dark and troubled,
And atheists will plead with God and the saints."   *(Nostradamus, Unpublished Quatrain)*

"For there are spirits of devils, working miracles, which go forth unto the kings of the Earth and of the whole world, to gather them unto the battle of that great Day of God almighty. And he gathered them together into a place called in Hebrew tongue Armageddon [Har-Megiddo, the mountain of Megiddo-the plain of Esdraelon, the great battlefield of Palestine] ... And their were voices, and thunders, and lightnings; and there was a great earthquake, such as was not since men were upon the Earth, so mighty an earthquake and so great."

"And the great city [Jerusalem] was divided into three parts, and the cities of the nations fell and great Babylon came into remembrance before God ... and every island fled away, and the mountains were not found."

"And there fell upon men a great hail out of heaven ... "   *(Revelation 16:14-31, Bible)*

The Jordan River and the Dead Sea occupy the northern end of an extensive series of related 'grabens' (a sheer-sided, flat bottomed valley) that include the Red Sea and rift valleys of East Africa.

There is a distinctive Y-shaped graben with Sinai in the center. To the east, the Gulf of Akaba is an extension of the greater Jordan graben with the Dead Sea and Lake Tiberias/Sea of Galilee both of which are well below sea level and will be 'swamped'. Farther south along this great 'East African' rift is the steep eastern wall in Ethiopia.

"On that day I will give Gog for his tomb a well-known place in Israel ... Gog shall be buried there, and it shall be named 'Valley of Hamon-Gog'." *(Ezekial 39:11, Bible)*

"Behold, the day of the Lord cometh, and thy spoils shall be divided in the midst of thee."

"For I will gather all nations against Jerusalem to battle ... Then shall the Lord go forth, and fight against those nations ... "

" ... The Day of the Lord! ... A day of wrath is that day, a day of anguish and distress, a day of destruction and desolation, a day of darkness and gloom, a day of thick black clouds, a day of trumpet blasts and battle alarm against fortified cities, against battlements on high ... Neither their silver nor their gold shall be able to save them on the Day of the Lord's wrath, when in the fire of his jealousy all the Earth shall be consumed. For he shall make an end ... of all who live on the Earth." *(Zephaniah 1:14-18, Bible)*

"The Archangel Michael will do battle with the Dragon ... the Archangel and the Dragon [Satan] are the two spirits that will contend for the kingdom of Jerusalem ... The Dragon has appeared in all countries and has brought terrible confusion everywhere. There is war everywhere. Individuals and nations will rise against each other. Wars! Wars! Civil wars, foreign wars! What terrifying clashes! Everything is dead or in mourning: and famine stalks the Earth." *(The Monk of Premol, 1783)*

"The Lord will shorten the days for the sake of the elect, and the Antichrist will be slain by the power of God through Michael the Archangel on the Mount of Olives ... " *(Excerpt from the 'Tiburtine Sibyl', 380 A.D.)*

"He spoke to them in parables ... The farmer sowing good seed is the Son of Man; the field is the world, the good seed the citizens of the kingdom. The weeds are the followers of the evil one and the enemy who sowed them is the devil. The harvest is the End of the World, while the harvesters are the Angels. Just as weeds are collected and burned, so will it be at the End of the World.

WHY THE END ?

The Son of Man will dispatch his angels to collect from his kingdom all who draw others to apostasy, and all evildoers. The Angels will hurl them into the fiery furnace where they will wail and grind their teeth." *(Matthew 13:34-42, Bible)*

"At the first blow of the sword of God which will fall, like lightning on humanity, the mountains and all nature will tremble because the disorder and the misdeeds of man will rise to the vault of heaven."

"The time is at hand. The abyss is opening: the king of the kings of darkness is watching, the beast is watching with his subjects who will proclaim him 'savior of the world'. He will rise into the air superbly to reach the sky, but the breath of the Archangel Michael will kill him. He will fall back and the Earth will shake without ceasing for three days. It will then open its womb full of fire and the beast and his followers will be allowed into the eternal abyss of inferno. Then water and fire will purify the Earth to destroy all human pride and everything will be renewed." *(Melanie Calvat, 1831-1940)*

"And at that time shall Michael stand up, the great prince which standeth for the children of the people; and there shall be a time of trouble, such as never was among the nations even to that time: and at that time thy people shall be delivered, every one that shall be found written in the book." *(Daniel 12:1, Bible)*

" ... Each person was JUDGED according to his conduct ... anyone whose name was not found inscribed in the book of the living was hurled into this pool of fire." *(Revelation 20:12-14, Bible)*

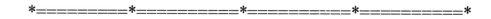

                                       Information Pioneers Publisher

261 Information Pioneers Publisher

WHY THE END ?

Information Pioneers Publisher

TRIAL BY FIRE

"Like moths to a flame, the armies of the world will go to Gehenna, on the day when the Earth will be changed into a different Earth, and the heavens as well." *(The Quran 14:48)*

"When things have reached a climax, and the hand of man can no longer do anything, affairs will be placed into the hands of Him, who will send down a punishment more terrible than anything seen before. God has already sent the flood, and he has sworn never to send another. Instead, what He will do will be something unexpected and terrible." *(St. Odile, 660-720 A.D.)*

"When that day shall come they shall be visited of the Lord of Hosts, with thunder, and with earthquake and with a great noise, and with storm and with tempest and with the flame of RAGING FIRE." *(Aton, 1989)*

"God will punish man more thoroughly than with the Flood. There will come the time of all times and the end of all ends. The great and powerful will perish together with the small and weak." *(The Third Prophecy of Fatima, Portugal, 1917)*

" ... The Heavenly Father is preparing to inflict a Great Chastisement on all mankind ... if men do not repent and better themselves, the Father will inflict a terrible punishment on all humanity. It will be a punishment greater than the deluge, such as one has never seen before. FIRE will fall from the sky and will wipe out a great part of humanity ... " *(Blessed Mary to Sister Agnes Sasagawa, Akita, Japan, October 13, 1973 in 'The Discernment of Visions and Apparitions Today' by Albert J. Herbert, 1994)*

" ... The deluge was not a myth, but a period when man had so belittled himself with the cares of the world ... as to require that there be a return to his dependence ... upon God."
"Will the entity see such occur again in the Earth? Will it be among those

who may be given these directions as to how, where the elect may be preserved for the replenishing again, of the Earth? Remember, not by water - for it is the mother of life in the Earth - but rather by the elements, FIRE." *(Edgar Cayce, 1944)*

"God gave Noah the rainbow sign, No more water; the FIRE next time." *(James Baldwin, 1963)*

"The present times are worse than at the time of Noah. The world was scourged by a deluge of water; now the world is going to be scourged by a deluge of FIRE." *(Blessed Mother to Anna of Seredne, Ukraine, December 20, 1954 in 'Prophecies! The Chastisement and Purification' by Albert J. Herbert, 1986)*

"The Eternal Father has given His promise to mankind, that the world shall never be made extinct again, as in the past with the time of the floods. However your world shall be cleansed with a 'baptism of FIRE'. Only a few, in the multitudes upon Earth, shall be saved. You have been asked to make a choice between the Cross and the Serpent." *(Blessed Virgin Mary to Veronica Lueken, October 2, 1979)*

"ARMAGEDDON to end by hailstorm/FIRE." *(John White in 'Poleshift', 1980)*

"After the U.N. building (seat of the Beast) and New York City ... are nuked (Revelation 16:16), the Beast itself (the Big four superpowers) is then thrown into ... 'LAKE OF FIRE' (Revelation 19:20)." *(Neal Chase, August 4, 1993)*

" ... On that day when Gog invades the land of Israel ... there shall be a great shaking upon the land of Israel ... Mountains shall be overturned, and cliffs shall tumble, and every wall shall fall to the ground."
"I will hold judgement with him in pestilence and bloodshed; flooding

rain and hailstones, FIRE AND BRIMSTONE, I will rain upon him, upon his troops, and upon the many peoples with him." *(Ezekiel 38:18-21, Bible)*

"Gog, chief prince of Meshech [Moscow] and Tubal [Yeltsin's birthplace] ... come up from the North parts and ... thou shalt fall upon the mountains of Israel ... And I will send FIRE upon Magog ... " *(Ezekiel 39:1-6, Bible)*

"This is the message of the end of the Age. The day of vengeance ... and the year of my redeemed is come ... behold the day ... that burneth as an oven." *(Phylos in 'Psychic & UFO Revelations in the Last Days', 1989)*

"In the days of Lot: they ate and drank, they bought and sold, they built and planted. But on the day Lot left Sodom, FIRE AND BRIMSTONE rained down from heaven and destroyed them all. It will be like that on the day the SON OF MAN is revealed." *(Luke 17:28-30, Bible)*

"Creator promised not to end in annihilation but will be cleansed by FIRE." *(Excerpt From 'Skeletons In the Closet', a Phoenix Journal, 1990)*

" ... Shall all the Earth be consumed." *(Zephaniah 3:8, Bible)*

"On that day says the Lord of Hosts, I will destroy the names of the idols from the land." *(Zechariah 13:2, Bible)*

"And when that day shall come they shall be visited of the Lord of Hosts, with thunder and with earthquake, and with a great noise, and with storm, and with tempest, and with the flame of DEVOURING FIRE." *(2 Nephi, 27 in 'The Book Of Mormon')*

"The FIRE of Heaven will fall and consume three great cities." *(Prophecy of La Sallette, 1846)*

WHY THE END ?

"Those nations which have rebelled against the law of Christ will perish by FIRE. Europe will then be too large for them who survived." *(Countess Francesca de Billiante, 20th Century, in 'Prophecies! The Chastisement and Purification' by Albert J. Herbert, 1986)*

" ... Two parts shall be cut off and die, but the third part shall be left therein. And I will bring the third part through the FIRE ... " *(Zechariah 13:8-9, Bible)*

"The present heavens and Earth are reserved by God's word for FIRE, they are kept for the DAY OF JUDGEMENT, the day when the godless will be destroyed ... The Lord does not delay in keeping his promise - though some consider it 'delay'. Rather, he shows you generous patience, since he wants none to perish but all to come to repentance."

"The day of the Lord will come like a thief, and on that day the heavens will vanish with a roar; the elements will be destroyed by FIRE, and the Earth and all its deeds will be made manifest."

"Since everything is to be destroyed in this way, what sort of men must you not be! How holy in your conduct and devotion, looking for the coming of the day of God and trying to hasten it! Because of it, the heavens will be destroyed in flames and the elements will melt away in a blaze." *(II Peter 3:7-12, Bible)*

" ... The Lord comes forth from his place, he descends and treads upon the heights of the Earth. The mountains melt under Him and the valleys split open, like wax before the FIRE ... " *(Micah 1:3-4, Bible)*

"For behold, the day is coming burning like an oven ... and the day which is coming shall burn them up ... " *(Malachi 4:1, Bible)*

"For the lord shall JUDGE by FIRE, and by his sword unto all flesh, and the slain of the Lord shall be many." *(Isaiah 66:16, Bible)*

"And He shall burn the great strength of men by FIRE ... " *(Excerpt from 'The Greek Sibyllae', 380 A.D.)*

"An unforseen FIRE will descend over the whole Earth, and a great part of humanity will be destroyed. This will be a time of despair for the impious: with shouts and satanic blasphemy, they will beg to be covered by the mountains, and they will try to seek refuge in caverns, but to no avail. Those who remain will find God's mercy in my power and protection, while all who refuse to repent of their sins will perish in a sea of FIRE!" *(Mother Mary to Mother Elena Leonardi, April 1, 1976 in 'Prophecies! The Chastisement and Purification' by Albert J. Herbert, 1986)*

"The day is not far off when the whole Earth will be covered with FIRE and the world will abound with corpses. Only one quarter of mankind will survive." *(Mother Mary to Enzo Alocci at Porto San Stefano in 'Prophecies! The Chastisement and the Purification' by Albert J. Herbert, 1986)*

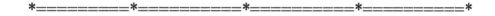

         Information Pioneers Publisher

WHY THE END ?

METEORS

"When the first angel blew his trumpet, there came a great hail and fire mixed with blood [meteors contain iron oxide, red in color], which was hurled down to Earth. A third of the land was scorched, along with a third of the trees, and every green plant." *(Revelation 8:7, Bible)*

"And I heard a great voice out of the temple saying to the seven angels ... pour out the vials of wrath ... and the first ... poured out his vial upon the Earth; and there fell a noisome and grievous sore upon the men who had the mark of the beast, and upon them which worshipped his image. And the second angel poured out his vial upon the sea; and it became as the blood of a dead man and every living soul in the sea died. And the third angel poured his vial upon the rivers and fountains of waters; and they became as blood. And the fourth angel poured out his vial upon the sun; and power was given to him to scorch men with fire. And men were scorched with great heat [solar flares]." *(Revelation 16:1-8, Bible)*

"And this is the Ninth and Last sign: You will hear of a dwelling-place in the heavens, above the Earth, that shall fall with a great crash. It will appear as a BLUE STAR. Very soon after this, the ceremonies of my people will cease." *(Native American Hopi Prophecy)*

"During the time of this ... confusion, look for another event which will distract the attention of the entire world. This is a celestial event, the coming of a light from the sky. This event will be so great in magnitude as to distract the attention of the world from war and fighting. It will give to all men common cause, greater than that which is the concern of the war. For it will seem to every man that the very existence of the Earth will be endangered ... Because of the magnitude, the sun will appear to turn black. It will be as if it had collapsed, giving its power to that which comes ... For that celestial body which comes ... having more similarity to a meteor than that you think of as a UFO. This will be the coming of His light in the sky, and will bring the dawning of a New Age, a

New Eden. The Earth will be renewed."

"Look toward the building of the temple as your most important sign of the coming of these events." *(Paul Solomon, September 16,1991)*

" ... A HUGE METEOR ... it's probable impact somewhere in the Nevada desert, upsetting faults and tectonic plates ... activates many volanoes ... " *(Lori Toye, 1995)*

"Your nation and others will try to deflect the incoming asteroids with nuclear bombs. This act will simply serve to affect the third of the skies, planets and the sun." *(Excerpt from 'Mary's Message to the World' by Annie Kirkwood, 1991)*

"When the great and the old enemy [Antichrist] who brings misfortunes poisoned,
The sovereigns [Americans] will be subjugated by innumerable [U.N. troops].
The METEORITES hidden in the comet's hair will rain down upon the Earth,
When the articles [Executive Orders] will be invoked in vain, concerning the nights of war." *(Nostradamus, Century II Quatrain 47)*

"Very near Auch, Lectoure and Mirande a GREAT FIRE will fall from the sky for three nights.
The cause will appear both stupefying and marvellous;
Shortly afterwards there will be an earthquake.
METEORITES hit south-western France and cause earthquakes." *(Nostradamus, Century 1 Quatrain 46)*

"When the SIGN OF FIRE will appear in the heavens, the time will have come close for these days to engulf humanity ... " *(Hepidanus, 11th Century)*

"And the second angel sounded, and as it were a great MOUNTAIN BURNING WITH FIRE was cast into the sea; and a third part of the sea became blood; and a third part of the creatures which were in the sea, and had life, died; and the third part of the ships were destroyed." *(Revelation 8:8-9, Bible)*

"The stars to all at midday will appear, with the two luminaries ... His heavenly chariot, and the three signs will show to all the world, of life to be destroyed."

"For a dark mist will wrap the boundless world, east, west, and south, and north; and from the heaven will flow a mighty STREAM OF BURNING FIRE, and every place consume - Earth, ocean, sky, and heaven's axis. And the lights of heaven will rush together, and take on a form all-desolate. For the STARS will fall into the sea, and all the souls of men gnash their teeth, burning in the stream below, that burns with brimstone and the force of FIRE. And then the elements of all the world shall be forsaken - air, Earth, sea, light, heaven and days and nights. No longer through the air will fiy the insatiate birds, nor swimming beasts pass through the sea, nor vessels sail the waves, nor cattle plow the field, nor sound of trees under the winds; but all things then will melt together, and will come out purified." *(Excerpt from the 'Sibylline Fragment', 2nd Century B.C.)*

"Then shall all the elements of all the world be desolate, air, Earth, sea, FLAMING FIRE, and sky and night, and all days to one FIRE and to one barren shapeless mass to come." *(Excerpt from the 'Sibylline Fragment', 2nd Century B.C.)*

"The sign of the doom: the Earth shall be moist with sweat; from heaven the king shall come to reign for ever ... At midnight in the hour when the angel made Egypt desolate, and when the Lord despoiled hell. In the same hour He shall deliver His elect from this world ... FIRE shall burn up Earth and sea and heaven ... The springs shall fail, and the everlasting flame consume; He shall cast down the hills, and raise up valleys from the depth ... from the heavens shall fall both FIRE and sulfur stream." *(Bede the Venerable, 672-735 A.D.)*

" ... And the FIERY POWER shall overflow on the Earth, then surely the universal elements of the world shall be dissolved, when God dwelling in the firmament shall roll up the heaven, which like a scroll shall be put away, and all the many shaped vault of heaven shall fall on the vast Earth, and on the deep shall flow a ceaseless torrent of GLOWING FIRE, and shall consume the Earth, consume the sea, and the pole of heaven, the nights, the days, and e'en the creation, and fuse all in one and set apart unto purification ... " *(Excerpt from the 'Sibylline Fragment', 2nd Century B.C.)*

"Before the universal conflagration shall happen so many great inundations that there shall be scarce any land that shall not be covered with water, and this shall last so long, that except for enthnographies and topographies all shall perish. Before and after these inundations in many countries there shall be such scarcity of rain and such a great deal of FIRE, AND BURNING STONES shall fall from heaven, that nothing unconsumed shall be left." *(Nostradamus in a letter to his son, March 1, 1555, in 'Nostradamus', Unpublished Prophecies')*

" ... The heavens shall pass away with a great noise, and the elements shall melt with fervent heat and the Earth also and the works therein shall be burned up." *(II Peter 3:10, Bible)*

"Fire will come from the sky and hit the Earth Mother in the water nursery of creation (oceans) and air, Earth, water and fire will be whole once again (before 2015)." *(Native American Cradleboard Prophecy)*

272   Information Pioneers Publisher

WHY THE END ?

Information Pioneers Publisher

COMET / BALL OF REDEMPTION

"And the third angel sounded, and there fell a great STAR from heaven BURNING as it were a lamp; and it fell upon the third part of the rivers, and upon the fountains of waters; and the name of the star is Wormwood [Comet Herculobus/The Ball of Redemption]; and a third part of the waters became wormwood [bitter/poisoned]; and many men died of the waters, because they were made bitter ... "

"And the fourth angel sounded, and the third part of the sun was smitten, and the third part of the moon, and the third part of the stars; so as the third part of them was darkened, and the day shone not for a third part of it, and the night likewise." *(Revelation 8:10-13, Bible)*

"There will come in the year 2000 the day of the Lord, who will judge both the living and the dead. Stars and COMETS will fall from above, the Earth will be set ablaze with lightning, and the old Earth will pass away." *(Prophecy of Warsaw, 1790)*

"The CHASTISEMENT will be great ... One will come from man, through the hands of man, a war so great that it will almost exterminate the Earth ... and the CHASTISEMENT of the BALL OF REDEMPTION." *(Blessed Virgin Mary to Veronica Lueken, November 20, 1978)*

"I beheld the menace of the BURNING SUN among the stars, and the dead wrath of the moon in her bright shining; the stars were in travail with warfare, and God gave the word for battle. Over against the sun great flames made combat, and the horned whirling of the moon was changed ... Capricorn smote ... the new risen Bull: and the Bull took from Capricorn his day of return ... the Virgin changed the fate of the Twins, in the Ram: The Pleiad shone no more; the Dragon refused the Girdle; the fishes swam up beneath the girdle of the Lion; Cancer stayed not in his place, for fear of Orion: the Scorpion crept under the tail of the Lion, and the Dog slipped away from the flaming of the sun; Aquarius was burnt up by the strength of the mighty Shiner. Heaven itself arose, and shook off the warring hosts, and cast them headlong in its wrath to the ground. And they, swiftly smitten down upon the waters of the ocean, set the whole Earth on fire; and the sky stood bare of stars." *(Excerpt from the 'Sibylline Fragment', III:512-531, 2nd Century B.C.)*

"From, Vysehrad comes a FIREBALL, blunders fly through the air and everywhere there is screaming, and a fire ocean. Everything that was the result of men, lies in disarray and ashes. Life is wiped out ... There, where the Dome once stood, I see only a ... FIREBALL." *(The Seeress of Prague, 17th Century)*

"A second 'sun' ... that which is labeled the BALL OF REDEMPTION ... now in transit ... It is guided by that which is outside your planet ... When it enters your atmosphere, hearts shall be gripped with fear! Many shall run to hide themselves, recognizing the wrath of their Lord."
"These events shall be gauged, measured and held in abeyance for the proper moment ... deemed by the Eternal Father for the cleansing of mankind - and it shall come in the twinkling of thine eyelid."
"The Creator has proclaimed that the Earth shall not end in annihilation for Creator has given His promise to mankind, that the world shall never be made extinct again, as in the past with the time of the floods. However, your world shall be cleansed with the baptism of fire." *(Excerpt from 'Skeletons In The Closet', a Phoenix Journal, 1990)*

"A METEOR/comet hits planet in Nevada and escalates these changes." *(Lori Toye, 1998)*

"I have seen a COMET strike our Earth ... earthquakes and tidal waves will befall us as a result of the tremendous impact of this heavenly body in one of our great oceans. It may well become known as one of the worst disasters of the twentieth century." *(Jeane Dixon, 1918-1997)*

"They shall make a little ball that will fall to the Earth, and the Earth will be devastated ... a GOURD OF MOLTEN ASHES falls from out of heaven."

(Native American Hopi Prophecy.)

"Your Earth, in due time, will be planet struck." *(Blessed Virgin Mary to Veronica Lueken, October 6, 1973)*

"A second sun lies out in your atmosphere: the BALL OF REDEMPTION. It is not a myth nor a story; it is a fact. The BALL OF REDEMEPTION nears!" *(Blessed Virgin Mary to Veronica Lueken, December 31, 1974)*

" ... A BALL OF FIRE ... It looks like a giant sun - it's so big! And it's spinning! There are two suns! ... it's like two suns in the sky ... The ball on the left, it's coming in very fast. It's an volute BALL OF FIRE and it's giving out ... trails of gases ... vapors ... they're not solid. It's like flames and smokes vapors." *(Veronica Lueken, September 7, 1974)*

"Now I see coming through the sky a tremendous huge BALL ... It's like a giant sun, but as it is travelling through the sky it seems to be turning colors, white and orange, and spinning so fast ... hurling through space ... it's going towards ... the world!" *(Veronica Lueken, April 13, 1974)*

"There has been much talk concerning a possible collision with Earth from another heavenly body ... The negative quality of Earth could magnetize it toward its location, but if the cleansing has already occurred for this planet, the other heavenly body would be diverted from its course. If it comes coincidental with nuclear action, it would be permitted as another form of cleansing." *(Kuthumi in 'Project World Evacuation', 1993)*

"In the year that Saturn and Mars are equally fiery,
The air is very dry, A LONG METEOR.
From hidden fires a great place burns with heat,
Little rain, a hot wind, wars and raids." *(Nostradamus, Century IV Quatrain 67)*

WHY THE END ?

"Listen, listen, white man, brother,
For the day is close upon us.
Will the great Massau'u return,
Or will there come the terrible one?
But if the sacred land is taken,
Then comes the changing of the seasons,
Earth will quake, and from the west wind,
There will come the Terrible One.
They shall make a little ball that will
Fall to the Earth, and the Earth will be
Devastated ... a GOURD OF MOLTEN ASHES
Falls from out of heaven.
So this day is close upon us,
When our world will shake and tremble
And the Old World, soon forgotten,
So our land will be no more."   *(Native American Hopi Prophecy)*

" ... The third war of your world ... a world aflame followed by the GREAT
COMET BALL OF REDEMPTION ... "   *(Excerpt from 'Phoenix Journal
Express', Volumes 1 & 2, 1990)*

" ... The BALL OF REDEMPTION ... will descend from the atmosphere
of your Earth: it will be from the heavens; it will not be man made; it will be
part of the universe." *(Blessed Virgin Mary to Veronica Lueken, October 2,
1979)*

"I see the moon of Mars [or a Comet with red dust] ... being pushed from
its orbit. It begins to spiral out into space ... I believe the Earth will intercept it
... I see a calendar that says three months [March]." *(Gordon-Michael Scallion,
June 1996, Earth Changes Report)*

"But first a COMET will pass by the Earth for a short time. This, however,
is only an interlude and can only be viewed as a forewarning ... "

"When the great time will come, in which mankind will have its last great trial ... finally, complete darkness will set in and last for three days and three nights. During this time, men ... will fall into a slumber-like sleep and not awaken, especially those who have no spark of spiritual life ... Of mankind there will be more dead than there have been casualties in all wars ... in the palaces of the church they will await the arrival of the great COMET." *(Johann Friede, 1204-1257)*

"One day before the COMET shines, a lot of people from need and misery will be wanting a home. The great empire in the sea ... will be devastated by earthquake, storm, and flood. This empire will suffer much misfortune from the sea. It will be divided into two islands and part of it will sink." *(St. Hilarion, 291-371 A.D.)*

"Before the COMET comes, many nations, the good excepted, will be scoured with want and famine. The great nation in the ocean that is inhabited by people of different tribes and descent by an earthquake, storm and tidal waves will be devastated. It will be divided, and in great part be submerged. That nation will also have many misfortunes at sea and lose its colonies in the east through a Tiger and a Lion. The COMET by its tremendous pressure, will force much out of the ocean and flood many countries, causing much want and many plagues. All seacoast cities wil be fearful and many of them will be destroyed by tidal waves, and most living creatures will be killed and even those who escape will die from a horrible disease. For in none of those cities does a person live according to the laws of God." *(Abbess Hildegard of Bingen, 1098-1179)*

"At first will come several terrestrial scourges, as great wars, through which many millions will run into destruction. After that will come the CELESTIAL SCOURGE in full severity, such as has never been. It will be short, but will cut off the greatest part of mankind." *(Maria Taigi, 1835)*

"Where all good is, everything right with the sun and the moon,
Is abundant, its ruin approaches

WHY THE END ?

From the sky it advances to vary your fortune,
In the same state as the seventh rock." *(Nostradamus, Century V Quatrain 32)*

"The moon shall be obscured in the deepest darkness,
Her brother [Comet] shall pass being of a ferruginous [red] color,
The great one long hidden under shadows,
Shall make his iron lukewarm in the bloody rain [iron oxide]."
(Nostradamus, Century I Quatrain 84)

"After great misery for mankind an even greater approaches
When the cycle of the centuries is renewed
It will rain blood, milk, famine, war and disease:
In the sky will be seen a fire, dragging a tail of sparks." *(Nostradamus, Century II Quatrain 46)*

"Mabus [Sadam reversed] will then soon die and there will come,
A dreadful destruction of people and animals.
Suddenly, vengeance will be revealed,
A hundred hands, thirst and hunger, when the COMET will pass."
(Nostradamus, Century II Quatrain 62)

"The COMET will appear towards ursa minor around 21 June.
Suse and Tuscany [Italy], Greece and the Red Sea will tremble.
The pope of Rome will die,
The night the COMET disappears." *(Nostradamus, Century VI Quatrain 6)*

"The GREAT STAR shall burn for the space of seven days,
A cloud shall make two suns [Sun and Comet] appear,
The big mastiff [Antichrist] shall howl all night,
When a great pope shall change his country." *(Nostradamus, Century II Quatrain 41)*

                           Information Pioneers Publisher

"For seven days and seven nights
Man will watch this awesome sight.
The tides will rise beyond their ken
To bite away the shores, and then
The mountains will begin to roar
And earthquakes split the plain and shore." *(Mother Shipton, 1488-1561)*

"When the great COMET is seen, the leader of the government [president] will be stricken by war, famine, plague: smoke of war and blood will be seen in all western countries with all their external signs, when a rebellion will be sparked off by the tonsured ones [traditionalists]." *(Nostradamus, Presage 52)*

"A fiery Dragon [Comet] will cross the sky
Six times before this Earth shall die
Mankind will tremble and frightened be
For the sixth heralds in this prophecy." *(Mother Shipton, 1488-1561)*

"His masked smile, his fate grandeur
Will serve the gods their anger stir.
And they will send the DRAGON back
To light the sky - his tail will crack
Upon the Earth and rend the Earth
And man shall flee, King, Lord, and serf." *(Mother Shipton, 1488-1561)*

"The DRAGON'S TAIL is but a sign,
 For mankind's fall and man's decline ... " *(Mother Shipton, 1488-1561)*

"Not every soul on Earth will die
As the DRAGON'S TAIL goes sweeping by.
Not every land on Earth will sink
But these will wallow in stench and stink
Of rotting bodies of beast and man
Of vegetation crisped on land." *(Mother Shipton, 1488-1561)*

WHY THE END ?

"But the land that rises from the sea
Will be dry and clean and soft and free [Atlantis]
Of mankind's dirt and therefore be
The source of mankind's new dynasty.
And those that live will ever fear
The DRAGON'S TAIL for many year
But time erases memory
You think it strange. But it will be." *(Mother Shipton, 1488-1561)*

"COMETS without tails, move silently
 Panic abounds, an offering rejected,
 A TAILED COMET glides among the bees, dies, and heads of state
Nonplussed.
 Signatures in the sand [Crop circles] ignored by all." *(Nostradamus, Unpublished Quatrain)*

"During the appearance of the BEARDED STAR
 Three great princes will be made enemies
 Struck from the sky, place earth quaking
 Po [France], Tiber overflowing [Italy], serpent placed on the shore."
(Nostradamus, Century II Quatrain 43)

"BURNING TORCH in heaven at night will be seen
Near the end and source of the Rhone:
Famine, steel, the relief provided late
The Persian turns to invade Macedonia." *(Nostradamus, Century II Quatrain 96)*

"A little before a monarch is killed,
Castor, Pollux, and a COMET in the sky appears,
The public brass, by land and sea shall be emptied,
Pisa, Asti, Ferra, Turin [Italy] shall be forbidden countries."
(Nostradamus, Century II Quatrain 15)

" ... The COMET pursues its course, and will appear on the scene at the right hour ... And then the Earth is purified and refreshed in every respect ... " *(Abd-Ru-Shin, 1930)*

" ... The major Earth Changes will be initiated by what I call the 'FIERY MESSENGER' [COMET/GREAT BALL OF REDEMPTION]. There is even now a star of great power proceeding towards our Solar body. The star at this moment is invisible to the human, or even telescopic eye, but is set on a path which will bring it in conjunction with our planetary system. As it passes by it will affect the motions of all the planets of our system ... changes on the surfaces of the planets themselves. The effect of the passage will be to set in motion the Earth Changes that are prophesied." *(Ramala Prophecy, 20th Century)*

" ... When the BALL OF REDEMPTION is sent upon you three-quarters of your world shall be gone." *(Blessed Virgin Mary to Veronica Lueken, November 1, 1977)*

"I will send my justice as a COMET to destroy and defeat the Antichrist and all his armies." *(Message to John Leary, June 4, 1998)*

Mayan and Hopi prophecy speak of a GREAT COMET [The 'Purifier'] heralding the beginning of time when Star Beings will return to set things right.

If a comet were to strike Earth we can expect red dust [iron oxide] and meteors to cover the planet. This has occurred in Earth's past as described in the Finnish 'Epos of Kale Vala'. Also when the Biblical Israelites left Egypt the 'Red Sea' was covered with red dust and they entered Edom (meaning 'red dust')

Other Ancient documents describe this event in the past:

"It rained, not water, but fire and red hot stones." *(Excerpt from the*

WHY THE END ?

Mexican 'Annals of Cuauhtitlan')

"It was not a flaming fire, but of a bloody redness." *(Servius)*

"Sun's motion was interupted ... the waters in the rivers turned to blood." *(Excerpt from the Mayan Manuscript 'Quiche')*

"The river is blood ... Gates, columns and walls are consumed by fire. The sky is in confusion." *(Excerpt from the Egyptian 'Papyrus Ipuwer')*

"All the waters that were in the river were turned to blood. There was blood throughout the land of Egypt ... Men shrink from tasting ... " *(Exodus 7:20-24, Bible)*

"Stones mixed with fire." *(Exodus 9:24, Bible)*

"People were drowned in a sticky substance raining from the sky ... there was a great din of fire above their heads." *(Excerpt from the 'Popol-Vuh')*

"Quiauh-tonatiuch (the sun of rain fire)." *(Excerpt from the 'Annals of Cuauhtitlan')*

"God sent a sea of fire upon the Earth ... The cause of the fire they call the fire-water." *(Voguls of Siberia)*

"Sengle-Das (Water of fire rained from the sky)." *(Aborigines of the East Indies)*

"River of fire ... " *(Daniel 7:10, Bible)*

"A stream of heaven-sent fire pours out from above and spreads over many places and overruns great places of the inhabited Earth." *(Plato in 'On the Eternity of the World')*

Comet 'Glacobini-Zinner' has a 13 year cycle - last seen 1985.
Comet 'Machholz II' has a 6.5 year cycle - last seen August 1994.
Comet '1998 C-J' was discovered in 1998 to be heading towards Earth.

See Internet site: www.enterprisemission.com and related links to obtain NASA's Soho satellite photographs of an intensely lighted object/planet entering our solar system.

WHY THE END ?

PLANETARY ALIGNMENT

Professor Hideo Itokawa has calculated the planets to be in a Grand Cross configuration on August18, 1999 that will initiate global cataclysms.

"All terrestrial things will be consumed when the planets shall coincide in the sign of Cancer [June/July] ... so placed that a straight line could pass through their orbs ... But the inundation will take place when the same conjunction of the planets shall occur in Capricorn [December/January] ... The first in Summer, the last in the Winter of the year." *(Berossus, Second Century A.D. Astrologer)[The year referring to the sidereal year, the precession of the equinoxes which takes 25,827 of our years - the time it takes the polar axis of Earth to return to its original position in space in relation to the zodiacal band.]*

A total eclipse on August 11, 1999 forms part of a Grand Cross [i.e. when 4 or more planets occupy positions at 90 and 180 degrees to the first position] involving the Moon, Sun, Uranus, Saturn and Mars. This is expected to trigger big changes on Earth's social systems, since Uranus in Aquarius emphasizes reform and radical social change. Neptune in Aquarius influences humanitarian revival and sudden reversals of fortunes.

"And the course of the winds will be confused and agitated, and innumerable meteors will flash through the sky foreboding evil. And the Sun will appear with six others [planets] of the same kind. And all around will be din and uproar, and everwhere there will be conflagrations ... and fires will blaze on all sides ... when the Yuga comes ... " *(Excerpt from the Hindu 'Mahabharata')*

Richard Noone's book '5/5/2000: Ice, The Ultimate Disaster' warns of a Grand Planetary Alignment [Mercury, Mars, Earth, Saturn, Jupiter & Pluto] on May 5, 2000 that will cause the Earth's axis/pole to wobble/shift causing a plantary catastrophe.

WHY THE END ?

"Watch the 5th day of May, 2000, for the time when again the planets will be aligned one behind the other across the sky, and the strain of magnetism will SHIFT the surface of the Earth until it takes a new shape and form." *(Paul Solomon, July 4, 1975)*

" ... Spoken by prophets ... on May 5, 2000, you will see a dawning of a new day." *(Paul Solomon, January 21, 1991)*

'The Jupiter Effect Theory' by Dr. John Gribbin and Dr. Stepen Plagemann predicts major earthquake activity around May 2000, due to the close grouping of the planets (Mercury, Mars, Earth direct allineation with Saturn, Jupiter, Pluto and Moon) which will exert a strong magnetic and gravitational influence upon Earth's crust and result in a possible Poleshift.

Information Pioneers Publisher

WHY THE END ?

Information Pioneers Publisher

POLAR AXIS SHIFT

" ... Magnetized solar flares ... in conjunction with the planetary alignment that is presently coming into its final position, combines to create a strong tendency to pull the Earth into untoward motion." *(Excerpt from 'Project World Evacuation', 1993)*

" ... Nations will be in confusion, and the courses of the stars will be changed." *(II Esdras 5:1-13, Apocrypha)*

"There are astrological signs foretelling that the Great POLAR SHIFT will come soon. There will be great cataclysms and geological changes ... The Great Shift will come at the time of atomic warfare, which will be of short duration." *(Michael X. Barton in 'Psychic & UFO Revelations in the Last Days', 1989)*

"The HEAVEN SHALL BE MOVED, the stars shall fall upon the Earth, the sun shall be cut in half like the moon, and the moon shall not give up her light." *(The Apocalypse of Thomas)*

"As there is the passing close of that red planet [Comet/Ball of Redemption], so will the crust of the Earth be attracted toward it, as it would be approaching; so ... the North Pole will point in the direction of its advance."

"Then ... at its point nearest the Earth, so then will the pole point directly upward ... and in the passing away of its presence from this planet, so then would the POLES SHIFT again a third time toward the opposite direction. So that there will be three separate temperature changes in this area, making near to impossible the survival of any animal species or plants, either in this area or upon ... most of the surface of this planet." *(Paul Solomon, 1973)*

[As another planetary body approaches, Earth would adjust its poles so that the same polar regions would tend to repel and align the opposing polarity, similar to two magnets.]

                              Information Pioneers Publisher

WHY THE END ?

"These are truly the final years as you see, for the next big happening will be the turning of the planet Earth onto its side, as it juggles and shakes the oceans out of their beds and new ground is brought up from the depths of the oceans."

"There will be much destruction of land before the TURNING OF THE AXIS ... Magnetic fields will play havoc on Earth in the last days. Machines will fail and science will not have answers."

"The planet ... is being bombarded with forces [photons] which will cause it to change its direction in relationship to the universe ... During this realignment, the Earth will be turned and shaken, and you will have many catastrophic effects ... " *(Excerpt from 'Mary's Message to the World' by Annie Kirkwood, 1991)*

"Before POLESHIFT ... land to rise off New York to Massachusetts."

"Last war to begin in 1998 [began with U.S. attacks on Iraq in December] and end in November 1999 then POLESHIFT." *(John White in 'Poleshift', 1980)*

" ... In the year 1999 or 2000 the Earth will tumble on its AXIS ... " *(Aaron Abrahamsen)*

"There shall occur in the month of OCTOBER a great upheaval, such that everybody will think the Earth has lost its natural motion and plunged into everlasting darkness. In the SPRING before this shall happen extraordinary changes, reversals of kingdoms and great earthquakes; all accompanied with the procreation of the New Babylon ... " *(Nostradamus in 'The Epistle to Henry II', 1555)*

"POLESHIFT of October 1999 or 2000 - preceded by a series of eclipses."
"Enormous tidal waves would roll across the continents as the oceans became displaced from their basins ... hurricane winds of hundreds of miles per hour would sweep the planet. Tremendous earthquakes and lava flows would wrack the land. Poisonous gases and ash would fill the skies. Geography would be altered as seabeds rose and land masses submerged. Climates would

change instantly ... Last of all, huge numbers of organisms would be destroyed ... with signs of their existence hidden under thick layers of debris, sediment and ice or at the bottom of newly established seas." *(John White in Pole Shift, 1980)*

"The Tribulation period spoken of in the Bible ... began February 2, 1992 and will end on March 21, 1999. This will be followed on October 19, 1999 by a tremendous ... POLAR FLIP." *(Excerpt from 'The Dark Side of the Force' by D.E.G., 1995)*

"EARTH AXIS FLIP ... end of fourth world ... and will be consummated after the appearance of a now invisible star, rushing toward Earth from space." *(Native American Hopi Prophecy)*

"Turtle Island could TURN OVER two or three times and the oceans could join hands and meet the sky." *(Native American Hopi Prophecy)*

"The world shall rock to and fro. The white man will battle against other people in other lands - with those who possessed the first light of wisdom. There will be many columns of smoke and fire ... Many of my people, understanding the prophecies, shall be safe. And soon - very soon afterward - Bahana will return." *(Native American Hopi Prophecy in 'The Book of the Hopi' by Frank Waters, 1963)*

" ... The AXIS WILL SHIFT and will cause a great deal of Earth Changes ... " *(Native American Hopi Elder 'Grand Father' on the Art Bell Radio Show, June 16, 1998)*

"There will be a SHIFTING OF THE POLES (so that where there have been those of a frigid or semitropical, it will become more tropical)." *(Edgar Cayce, 1934)*

WHY THE END ?

" ... Perhaps half the plate structure of the Earth, SHIFT as if in a single moment. They do not go down or up, but rather, they slip ... something akin to twenty-five or thirty degrees of slippage." *(Gordon-Michael Scallion, June 1996, Earth Changes Report)*

" ... The Great Lakes ... flooding ... through the Mississippi River as the Earth TILTED into its new axis position." *(Mary Summer Rain)*

"The Earth will SHIFT between 23 and 24 degrees ... Reposition North Pole on border of Finland and Sweden. The South Pole on the Arctic Circle just to the left of 150 degrees." *(Excerpt from 'Daybreak: The Dawning Ember' by Mary Summer Rain, 1991)*

" ... The approach ... after the year two thousand, of the passing of Mars [or Wormwood] ... close enough to have magnetic influence ... And if the Earth ... is shifted even slightly out of its normal movement and rotation ... you shall have the SHIFTING OF THE POLES." *(Paul Solomon, April 3, 1988)*

"Atomic energy bursts would ignite the radiation belt, heat ice caps and the water would throw you off balance - Earth will SHIFT at least another 13 degrees." *(Hatonn, April 26, 1992)*

[First line obliterated]
"Darkens descends. Eclipses great. NORTH AND SOUTH CHANGE.
War and nature unite against the peace. Heavenly holocausts
Rain blood on the rocks and our face is mutilated." *(Nostradamus, Unpublished Quatrain)*

"The Celtic River will CHANGE ITS COURSE
No longer will include the city of Agrippina:
All transmuted except the old language;
Saturn, Leo, Mars, Cancer in rapine." *(Nostradamus, Century VI Quatrain 4)*

 Information Pioneers Publisher

"For the stars of heaven and their constellations will not give their light. The sun will be darkened ... moon will not cause its light to shine. Therefore I will shake the heavens, and the Earth will MOVE out of her place ... " *(Isaiah 13:13, Bible)*

" ... The Lord makest the Earth empty, and makest it waste, and turneth it UPSIDE DOWN, and scattereth abroad the inhabitants thereof." *(Isaiah 24:1, Bible)*

"The Earth mourneth and fadeth away ... " *(Isaiah 24:4, Bible)*

"The Earth is utterly broken down, the Earth is clean dissolved, the Earth is MOVED exceedingly." *(Isaiah 24:19, Bible)*

"The Earth shall reel to and fro like a drunkard and it will sway like a hut." *(Isaiah 24:20, Bible)*

"There was a great earthquake: and the sun became black as sackcloth of hair, and the moon became as blood."
"And the stars of heaven fell unto the Earth, even as a fig tree casteth her untimely figs, when she is shaken of a mighty wind."
"And the heaven departed as a scroll when it is rolled together: and every mountain and island were moved out of their places." *(Revelation 6:12-14, Bible)*

"Immediately after the tribulation of those days shall the sun be darkened, and the moon shall not give her light, and the stars shall fall from heaven, and the powers of the heavens shall be shaken." *(Matthew 24:29, Bible)*

"Before them the Earth trembles, the heavens shake ... the sun and moon are darkened and stars withhold their brightness." *(Joel 2:10, Bible)*

<u>WHY THE END ?</u>

"I will shake the heavens and the Earth, the sea and the dry land." *(Haggai 2:6, Bible)*

"Mountains shall be overturned, and cliffs shall tumble, and every wall shall fall to the ground." *(Ezekial 38:19-20, Bible)*

"There followed lightning flashes and peals of thunder, then a violent earthquake. Such was its violence that there never has been one like it in all the time men have lived on the Earth." *(Revelation 16:17, Bible)*

"Many people will not survive this SHIFT, but others will, because after a period of churning seas and frightful wind velocities the turbulence will cease, and those in the north will live in a tropical clime, and vice versa. Before the year 2000 it will come to pass." *(Ruth Montgomery, 1971)*

"As we near the last decade of this Century, we will encounter evil beings who are intent on taking advantage of everyone ... This is the last desperate attempt by evil forces to control the Earth before they realize that their power will be eclipsed by the SHIFT and the new age." *(Spirit Guides of Ruth Montgomery, 1986)*

Ancient documents describe Earth's previous Pole Shift:

"Earth turned upside down." *(Excerpt from the Egyptian 'Papyrus Ipuwer')*

"The south becomes north, and the Earth turns over." *(Excerpt from the 'Papyrus Harris')*

                             Information Pioneers Publisher

WHY THE END ?

MESSENGERS / MASTER TEACHERS

On November 28, 1996 Radio Show Host Art Bell spoke of a photograph taken on November 14, 1996 by Houston Astronomer Chuck Shramek of Comet Hale-Bopp with a 'mystery object' which was actually a spacecraft 4 times larger than Earth and sending radio transmissions which were picked up by radio telescopes on Earth.

" ... A blue star [Spaceship Phoenix - previously known as the 'Star of Bethlehem'] ... has moved through the heavens at various cycles ... Each time the star came because it was called and its assistance was needed during the transitions. Once again the blue star returns ... " *(Gordon-Michael Scallion, March 1993, Earth Changes Report)*

" ... The blue star [The Phoenix] shall be visible for 1,800 years ... will appear as a silvery light 100 times brighter than any morning star ... During the evening, it will appear as a moon ... " *(Gordon-Michael Scallion)*

"We are now visible all over your places. Each one of you can look into the heavens and see us in your night sky. We will be strategically stationed for easy viewing of multi-light rotation ... There are millions of us out here waiting your petition." *(Excerpt from 'Aids The Last Great Plague', a Phoenix Journal, 1989)*

"You want proof of who we are ... Look around you. See the truth of your circumstances and the ponder as to whether or not that God in which you trust and unto whom you pray would not send MESSENGERS to assist you in answer to your petitions? However for your more sensitive senses - go without on a clear night and search, briefly, the sky. Wait until you see a seemingly 'strobing' rainbow of color emitting from many of those twinkling lights out there. Pleiades craft will always show you the rainbow spectrum ... man wants facts and figures, and lots of them ... but then ... cast them into a pile, and go right on doing what he has been doing anyway." *(Tomeros Maasu Korton in*

WHY THE END ?

'The Wisdom of the Rays', Volume 1, 1997)

"Comets without tails [Spaceships], move silently
Panic abounds. An offering rejected, a tailed comet
Glides among the bees, dies, and heads of state
Nonplussed. Signatures in the sand [crop circles] ignored by all."
(Nostradamus, Unpublished Quatrain)

"The bees sting amid thunderclaps and lightning bolts,
Confusion. Fear. Awe. The fish trembles,
Governments are strangely silent while the HEAVENS
FLASH OMINOUS MESSAGES to the populace. East and West darken."
(Nostradamus, Unpublished Quatrain)

"Your world is at the brink of a 'new' reality. There is fast approaching a time when your world will no longer quibble over such trite subjects, 'Are We Alone in the Universe?' ... "

"'Your learned Brothers from afar' will be openly announcing their presence to your world, and along with their announcement will eventually come an acceptance of who they are and their true knowledge will be shared with you who are of Godly intent."

"There will be a brief time of confusion as ones effort to come to grips with the 'lies' that they have not only held onto, but have actually worshipped."

"However, there will also be a step up of manmade tamperings to try to get you ones convinced that these 'planetary visitors' mean you-the-people harm. The desperate elite controllers, who have been your behind the scenes masters for so long do not wish to give up their control and perceived positions of power."

"Eventually, after great 'catastrophe', these manipulators will only succeed at exposing themselves for who they really are." *(Volinio Saint Germain, May 1, 1998)*

"Before long all will be arranged.
We will expect a very sinister century,

300   Information Pioneers Publisher

The state of the masked and solitary ones [Illuminati/Bilderberger/Trilateral Commision/Council On Foreign Relations] much changed,

Few will be found who want to be in their place." *(Nostradamus, Century II Quatrain 10)*

"You will witness many stories that will try to convince you - the - people that the 'alien invaders' mean to do you harm. These stories will only serve to expose the true criminals for who they are. Mainstream religious leaders and politicians will be the greatest offenders and will effort greatly to hold onto their control over you-the-masses."

"As the time of truth draws ever nearer there will be greater and greater efforts made to persuade the masses that these so called 'invaders' mean to destroy you-the-people of the Earth. Some of the events planned by your elite controllers will appear so real in presentation, due to their technological sophistication [Area 51 projects/Project Blue Beam Holographs], that many will fall victim to the lies ... "

"There are likely to be millions of people sacrificed by your 'united one-world government' in order to convince those remaining that the deception is the truth. There will be a call to defend your planet from these 'evil invaders'."

"At the same time, however, there will be overwhelming evidence which will show that these higher evolved beings mean you no harm ... "

"You live in perhaps the most unique time that your planet will ever experience - coming out of ignorance (darkness) and into knowledge (light)." *(Sanat Kumara, May 23, 1998)*

"A salver flies [spaceship], comes to rest in the New City
Hate flourishes for the entity within [Commander Hatonn].
Battle lines Drawn. Fears of disease mask truth while three
Leaders in secret, unite against a false threat." *(Nostradamus, Unpublished Quatrain) [Government propaganda that space brotherhood visitors are carrying disease.]*

WHY THE END ?

"Twenty plus two times six [2012] will see the lore of the heavens
VISIT THE PLANET in great elation. Disease, pestilence,
Famine die. Rome rejoices for souls saved. The learned
Smile in awe.   Astrology confirmed.   For science a new beginning."
(Nostradamus, Unpublished Quatrain)

"And before the race is built anew
A silver serpent [spaceship] comes to view
And spew out men of like unknown
To mingle with the Earth now grown
Cold from its heat, and these men can
Enlighten the minds of future man
To intermingle and show them how
To live and love and thus endow
The children with the second sight.
A natural thing so that they might
Grow graceful, humble, and when they do
The Golden Age will start anew."   *(Mother Shipton, 1488-1561)*

"A revolution without bloodshed [war of ideologies], without strife
Men in unhappy confusion strive for perfections
Beyond their ken. Failure. Then elation. The
Earth's forces give way to a new power ABOVE THE CLOUDS."
(Nostradamus, Unpublished Quatrain)

"My people have a legend that ... our teachers came down from the sky in
a silver or white clamshell. When it settled onto the ground, the clamshell
opened up and the teachers came out. This describes a spaceship perfectly."
(Sun Bear in 'Black Dawn/Bright Day', 1992)

*Erich Von Daniken visited a South American tribe that has an object
given to them thousands of years ago by 'sky people'. They were instructed to
keep it clean and, 'When it hums like thousands of swarms of bees, we will*

return'. It began humming in 1978.

"The star people will return in the latter part of the 1990's. Changes will happen as their time draws near." *(Floyd Hand, Oglala tribe)*

"All things will be possible in the New Age. The race of humanity that will walk the Earth in the Aquarian Age will differ in many respects from today. The human form will be different and will vibrate to a different note. The Angels and the Great Masters will actually be present on the Earth in physical appearance, and will walk and talk with you. The whole structure of matter, the frequency range in which you live, vibrate ... will be altered." *(Ramala Prophecy, 20th Century)*

"During and after the cleansing, many of the great spirit teachers will take human form and walk among us." *(Sun Bear)*

"They shall all see the men who were taken up into heaven without ever knowing death. Then shall men on Earth feel a change of heart and come to a better mind. Wickedness shall be blotted out and deceit destroyed, but fidelity shall flourish, corruption be overcome, and truth, so long unfruitful, be brought to light." *(II Esdras 6:18-28, Apocrypha)*

" ... You shall see heaven opened and the Angels of God ascending and descending upon the Son of Man." *(John 1:47-5, Bible)*

" ... Angels of God ... will come to answer questions and give advice. Many will think them devils, and many of your religious leaders will confuse the people and give wrong advice. They will denounce the spiritual realm which will show itself to mankind ... It will not be in outer guidance, but in inner guiding that these Angels will come to assist." *(Excerpt from 'Mary's Message to the World' by Annie Kirkwood, 1991)*

WHY THE END ?

"People gonna see new beings ... They no gonna hide, play games. It be time they show they really be here all 'long." *(No-Eyes in 'Phoenix Rising' by Mary Summer Rain, 1993)*

"When the swords upon the star-lit heavens [missles] appear at even and at morn, then will come the whirlwind [space ship] from heaven upon the Earth ... " *(Excerpt from the 'Sybilline Fragment', 2nd Century B.C.)*

"Not before the time when machines project themselves into the sky will truth breakthrough and false teachings will slowly become shaky ... This will be the time when we Celestial Sons will begin to reveal ourselves anew to the human races because they will have become knowing and will threaten the order of heaven with the power [scalar weapons] they will have gained." *(Hatonn)*

" ... And if not at that time the Celestial Sons would not appear in order to bring it to a stand still [WW III] ... not one person would survive on the face of the Earth." *(Excerpt from 'And They Called His Name Immanuel', a Phoenix Journal, 1989)*

"For, behold, the Lord will come with fire, and with his chariots like a whirlwind." *(Isaiah 66:15, Bible)*

"The chariots of God are twenty thousand, even thousands of angels." *(Psalm 68:17, Bible)*

"In that day shall MESSENGERS go forth from me in ships." *(Ezekial 30:9, Bible)*

" ... A whirlwind came out of the north, a great cloud, and a fire infolding itself, and a brightness was about it ... " *(Ezekiel 1:4, Bible)*

"A day of clouds and whirlwinds ... hath not been from the beginning ..." *(Joel 2:2, Bible)*

" ... A day of tribulation ... a day of clouds and whirlwinds ... " *(Zephaniah 1:15, Bible)*

"And behold the mountain was full of horses and chariots of fire ... " *(2 Kings 6:17, Bible)*

"And thou shalt come upon my people ... like a cloud, to cover the Earth." *(Ezekiel 38:16, Bible)*

"They shall leap like the noise of chariots upon the tops of mountains ... " *(Joel 2:5, Bible)*

" ... And behold a white cloud and upon the cloud one sitting like to the Son of Man ... " *(Revelation 14:14, Bible)*

"Behold, he shall come up like clouds, and his chariots like a whirlwind. His horses are swifter than eagles ... " *(Jeremiah 4:13, Bible)*

"Behold, the whirlwind of the Lord goes forth in fury, a continuing whirlwind ... " *(Jeremiah 30:23, Bible)*

Late night radio show host Art Bell had as guests 'remote viewers' that said Planet Niburu is heading toward Earth with advanced and peaceful intelligences to awaken us and bring word that we are not alone. And that there is a great Galactic Federation Fleet and Cosmic Council which would like to welcome us to the greater community of cosmic brotherhood of which we are all a part.

'Newsweek' magazine July 13, 1987 reported John Anderson and Kenneth Seidelmann calculated that a distant planet five times the size of Earth, traveling in a very elongated elliptical orbit, possibly perpendicular to the orbits of the known planets, could have caused the irregularities in the orbits of Uranus and Neptune during the 19th century.

WHY THE END ?

" ... Uranus and Neptune continue to wobble in their paths around the sun. Something must be disturbing them." *(Excerpt from 'Omni' magazine June 1985)*

"Discrepancies in the motions of Uranus and Neptune persist, which causes some astonomers to search for an unseen Planet-X that lies far beyond Pluto." *(Excerpt from 'Astronomy' magazine August 1988)*

"Pluto, the ninth planet ... was found in 1930 ... showing up slightly out of its expected position." *(Excerpt from 'Science News' July 11, 1987)*

"Pluto's orbit makes an angle of 17 degrees with the ecliptic, and its eccentricity is so great that near perhelion Pluto lies closer to the Sun than Neptune does." *(Excerpt from 'Astronomy' magazine August 1988)*
[Pluto crossed the orbit of Neptune on February 11, 1999 to once again become farther from the Sun than Neptune, where it will remain for 228 years.]

"If Planet-X does exist, its gravity must pull the outer planets from their predicted paths. The more massive Planet-X is and the closer it lies to another planet, the more it pulls that planet off course." *(Excerpt from 'Astronomy' magazine August 1988)*

Niburu is the '12th Planet' [Planet-X] of our solar system according to Zecharia Sitchin in 'Genesis Revisited'. Comet Herculobus [The Ball of Redemption] is a harbinger for Niburu now approaching on its course toward and by Earth once again on its 3,600 year orbit.

'Science News' January 19, 1985 reported Daniel P. Whitmire and John J. Matese theorized that Planet-X periodically crosses a belt of comets in the past which disrupted the Earth's atmosphere and spelled doom for the dinosaurs.

" ... Planet-X may be in an orbit tilted 30 degrees or more from the paths of the known planets, so that sometimes it is too far away to affect them."

Two Millennia Of Prophecy And It's Fruitless Attempt To Awaken Humanity

(Excerpt from 'Science News' July 11, 1987)

The 12th Planet 'Nibiru' (Planet-X) was deduced by researcher Zecharia Sitchin to come from the direction of the Constellation of Sagittarius, where comet Herculobus was also first discovered.

Niburu means 'Planet of the Crossing' in ancient Sumerian texts because of its elliptical orbit between Mars and Jupiter. This planet only needs to pass by Earth to cause a tilt/poleshift and Earth Changes, or it may have satellites/ moons collide with Earth.

During 1998, NASA'S Soho satellite obtained pictures of a new 'planet' and another object within our solar system. (See Richard Hoagland's website: www.enterprisemission.com)

Native American Hopi Prophecy states that the appearance of a long-tailed comet which is surrounded in mystery is to be followed by Bahana [Niburu?] seven seasons later [1 and 3/4 years].

Nibiru is the home to the Annunaki (called the Nefilim in Genesis, Chapter 6, of the Bible) and is known as the planet of God. The Nefilim are 'Those who came from heaven to Earth' about 445,000 years ago.

The Annunaki are called the Watchers in the 'Book of Enoch'.

"I saw in the vision upon my bed, behold, a Watcher and a holy one came down from heaven." *(Daniel 4:13, Bible)*

"In the vision of my brain in bed I looked, and there was one of the angel-guard!" *(Daniel 4:13, Moffat Bible)*

<u>WHY THE END ?</u>

The Annunaki are called Anakim in the Bible:

" ... We have seen the sons of Anakim ... "   *(Deuteronomy 1:28)*

" ... The Anakim, a people great and tall."   *(Deuteronomy 9:2)*

" ... The Anakim were a race of giants ... "   *(Numbers 13:32)*

"As of August 17, 1987 you entered a new millennium ... and the ancient aboriginal calendars ended ... and ... the aboriginal people ... are waiting for two things (1) Their (and your) extraterrestrial brethren to return, along with the Great Spirit, and (2) to see if and how far man will fall during this time of kali (chaos)."   *(Korton, March 2, 1999)*

Information Pioneers Publisher

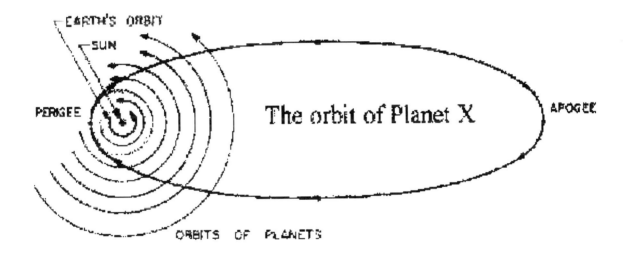

WHY THE END ?

EVACUATION / LIFTOFF

"I am going to prepare A PLACE for you. And then I shall come back to take you with me ... " *(John 14:3, Bible)*

"What neither eye has seen, nor ear heard, God has prepared." *(1 Corinthians 2:9, Bible)*

"And then shall He send His Angels, and shall gather together His Elect from the four winds, from the uttermost part of the Earth to the uttermost part of heaven." *(Mark 13:27, Bible)*

"In that night ... one shall be taken and the other shall be left ... two women shall be grinding together; the one shall be taken, and the other shall be left; two men shall be in the field, the one shall be taken, and the other shall be left." *(Luke 17:34-36, Bible)*

"Two men will be out in the field; one will be taken and one will be left ... " *(Matthew 24:40, Bible)*

"Hachkyum, our true Lord, will ... gather all of us ... when the world's end is coming." *(Lacandone, Mayan Prophecy)*

"This is His promise: He would send the word of truth unto you and you will do with it that which you will - and we will remove, unto his places, those who choose his way!" *(Excerpt from 'Murder By Atomic Suicide', a Phoenix Journal, 1991)*

" ... Reason that ... Earth must be EVACUATED, is the planetary lineup, followed quickly by the bypass of a larger planet [Niburu]."
" ... Planet would go into the flip on the axis, which in turn would end a war of any kind, and wash the whole Earth, and begin its purification."
"If that happened, it would only be a matter of minutes -- an hour at the

most -- during which we can pick up the persons to be saved ... those who would be proper to populate the Earth in the New Age, when you will have 'Heaven on Earth'."

"Approximately ten percent of the planetary population is to be taken aboard for eventual return to the planet after 5 to 7 years. Some will remain aboard ships. The boarding pass for all will be 'love in the aura', for without that, one cannot withstand the higher vibrational frequencies which will be necessary." *(Monka, in 'Project World Evacuation', 1993)*

"Earth Changes will be the primary factor in mass EVACUATION of this planet ... " *(Korton, in 'Project World Evacuation', 1993)*

"If atomic warfare does become activated, that will be the point of immediate mass EVACUATION ... " *(Excerpt from 'Project World Evacuation', 1993)*

"When the day of reckoning comes, you will be picked up by ... high frequency light beam - that is ascension - if you ask for it." *(Hatonn, June 2, 1992)*

"When your planet has been healed, you will be returned to it and all of your needs for reconstruction will be given. Higher intelligences shall walk with you to assist you in a speedy reclaiming of the Earth in Universal Love." *(Hatonn in 'Project World Evacuation', 1993)*

"The heaven shall be moved [poleshift], the stars [space ships] shall fall upon the Earth, the sun shall be cut in half like the moon, and the moon shall not give up her light." *(The Apocalypse of Thomas)*

"And the stars [space ships] of heaven fell to Earth, even as a fig tree casteth her untimely figs, when she is shaken of a mighty wind." *(Revelation 6:12-14, Bible)*

" ... The Lord himself will come down from heaven at the word of command, at the sound of the archangels voice and God's trumpet; and those who have died in Christ will rise first. Then we the living, the survivors, will be caught up with them in the clouds to meet the Lord in the air. Thenceforth we shall be with the Lord unceasingly." *(1 Thessalonians 4:16-17, Bible)*

"Every being who is of God will be offered removal from this place into security and safety - just as the prophecies foretold."

"Always before the cycle change of planet, civilization or species, the MESSENGERS come to set the record straight and to retrieve the people of God." *(Hatonn, October 24, 1992)*

"If you have done that which is required and move within the laws of God and Creation ... then you will come ... right aboard our craft. Those ones who choose other and to remain in the actions of physical Earth plane -- will perish by their own actions. If they are not atomized by atomic murder or suicide, they will simply make transition ... " *(Excerpt from 'Murder By Atomic Suicide', a Phoenix Journal, 1991)*

"It is the time of cycles in which the planet will either be shaped up or EVACUATED to allow for rebirthing and healing ... This is why you will find craft and beings from myriads of galactic locations here at this time - to tend the flocks and participate in the transitional change." *(Excerpt from 'God Said: Let There Be Light', a Phoenix Journal, 1991)*

" ... The job of the Christ, the Masters, etc., efforting to make this separation, EVACUATION, Transition, Transmutation and bring the unruly flocks within goodness." *(Excerpt from 'Phone Home, E.T.', a Phoenix Journal, 1991)*

"Beings from other worlds ... will come to lift many of you off the planet ... " *(Excerpt from 'Mary's Message to the World' by Annie Kirkwood, 1991)*

WHY THE END ?

"We of the lighted brotherhood ... are ready to make our presence upon your place. We travel and act in the direct service and under command of Esu 'Jesus' Sananda. Sananda is aboard my command craft, from whence he will direct all EVACUATION and transition activities as regards the period you ones call the End Prophecies of Armageddon. He has organized placement for his peoples and will oversee all operations as regards his people."

"This document is offered in response to ones who continue to ask me, 'When?' and 'What do we do?' ... you are in the ending times upon a planet in rebirthing and reberthing into a higher existence. You have reached the time of Armageddon! ... Those things which the prophets wrote, will come upon you within this generation of your elderly ones. All the signs are in place ... We also come in service and love unto you ones to assist you through the times of tribulations and bring you home. He went forth before you to prepare A PLACE for you. He has done so. Are you ready? We now prepare you to receive of him, that you be not frightened ... How did you think he would come? ... You will be taken up into craft, those of you who are prepared and into safety. The transition will be most hard on your physical bodies to change dimension so rapidly." *(Hatonn in The 'Wisdom of the Rays', Volume 1, 1997)*

"After the Great War ... we will send ships down that will clear the air of any radioactivity. The volcanic eruptions will probably simmer down for awhile. The earthquakes will also become less frequent because there will be a shifting ... of the entire Earth's axis. So the whole land mass will be reshaped entirely. There will be very few areas that will be able to stand the force of the holocaust ... But, it is from these areas that a good many of the people that will be ... lifted off the Earth."

"There will be several large cities in space ... These ships which can house many, many thousands of people will be put in orbit ... as if they were planets themselves. Then at the time the Earth is made stable again, the people will be brought back." *(Excerpt from 'Psychic & UFO Revelations in the Last Days', 1989)*

"There will be several large cities in space ... These ships which can house many, many thousands of people will be put in orbit ... as if they were planets themselves. Then at the time the Earth is made stable again, the people will be brought back." *(Excerpt from 'Psychic & UFO Revelations in the Last Days', 1989)*

" ... As the flame [light beam] rose to the sky ... the angel of the Lord ascended in the flame [light beam] ... " *(Judges 13:20, Bible)*

"A select number will be EVACUATED and will not be seen until after the catastrophes are over ... The American Indians and other knowledgeable individuals will assist in the EVACUATION." *(Robert Short)*

" ... Wonders in the heavens and on the Earth, blood, fire, and columns of smoke; the sun will be turned to darkness, and the moon to blood, at the coming of the DAY OF THE LORD. Then everyone shall be RESCUED who calls on the name of the Lord; for on Mount Zion there shall be a remnant." *(Joel 3:4-5, Bible)*

" ... Our sky is going to be filled up with spaceships ... there will be much turmoil and confusion and there will be buildings collapsing ... " *(Jane Allyson, 1978 in 'Psychic & UFO Revelations in the Last Days', 1989)*

"People who will be EVACUATED will be allowed to take their pets ... also their family members ... and their family will have an abode to live in ... within the mothership quarters." *(Diane Tessman in 'Psychic & UFO Revelations in the Last Days', 1989)*

"There is quietness, cooperation and dignity ... courtesy and devotional awareness within each being. This is the only attitude capable of continuance in the vibrational atmosphere present within our craft. The frequencies are so high that they would destroy any vibration of a lesser nature. It is not a matter of saying, 'This one may come, or this one must stay', it is of frequencies and

WHY THE END ?

"Those who refuse to be enlightened and infused with the light of God will be taken to other planets that are uninhabited, but inhabitable, and there they will make a new start." *(Artemis' message to Anthony Volpe, 1981)*

"At the same hour when the angel made Egypt desolate, and when the lord despoiled hell, in the same hour He shall DELIVER HIS ELECT from the world." *(Bede the Venerable, 672-735 A.D.)*

⚬ "I myself will gather the remnant of my flock from all the lands ... " *(Jeremiah 23:1-6, Bible)*

⚬ "On that day, The Lord shall again take it in hand to reclaim the remnant of his people ... " *(Isaiah 11:11, Bible)*

"As your holy prophecy so states, we shall save the elect. We stand by with our craft of all types and sizes ... should it become necesary to EVACUATE the elect to new homes on nearby planets where they will be our guests until your planet has been completely washed and cleansed and and made fit once more to dwell upon." *(Message received by Carl A. Anderson)*

" ... To them which find and shall be delivered up ... they shall be placed within safety where abides peace ... unto those which find not peace, they shall be put into a place wherein they may labor for their bread and wherein they may begin anew. They shall have for their tools only their bare hands for they shall be again as in the beginning." *(Aton, 1989)*

" ... EVACUATE any and all who wish to go ... no coercion - just plain old 'Do you want to go or stay?' You are now being given your final lessons - changes for reversing are all gone. You are to final decision time." *(Excerpt from 'Space Gate: The Veil Removed', a Phoenix Journal, 1991)*

"The man was lifted beyond the Earth. No longer he saw the Age of Destruction. Gone was the horrible Age of Warfare. He was looking beyond the Age of Carnage."   *(Kate-Zahl)*

"When it [Comet Herculobus/Wormwood/Ball of Redemption] gets close enough we have to get our people off or you are going to have to making enough of a turnaround to warrant diverting it ... "   *(Hatonn)*

"The onset of war ... would precipitate intervention ... Geological factors ... within the orb itself are part of triggering action. The combination of both of these events would trigger the first two phases of EVACUATION immediately in a secret manner. For the third phase is a public occurrence, while the first two are covert maneuvers, to insure their completion. Time-wise, it is impossible to yet tell precisely how the nations will go or when they will yield to the crisis situation and blow the world apart."

"Destination will depend on age as well as enlightenment level. Some will be put to sleep to lessen the trauma. Some will remain on the ships, depending on their ability to continue in service. Some will be escorted to other planets where acclimation is possible, while others may be transferred to the tremendous city like ships. Destination depends upon the individual survivor, his life patterns and spiritual evolvement. Some who qualify to be lifted up will be in need of treatment. This will be provided. Others will be on the right level, but will require education and training in areas designed for that purpose. The length of time involved in removal will depend on the nature of what has taken place upon the Earth. In some cases where Earth devastation is present locally, some may merely be relocated to another area ... "

"The Space Confederation has announced that the coming EVACUATION will not necessarily involve landings except in rare isolated areas. They have measured the hostility factor within ... your local and national military ... It was determined that in most cases, a large majority of these forces would openly attack us and fire upon us in the event of our appearing. This they would do even in disastrous circumstances and disrupt rescue, thinking it to be some form of invasion."

"We are therefore forced to forsake almost all landings that had been planned and to resort to the invisible levitation plan. This means that those

317   Information Pioneers Publisher

whom are calling for our assistance will need to believe we are there. Those with the vision to see us, our ships and those who are being lifted, will be of great benefit to those who do not see. It is still hoped throughout the Confederation that this material will fall into many hands who are a part of these policing groups and military reinforcements, and that this information will gentle the hostile spirit when these events do come to pass. For to openly offer our rescue assistance would be far less complicated than to enter your atmosphere incognito and invisible ... "   *(Kuthumi)*

"This will be a mass hovering in the skies for whoever is unafraid to join us to be rescued. The ultimate destination of these will be determined later. The moment at hand will require only that they be without fear and of sufficient vibratory frequency to withstand the levitating beam around them. Phase III makes up the invitation to the multitudes to welcome whomsoever can withstand the activities of rescue and accept our call, in whatever few moments are left, for we cannot linger in your atmosphere when the turbulence gets underway. This final lift-off will ... also include those faithful Earth Commanders who have borne the heavy responsibility of Earth details in preparation for our coming ... "

"The Great EVACUATION will come upon the world very suddenly. The flash of emergency events will be as lightning that flashes in the sky. So sudden and so quick in its happening that it is over almost before you are aware of its presence. And so it will be when the events that warrant this action have come to the planet. It is not possible to totally describe these events, but it is possible to instill at this time into the hearts of humanity the hope and the knowledge of our vigilance and emergency actions on their behalf."

"Our rescue ships will be able to come in close enough in the twinkling of an eye to set the lifting beams in operation in a moment. And all over the globe where events warrant it, this will be the method of EVACUATION. Mankind will be lifted, levitated ... by the beams from our smaller ships. These smaller craft will in turn taxi the persons to the larger ships overhead, higher in the atmosphere, where there is ample space and quarters and supplies for millions of people."

"There is a certain amount of preparedness necessary because of exposure to this powerful beam which will be operating in these circumstances. The frequency of it will be higher than most of your known electrical ... exposures. Those of extreme density and extreme selfish dispositions - especially at the expense of others - or causing suffering to others, will find extreme physical difficulty in surviving in the frequency of our beams ... Those who have lived closely aligned to the Father's will in their lives and have let the love of the Father flow through them, will have no problem with the frequency of the evacuation rays. For a high state of love in the human heart reacts upon the human force-field surrounding the physical form, giving it an electrical sheath of protection and a blending with the incoming vibrations between now and that time. Indeed, if enough souls could experience perfect love, there could very well be no need for a removal of humanity."

"There is nothing to be feared in coming into our midst. We are loving, normal persons, as yourselves, with the attitude of good neighbors and helpers in a time of crisis. We are prepared with clothing ... foods, and the needs to which you have accustomed yourselves."

"Those beamed up in physical form will be accelerated and quickened within that physical form to a more spiritual essence within the body, into what has been termed 'Light' bodies. The physical form will remain the same in appearance to most, but that higher blending of the etheric with the physical will bring about change, and eliminate sickness and physical disharmony among you."

"There will be a period of time to be spent with us, for your beautiful Earth must be healed in its cleansing, and given time to return to its true glory. Then those who have been lifted in the body will be returned to reconstruct a New World ... you will be given the opportunity to attend classes and training for the work which will need to be done. You will be given our constant help in doing this; our advice and our technology will be at the disposal of these returning ones. Many others who have been lifted through natural transition will be returned in new bodies to participate in the new awakening. Those who could not participate in the lifting off rescue will be transported, following their natural transition, to locations with a vibration and frequency equal to their own, where they may grow and learn at a pace slower than the new vibration of planet

Earth. For the Earth will be in an accelerated and very high frequency as it finds expression in the Aquarian Age."

"In the beginning of this great occurrence, time will be of the essence ... We ... must work speedily in the Phase III portion of the rescue of the multitudes who consciously choose to be included. You must understand that this great activity will only be set into motion when events on Earth have reached a crisis. We may not interfere with your lives in any way unnecessarily or too soon. But only in that last moment of danger to the masses will the final stages of EVACUATION be set into motion ... This phase will continue as long as the situation allows, WHICH AT BEST, WILL BE BRIEF!" *(Andromeda Rex)*

❧ "We have millions of ships stationed in the skies above your planet, ready to instantly lift you off at the first warning of your planet's beginning to tilt on its axis. When this occurs, we have only a very short period of time in which to lift you from the surface before great tidal waves will lash your coastlines - possibly five miles or more high! They will cover much of your land masses!"

"These tidal waves will unleash great earthquakes and volcanic eruptions and cause your continents to split and sink in places and cause others to rise."

"We expect to complete the EVACUATION of Earth of the Souls of Light in some fifteen minutes - even though they are of a tremendous number ... "

"After the souls of light have been EVACUATED, then the children will be lifted off ... to special ships to be cared for until they can be reunited with their parents ... There will be people specially to handle their trauma."

"After the EVACUATION of the children, the invitation will be extended to all remaining souls on the planet to join us. However, this will be for only a very short time ... fifteen minutes ... because the atmosphere by this time will be full of fire, flying debris, poisonous smoke, and because the magnetic field of your planet will be disturbed, we will have to leave your atmosphere very quickly or we, also with our craft, would perish."

"Therefore, he who steps into our levitation beams first will be lifted first. Any hesitation on your part would mean the end of your third dimensional existence you call the physical body."

"Which brings us to the most serious and difficult part of the

EVACUATION ... Souls of Light have a higher vibration frequency than do those who are more closely tied to the Earth and its ways."

" ... Those of low vibrational frequency may not be able to withstand the high frequency of the levitation beams without departing their third dimensional bodies."

"If you do not decide to step into the levitation beams to be lifted up, you might be one of the few who survive the 'cleansing' of the planet for the New Golden Age. However, during this period of cleansing, there will be great changes in climate, changes in land masses, as the poles of the planet will have a new orientation. This alone will create untold hardship for the survivors."

"The most important point for you to remember is this: Any show of fear lowers your frequency of vibration, thus making you less compatible with our levitation beams!! Therefore, above all else, REMAIN CALM. DO NOT PANIC. Know that you are in expert hands, hands which have extensive experience in EVACUATION of planets! WE CANNOT OVEREMPHASIZE THIS; REMAIN CALM! RELAX! DO NOT PANIC WHEN YOU STEP INTO OUR LEVITATION BEAM."

"What is to happen to you if you survive the lift off? First you will be taxied to our 'mother ships' high above the planet where you will be taken care of during your trauma. Some of you may need medical attention. Our expert medical staff will be there to treat you with our highly advanced medical equipment. You will be fed and housed until such time as transfer elsewhere is advisable."

"Some of you will be taken to cities on other planets to be trained in advanced technology before being returned to the planet Earth to start the TIME OF RADIANCE."

"The cataclysms will begin without warning! Everything will happen so fast you will not have any time to think! THINK ON THESE THINGS NOW!"

"Think; picture yourself standing with all the havoc around you: people screaming and running, others on their knees praying, automobiles crashing, glass breaking, buildings falling, ground shaking and gaping with huge cracks, debris falling all around you! THINK NOW!! ... REMAIN CALM AND WITHOUT FEAR. MAINTAIN AN INNER PEACE OF MIND AND STEP

WHY THE END ?

INTO THE LEVITATION BEAMS WHICH FLOW FROM THE UNDERNEATH CENTER OF OUR SPACE CRAFT." *(Excerpt from 'Sipapu Odyssey', by Dorushka Maerd, 1989)*

"It appears all probabilities of avoiding this untoward event are past. We see no changes in magnitude of perceptions of such proportions that would alter the course of events." *(Excerpt from 'From Here To Armageddon', a Phoenix Journal, 1990)*

"The hour when the call is extended to mankind, while very broad and universal, will come very quickly and will not be extended but for a very short period of time. At that point in time, the atmosphere will be dangerous to us as well as to you ... and to linger in it would destroy us both. Therefore ... humankind cannot wait until that moment to decide what they will do, for the time will be well for mankind to think on these things now, and ask himself what he will do in that eventuality. Not only that, but to ask himself also whether or not he would qualify for survival of the operation, in terms of personal frequencies and attitudes. There will be no time then to set about changing oneself, or beginning then to attempt personal change ... What a man is within himself will be revealed by all to see when he steps into those levitation rays. Density and low vibrations will not survive them, only the higher aspired mind and the pure heart will be immune to them."

"It is not the materialistic accumulations of a lifetime that matter at all in the hour when you face your rescue. Human opinions and the perils of pride, the falsity of ego-centered thought and activity, will all perish in the twinkling of an eye. Only love for others will make the ascension, service to others will lay up treasures in heaven, but selfishness and guile will be destroyed in that hour."

"Therefore, we plead with all souls now, to think on these things ... and judge yourselves that ye be not judged ... How will you feel ... when your eyes behold the sky black with craft over your head? ... This final massive maneuver of Phase III will be humanity's last opportunity to retain the present physical form and be kept within our ships until the calamities be passed." *(Hatton in 'Project World Evacuation', 1993)*

"When the trumpet sounds I will gather my elect from the four corners of the world. Then will be rendered to all a just judgement." *(Message to M.E., 1977, in 'Prophecies! The Chastisement and the Purification' by Albert J. Herbert, 1986)*

"Earth - as a playground and educational institution - is CLOSING DOWN FOR A PERIOD. After a cleansing and remodeling has transpired, it will be reopened, but with a greater curriculum and staff to challenge the eager students of life into more preparations for even greater horizons that will challenge them after graduation. After successful preparations, those returning to Earth will know the laws and be prepared to live in harmony with them." *(Excerpt from 'Project World Evacuation', 1993)*

" ... Many shall be taken from your Earth before the GREAT CHASTISEMENT ... " *(Blessed Virgin Mary to Veronica Lueken, December 7, 1976)*

"Either way, Earth ... will be emptied that she can be reclaimed to her wholeness ... Tribulation is the allowance of sorting and the Earth Mother is cleansing ... birthing of new mountains and valleys ... Then once again man can live in harmony and move in radiance and balance ... " *(Sananda, March 7, 1989)*

"Mine ones shall be lifted unto the craft for their work is done, the word is being sent forth as requested ... " *(Excerpt from 'Aids The Last Great Plague', a Phoenix Journal, 1989)*

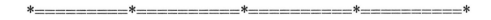

===================*==========*==========*

WHY THE END ?

Information Pioneers Publisher

THE REMNANT

"And except those days be shortened, there should no flesh be saved. But for the elect's sake those days shall be shortened." *(Matthew 24:22, Bible)*

"Thus saith the Lord God, although I have scattered them among the countries, yet will I be to them a little sanctuary in the countries where they shall come." *(Ezekiel 11:16, Bible)*

"In all the land, says the Lord, two thirds of them shall be cut off and perish, and one third shall be left. I will bring the one third through the fire, and I will refine them as silver is refined, and I will test them as gold is tested. They shall call upon my name, and I will hear them." *(Zechariah 13:8-9, Bible)*

"People will know that their survival came about because they made a good effort to live in love and harmony." *(Sun Bear)*

"After the greater changes occur between 1998-2001, the vibration on the physical Earth as well as the inner Earth will change ... only those whose spiritual vibration matches the new Earth will find entrance ... thus the millennium of peace as so prophecied." *(Gordon-Michael Scallion)* ⊖

"Because you have kept my word of patient endurance, I will keep you from the hour of trial (tribulation) which is coming on the whole world to test the inhabitants of the Earth." *(Revelation 3:10, Bible)*

"To him that overcometh will I grant to sit with me on my throne." *(Revelation 3:21, Bible)*

"Believers be already ready - they be in safe groups." *(No-Eyes in 'Spirit Song' by Mary Summer Rain, 1987)*

" ... Only few will be left to rebuild the world." *(Seeress Regina)*

WHY THE END ?

" ... The number of those who were so marked - one hundred and forty-four thousand (144,000) from the tribe of Israel ... " *(Revelation 7:4, Bible)*

"The 144,000 who were found blameless are those who have found their connection to God." *(Excerpt from 'Mary's Message to the World' by Annie Kirkwood, 1991)*

"Evil shall rise against itself and the clash shall be to the point of total devastation and Mother shall cleanse herself. Man will destroy man to the extent that it shall be but REMNANTS of civilization which shall be ultimately preserved." *(Excerpt from 'Footsteps Into Truth', a Phoenix Journal, 1994)*

"The planet ... will enter a period of cleansing to prepare itself for its Golden Age. You are part of that heritage and you shall inherit the Earth and its glory." *(Korton, in 'Project World Evacuation', 1993)*

"A great lament will come over all of mankind and only a small batch will survive the storm, the pestilence and the horror. And neither of the two adversaries will conquer or be vanquished. Both mighty ones will lie on the ground, and a new mankind will come into existence." *(Barthalomew Holzhauser, 1612-1658 A.D.)*

" ... For on Mount Zion there shall be a REMNANT." *(Joel 3:5, Bible)*

"I will plunge the Earth into darkness for three days and nights ... when the sun rises after ... the purified Earth shall shine ... My REMNANT shall experience it." *(Message to L.G.A., February 23, 1986)*

" ... There will remain a REMNANT - untouched by the chaos who, having been faithful in following me and spreading my warnings, will gradually inhabit the Earth again with their dedicated and holy lives." *(Our Lady of America to Sister M, January 3, 1984 in 'Prophecies! The Chastisement and the Purification' by Albert J. Herbert, 1986)*

"The man who holds out to the end ... is the one who will see salvation." *(Matthew 24:13, Bible)*

" ... Pray always that ye may be accounted worthy to escape all these things that shall come to pass." *(Luke 21:36, Bible)*

" ...Though the Earth be shaken and the mountains plunge into the depths of the sea; though its waters rage and foam and the mountains quake at its surging, the Lord of Hosts is with us." *(Psalm 46:3-4, Bible)*

"If you want to survive the coming changes, remember this: the only people who are going to survive, Spirit says, are the people who are willing to make a conscious change in the way they look at life, in the way they understand things, and in their actions toward all of creation ... " *(Sun Bear in 'Black Dawn/ Bright Day', 1992)*

"There will be a REMNANT of God's people who will move through this transition and all who will come with us are welcome and blessed." *(Esu 'Jesus' Sananda, June 5, 1991)*

" ... Every believer shall ... not be alarmed at anything that may happen in the coming years. If he can look up with confidence to God, no harm will come to him." *(Dr. Richard Steinpach, The Grail Message Prophet)*

"And not a person shall be left which is not prepared for that which shall be. And there are many called but few are chosen, for there are none which have been chosen which have not been carefully prepared, and they have been unto themselves true, and they have given credit where credit is due. And now its given unto them to be the seed of the New Civilization which shall come upon the Earth ... and within the time which is left before this shall come upon the Earth, it shall be that many will be called and they shall doubt and they shall fear and they shall faint, and they shall fall by the way, and they shall be in no wise, wise, for it is given unto man to fear that which he does not understand ... "

WHY THE END ?

(Excerpt from 'Sipapu Odyssey' by Doruska Maerd, 1989)

"Only the pure in heart, those who follow God's laws, the Natural Order, will survive to see the dawning of the New Age." *(Ramala Prophecy, 20th Century)*

"And he that overcometh and keepeth my words unto the end, to him will I give power over the nations, and he shall rule them with a rod of iron." *(Revelation 2:26-27, Bible)*

"For those who have been mindful of the law and the light, and worked therein, they shall be brought into a place of newness wherein is total light. They shall be relieved of all stresses, for it is lawful to say that they shall be brought into the places wherein I am, for I have prepared for them a place and I have provided well; and for this day I have provided." *(Aton in 'The Wisdom of the Rays', Volume 1, 1997)*

"The time of the Tribulation is upon you ... In this last great upheaval of the results of humanity's evil to itself, called 'karma' of cause and effect, be sure you stay in daily contact with your soul ... only those who are of the higher consciousness will be brought back for the thousand years of peace." *(The Christ in 'New Teachings For An Awakening Humanity', 1994)*

"Nations will rise against nation and kingdom against kingdom. There will be great earthquakes, plagues and famines in various places - and in the sky fearful omens and great signs ... all will hate you because of me, yet not a hair of your head will be harmed. By patient endurance you will save your lives." *(Luke 21:10-11, 17-19, Bible)*

" ... Those who put their trust wholly in the Lord will not come up missing but will find conditions, circumstances, activities, someway and somehow much to be thankful for." *(Edgar Cayce, 1944)*

328Information Pioneers Publisher

"The only protection we will have will be c   sciousness ... Only those with raised consciousness will understand and ⌐   ." *(Jane Allyson)*

"As the final scenes of this current play unfold,   shall increase exponentially, <u>and only those who are well grounded in</u>   her reality of <u>creator shall</u> be able to function without the emotional traui.   <u>ie impacting</u> <u>'rea</u>lity' of change."

"You ones are fast approaching a time when the need foι   ventional solutions to problems will be needed. <u>The past ways of doing e\</u>   <u>v things</u> <u>will soon be gone.</u> Your very <u>survival may depend upon each pers</u>   <u>'ity to</u> <u>hear or feel the creative nudge to survive."</u> *(El Morya in 'The Wι.   `the Rays', Volume 1, 1997)*

"These survivors will be the seed bed for a new human race - a humanity - which will evolve in an accelerated fashion. The new rac know from first hand experience what the terrible consequences are for fa. to walk in balance upon the Earth Mother. The new race will know how to li in harmony with the cosmos and they will inherit the Earth." *(John White)*

"You made of them a kingdom ... and they shall reign on the Earth." *(Revelation 5:10, Bible)*

"I myself will gather the REMNANT of my flock from all the lands ... " *(Jeremiah 23:1-6, Bible)*

"On that day, The Lord shall again take it in hand to reclaim the REMNANT of his people ... " *(Isaiah 11:11, Bible)*

"He that overcometh shall inherit all things." *(Revelation 21:7, Bible)*

———————————————————————

WHY THE END ?

THE GOLDEN AGE

"In the end my Immaculate Heart will triumph ... And there will be an era of peace." *(Mother Mary, Fatima Prophecy, 1917)*

"When I renew the world, it will be a world you never knew, nor could have imagined ... The new world ... will be the abode for those, who have survived the cleansing and purging fire ... " *(Message to L.G., September 11, 1983 in 'Prophecies! The Chastisement and Purification' by Albert J. Herbert, 1986)*

"And in this last era all the kingdoms of Christianity and also of the unbelievers shall quake for the space of years, and there shall be more grievous wars and battles ... After this shall have lasted for a good while, there shall be renewed a reign of Saturn and a GOLDEN AGE. God the Creator shall say, hearing the affliction of His people, Satan shall be put and tied in the bottom of the deep, and there shall be an age of universal peace between God and man. The ecclesiastical power shall return in force and Satan shall be bound for the space of a thousand years ... " *(Nostradamus, 'The Epistle to Henry II', 1555)*

"The GOLDEN or Aquarian Age is a time of energy change and uplifting for all of humanity. It is a time when things formally invisible are made real to you; it is a time of joining Heaven and Earth together in open communication and cooperation ... much will be revealed ... many universal laws will be given the peaceful scientists. Many mysteries will be explained ... " *(The Christ in 'New Teachings For An Awakening Humanity', 1994)*

"The GOLDEN AGE prophecies have foretold - every Earth human will have opportunity to become all that he/she was meant to be, to understand the planet's true history and recover lost full consciousness abilities ... " *(Excerpt from 'You Are Becoming A Galactic Human' by Virginia Essene and Sheldon Nidle, 1994)*

WHY THE END ?

"This is the initial phase of the 'GOLDEN AGE', the transition phase of the two centuries. The culmination of this period will come in time -- it is said to be around 2028 in calculation of your years."   *(Excerpt from 'Pleiades Connection', Volume 1, a Phoenix Journal, 1991)*

" ... I see nothing else before us but union and universal fraternity. All men are in reciprocal love. One helps the other. They are all happy." *(Magdalene Porzat, 19th Century)*

" ... The Age of Aquarius is to be an age of great evolution ... In this New Age, man will progress and evolve beyond your wildest dreams. The Earth will become what it should be: a vibration of Universal Love fulfilling its purpose in the solar body ... giving out its emanations ... to the Creation beyond." *(Ramala Prophecy, 20th Century)*

"Later in the epoch ahead of us called Aquarius or the GOLDEN AGE the highest teaching will be brought forward."   *(The Christ in 'New Teachings For An Awakening Humanity', 1994)*

"Whoever will survive this settlement will see an entirely new Earthly existence manifested. For a long, very long time the word war will be crossed out from the dictionary of mankind, perhaps even for all time. Christmas, the festival of Christianity, will be accepted by all religions as the true festival of peace. Blessed be who will live to see this epoch!" *(Mahatma Ghandi)*

"Lo, I am about to create new heavens and a new Earth ... "   *(Isaiah 65:17, Bible)*

"What we await are new heavens and a new Earth where, according to his promise, the justice of God will reside." *(II Peter 3:13, Bible)*

"The God of heaven will set up a kingdom that shall never be destroyed or delivered up to another people." *(Daniel 2:44, Bible)*

"Then I saw new heavens and a new Earth. The former heavens and the former Earth had passed away, and the sea was no longer. I also saw a new Jerusalem ... He who wins the victory shall inherit these gifts ... " *(Revelation 21:1-2,7, Bible)*

"In days to come the mount of the Lord's house shall be established higher than the mountains; it shall rise high above the hills, and people shall stream to it ... For from Zion shall go forth instruction and the word of the Lord from Jerusalem. He shall judge between many peoples and impose terms on strong and distant nations; they shall beat their swords into plowshares, and their spears into pruning hooks, One nation shall not raise the sword against another, nor shall they train for war again." *(Micah 4:1-5, Bible)*

"A good, noble man with red hair will be sitting on the throne of the world ... Blessed are those who will live to see him, because the red-haired man will bring happiness to all." *(Mitar Tarabic, 1829-1899)*

" ... The Lord, for he comes ... to rule the Earth. He shall rule the world with justice and the peoples with his constancy." *(Psalms 96:13, Bible)*

" ... Only those shall enter whose names are inscribed in the book of the living kept by the lamb." *(Revelation 21:10, 26, Bible)*

" ... Do you not know that the unjust will not possess the kingdom of God? ... neither fornicators, nor idolators, nor adulterers, nor the effeminate, nor sodomites, nor thieves, nor the covetous, nor drunkards, nor the evil-tongued, nor the greedy will possess the kingdom of God." *(1 Corinthians 6:9-10, Bible)*

"Never again will there be in it an infant that lives but a few days, or an old man who does not live out his years; he who dies at a hundred will be thought a mere youth; he who fails to reach a hundred will be considered accursed." *(Isaiah 65:20, Bible)*

WHY THE END ?

"There will be no more death or mournings, or crying or pain, for the old order of things has passed away." *(Revelation 21:4, Bible)*

"Those ... that are come into the new life, the new understanding - the new regeneration there is then the new Jerusalem ... not a place, alone, but a condition, as an experience of the soul." *(Edgar Cayce, 1944)*

"In the new era you will have 1000 years of peace because the devil consciousness has been eliminated. There will be no fear, anger or hostility."
"The new Jerusalem is the new era. It is the time of peace on Earth. It will be a new and mighty time on Earth. This will be the time of completions. It will be the time of great progress on Earth and in the spirtual realm. That is the reason it is a time of celebration ... I will be a glorious time. These will be wonderful, peaceful lives you will lead on Earth." *(Excerpt from 'Mary's Message to the World' by Annie Kirkwood, 1991)*

"After a Great Cleansing and rearrangement ... a new government under the Law of One will come forth to empower peace." *(Excerpt from 'New Cells, New Bodies, New Life!' by Virginia Essene, 1991)*

"Come to the city of the future. Here are the buildings unlike those we build, yet they have breathless beauty. Here people dress in materials we know not, travel in manners beyond our knowledge, but more important than all this difference are the faces of the people. Gone is the shadow of fear and suffering, for man no longer sacrifices, and he has outgrown the wars of his childhood. Now he walks in full stature toward his destiny - into the GOLDEN AGE of Learning." *(Kate-Zahl, 1st Century A.D.)*

"It is not for them, which are the remnants, to communicate by water; for it shall be with a new science and a new method shall be given unto them. For there is not a place which is that shall remain the same in its present state." *(Excerpt from 'Sipapu Odyssey' by Dorushka Maerd, 1989)*

"After the cleansing, we will see only people who know how to reach out and learn. We'll see people who are always seeking spiritual knowledge. People will know that their survival came about because they had made a good effort to live in love and harmony."

"As human beings relearn their balance with nature, they will become healthier in body as well as spirit. When people are no longer in stress and out of balance, Spirit will let them live longer. We are told that after the changes, we'll be learning how to rejuvenate our bodies. This will be easier because we will no longer have people around who are polluting the air, water and Earth ... " *(Sun Bear, 1992)*

" ... Then shall Eden bloom again, and man live in harmony and there shall be no more war." *(Paul Solomon, 1991)*

"Then all nations will follow Michael and the world will become a real garden of Eden. There will be food everywhere, in rivers, seas, and forests. Those who will be born then will live happily and for so long that they will forget when they were born." *(Mitar Tarabic, 1829-1899)*

"It is the seedtime of peace: the vine shall yield its fruit, the land shall bear its crops, and the heavens shall give their dew; all these things I will have the remnant of the people possess." *(Zechariah 8:12, Bible)*

" ... When the twentieth century have passed away, and the sign of the God-man is in the sky; peace shall reign upon the Earth and no man shall hate his brother."

"Neither shall there be war, nor pestilence, nor poverty, nor any other of the shameful things which man has done unto himself ... "

"Then wisdom shall sit in the palaces of cities, and on the mountain tops ... " *(Edgar Cayce, 1877-1945)*

"The Kingdom of God shall come upon good men for the Earth ... shall yield to men the best, and infinite fruits ... and the cities shall be full of good

WHY THE END ?

men, and the fields shall be fruitful, and there shall be no war in the Earth, nor
tumult, nor shall the Earth groan by an earthquake; no wars, nor drought, nor
famine; nor hail to waste the fruits; but there shall be real peace in all the Earth,
and one king shall live in friendship with the other, to the end of the age: and the
immortal, who lives in the heavens adorned with stars, shall give a common law
to all men in all the Earth, and instruct miserable men what things must be done;
for he is the only God ... and He shall burn the great strength of men by fire."

"Then He shall raise a kingdom for ever over all men, when He hath
given a Holy Law to the righteous ... and the world of the blessed, and all joys,
and an immortal mind, and eternal cheerfulness .. and there shall be just riches
for men, for the government of the great God shall be a just judgement ..."
(Excerpt from the 'Sibylline Fragment', 2nd Century B.C.)

"There will be no religious beliefs in the new world, but there will be the
code of right thinking, which will reward the race with peace ... " *(C.H. Kramer,
1946)*

"Mankind will be glad to have the new era to correct the errors of your
civilization's past. Humanity will remember what these errors were. Future
generations will learn from your mistakes ... "
"New cells will blossom in the physical body. Humanity will have
communication with the spiritual world ... you will be able to use more of your
mind. Mankind will have powers that are not known now. There will be the
ability to communicate with all worlds by your mind ... also with the animals by
this method."
"The atmosphere will change in components. The solar system will be
different. A new sun will be added. This will be a binary solar system. The two
suns will activate cells which will draw nourishment from the sun's rays."
" ... Intuition will be strongly activated in all mankind ... Today mankind
hides his feelings and thoughts. In the aftertime, man will not be able to hide his
feelings or random thoughts. Motives will be known ... All feelings, all thoughts
will be sensed and heard by everyone. People will learn to live in peace ...
forgiveness will be the accepted mode of conduct." *(Excerpt from 'Mary's*

                           Information Pioneers Publisher

Message to the World' by Annie Kirkwood, 1991)

"No longer shall the sun be your light by day nor the brightness of the moon shine upon you at night; the Lord shall be your light forever ... no longer shall your sun go down, or your moon withdraw, for the light shall be your light forever ... " *(Isaiah 60:19-20, Bible)*

" ... I assure you once more of the hour of cleansing after which a new sky, a new Earth, and a new Church will arise ... A new epoch in the history of man will have its beginning." *(Our Lord to Msgr. Ottavio Michelini, June 21, 1978)*

"Then the Earth will sit in peace and there will be great peace and tranquility upon the Earth such as has never been nor ever will be any more since it is the final peace at the end of time ... " *(The Pseudo-Methodius, 680 A.D.)*

"The True White Brother and his helpers will show the people of Earth a great new life plan that will lead to ever lasting life. The Earth will become new and beautiful again, with an abundance of life and food. Those who are saved will share everything equally." *(Native American Hopi Prophecy)*

"For the end of the world will bring not nothingness, but the Kingdom of Heaven for you are long from the time of 'voidance' ... The Kingdom of Heaven: this signifies the era in which God alone will govern. Inevitably it will come, not through any human acts but solely through Divine action ... Thus the end is not a kind of threat upon Man and/or the destruction of a world, but it is a Promise: the Kingdom of God." *(Esu 'Jesus' Sananda, June 5, 1991)*

"The year seven of the great number being past [Year 2007, Age of Aquarius begins]

    There shall be seen the sport of the ghostly sacrifice,

    Not far from the great age of the millennium,

              Information Pioneers Publisher

That the buried shall come out of their graves." *(Nostradamus, Century X Quatrain 74)* *[Graduation into higher awareness/consciousness]*

"A new ruler anointed, rises from the 50th Latitude;
Renews this once-great fish. PEACE FOR A MILLENNIUM.
Rome rebuilds and the divine hand at the ruler's side
Departs. Earth in renewal, but the scars heal slowly." *(Nostradamus, Unpublished Quatrain)*

"Twenty plus two times six [2012] will see the lore of the heavens
Visit the planet in great elation. Disease, pestilence,
Famine die. Rome rejoices for souls saved. The Learned
Smile in awe. Astrology confirmed. For science, a new beginning."
(Nostradamus, Unpublished Quatrain)

The Earth completes one revolution around its sun in one year of twelve months. But our whole solar system revolves around the central sun-star Alcione in an orbit that requires approximately 25,827 of our Earth-years.

The solar system year is divided into months (called houses), each one taking approximately 2,152 years. As the change from one House into another occurs it is known as 'Passover' with each House being identified by its 'sign' (i.e. Pisces, Aquarius, etc.). Earth has been in the house/sign of Pisces for the last 2000+ years, and will enter the Sign of Aquarius in the year 2007, prophesied to be the Golden Age.

==================*=========*=========*

THE END IS UP TO YOU

"The ending does not need to be as projected in the past ... You are given scenes which causes collective thought to focus on fulfillment of that which is desired for you to achieve ... " *(Excerpt from 'I And My Father Are One', a Phoenix Journal, 1991)*

We as individuals, perceive and shape the reality around us - by relying on our own experiences, knowledge, beliefs, decisions, and actions. If you look at the world through rose-colored glasses - all seems well, or so the media deceives us. Yet look deep inside yourself - a force stirs within us - change is on the horizon - a threshold approaches.

If one studies the constellations as a grand cosmic clock - humanity too, is part of the natural cycles. The new millennium brings a new cycle upon the Earth. Feelings of ecstasy or fear of the unknown abound and flow through us like an emotional tape. The underlying current tells us something is afoot. We may not be able to grasp the future, but if one looks at the past, today's events are the result. The prophets have warned us, but it appears not enough have listened to their visions and words of wisdom, as most were misunderstood or neglected altogether - after all, who wants to hear doom and gloom anyway?

But the visions of seers have survived to this day, and for the first time they are organized by obvious categories, painting a coherent sequence of events, a rational step-by-step progression of the much-debated "End Time", or "End of the World", as some describe the imminent transformation.

The real question is, "Why the End?" What is the reason that life as we know it, has to end? Is it divine providence, or is it man's creation? As one lives day-to-day, we may not be aware that our awareness (consciousness) is knowingly or unknowingly involved in the events playing out on Earth. Pure thoughts are real things that can influence and affect the outcome of events and lives. The sum of the existing wavefields of consciousness equals the existing reality in the world. Be careful of what you think, and think positively, because your thoughts form the reality you will create and experience. As you acquire more information of truth, beauty and goodness, you can expand beyond the limited mental boxes within which many persons have allowed themselves to be relegated and confined by the narrow-minded controllers. Hopefully, by awakening - you can refocus your conscious thoughts and change projections.

Have no fear, worry or confusion because what you put out, is what you reap on a personal and collective level. Transform from selfishly being part of the problem, to altruistically becoming the long-overdue solution of accelerated physical, mental, and spiritual growth, opportunity, and progress. The path may be challenging, the doorway narrow, but throughout the adventurous journey, the brilliant enduring light and life-spirit of survivors ushers in the Golden Aquarian Age of peace and prosperity for freemen. Every great achievement and transformation was once impossible, but is now within the reach of every conscious person. Will you choose to do your part?

WHY THE END ?

342   Information Pioneers Publisher

BIBLIOGRAPHY

Bear, Sun and Wabun, Wind: <u>Black Dawn, Bright Day.</u> New York: Simon and Schuster, 1992.

Beckley, Timothy Green: <u>Secret Prophecy of Fatima Revealed.</u> New Brunswick, New Jersey: Inner Light Publications, 1991.

Bernard, Raymond: <u>The Hollow Earth.</u> Secaucus, New Jersey: Citadel Press, 1969.

Beckley, Timothy Green: <u>Psychic & UFO Revelations in the Last Days,</u> New Brunswick, New Jersey: Inner Light Publications, 1989.

Beckley, Timothy Green: <u>Nostradamus, Unpublished Prophecies.</u> New Brunswick, New Jersey: Inner Light Publications, 1991.

Boyles, Nora: <u>The Garden of Aton.</u> Las Vegas, Nevada: Phoenix Source Distributors, 1993.

Cannon, Dolores: <u>Conversations with Nostradamus: His Prophecies Explained Vol.I.</u> Tehachapi, California: America West Publishers, 1989.

Cannon, Dolores: <u>Conversations with Nostradamus: His Prophecies Explained Vol.II.</u> Tehachapi, California: America West Publishers, 1990.

Christ, The: <u>New Teachings for An Awakening Humanity.</u> Santa Clara, California: S.E.E. Publishing, 1994/1995 Update.

Dixon, Jeane: <u>My Life and Prophecies.</u> New York: William Morrow and Co., 1969.

WHY THE END ?

Driscoll, Brother Craig: <u>The Coming Chastisement.</u> Santa Barbara, California: Queenship Publishing, 1995.

Duduman, Dumitru: <u>Dreams and Visions From God.</u> Mineola, Texas: Hand of Help Publishing, 1996.

Essene, Virginia, ed.: <u>New Cells, New Bodies, New Life!</u> Santa Clara, California: S.E.E. Publishing, 1991.

Essene, Virginia and Nidle, Sheldon: <u>You Are Becoming A Galactic Human.</u> Santa Clara, California: S.E.E. Publishing, 1994.

Garrison, Omar V.: <u>The Encyclopedia of Prophecy.</u> Secaucus, New Jersey: Citadel Press, 1978.

Herbert, Albert J.: <u>The Three Days Darkness: Prophecies of Saints and Seers.</u> Paulina, Louisiana, 1986/1996.

Herbert, Albert J.: <u>Signs, Wonders and Response.</u> Paulina, Louisiana, 1988/1993.

Herbert, Albert J.: <u>The Discernment of Visionaries and Apparitions Today.</u> Paulina, Louisiana, 1994.

Herbert, Albert J.: <u>The Visionaries - U.S.A. - Today!</u> Paulina, Louisiana, 1993.

Herbert, Albert J.: <u>Prophecies! The Chastisement and Purification.</u> Paulina, Louisiana, 1986.

Hogue, John: <u>The Millenium Book of Prophecy: 777 Visions and Predictions from Nostradamus, Edgar Cayce, Gurdjieff, Tamo-San, Madame Blavatsky, The Old and New Testament Prophets and 89 others.</u>

San Francisco, California: HarperSan Francisco, 1994/1997.

Hogue, John: <u>Nostradamus, The Complete Prophecies.</u> Rockport, Massachusetts: Element Books, 1997.

Kay, Tom: <u>When the Comet Runs: Prophecies for the New Millennium.</u> Charlottesville, Virginia: Hampton Roads Publishing, 1997.

Kirkwood, Annie: <u>Mary's Message to the World.</u> Nevada City, California: Blue Dolphin Publishing, 1991.

Kirkwood, Brian: <u>Survival Guide to Earth Changes.</u> Nevada City, California: Blue Dolphin Publishing, 1994.

Leary, John: <u>Prepare for the Great Tribulation and the Era of Peace Volume XI.</u> Santa Barbara, California: Queenship Publishing, 1998.

Mihalik, Paul A.: <u>The Final Warning and a Defense Against Modernism.</u> Santa Barbara, California: Queenship Publishing, 1997.

Noone, Richard W.: <u>5/5/2000: Ice The Ultimate Disaster.</u> Dunwoody, Georgia: Genesis Publishing, 1982.

Noorbergen, Rene: <u>Invitation To A Holocaust: Nostradamus Forecasts World War III.</u> New York: St. Martin's Press, 1981.

Nostradamus, Michel: <u>Prophecies of Nostradamus.</u> Crown Publishing, 1975.

Paulus, Stephan: <u>Nostradamus, 1999: Who Will Survive?</u> St. Paul, Minnesota: Llewellyn Publishing, 1996.

Phoenix Journals: Las Vegas, Nevada: Phoenix Source Distributors, 1989-1998.

Rex, Moebius: Prophecy: A History of The Future. Jean, Nevada: Rex Research, 1986.

Roberts, Henry C.: The Complete Prophecies of Nostradamus. New York: Oyster Bay Press, 1969.

Scallion, Gordon-Michael: Notes From the Cosmos. W. Chesterfield, New Hampshire: Matrix Institute, 1987/1997.

Shaw, Eva: Eve of Destruction - Prophecies, Theories and Preparations for the End of the World. Chicago, Illinois: Contemporary Books, 1995.

Sitchin, Zecharia: Genesis Revisited. New York: Avon Books, 1990.

Stearn, Jess: Edgar Cayce: The Sleeping Prophet. Garden City, New York: DoubleDay and Co., 1969.

Summer Rain, Mary: Phoenix Rising: No-Eye's Vision of the Coming Changes. Norfolk, Virginia: Hampton Roads Publishing, 1987.

Summer Rain, Mary: Spirit Song: The Visionary Wisdom of No-Eyes. Westchester, Penn: Donning Co., 1987/1993.

Summer Rain, Mary: Daybreak: The Dawning Ember. Norfolk, Virginia: Hampton Roads Publishing, 1991.

The New American Bible, Encino, California: Benziger a division of Glencoe Publishing, 1970.

Tuella: <u>Project World Evacuation.</u> New Brunswick, New Jersey: Inner Light Publications, 1993.

Vanjaka, Zoran and Sever, Jura: <u>The Balkan Prophecy.</u> New York: Vantage Press, 1998.

Velikovsky, Immanuel: <u>Worlds In Collision.</u> Garden City, New York: Doubleday and Co., 1950.

Wheeler, W. Alexander: <u>Prophetic Revelations of Paul Solomon: Earthward Toward a Heavenly Light.</u> York Beach, Maine: Samuel Weiser, 1994.

White, John: <u>Poleshift.</u> Virginia Beach, Virginia: A.R.E. Press, 1980.

<u>Wisdom of the Rays: The Masters Teach Vol.1.</u> Champlain, New York: America East Publishers, 1997.

Publications:

Gordon-Michael Scallion's Earth Changes Report & Future Map of the United States: Matrix Institute, Inc., P.O. Box 336, Chesterfield, New Hampshire 03443-0336

Contact Newpaper, as of April 1999 changed to "Spectrum" c/o Wisdom Books and Press, Inc., 9101 West Sahara Avenue, Suite 105-158, Las Vegas, Nevada 89117

Nexus Magazine, P.O. Box 177, Kempton, Illinois 60946-0177

Preparedness Journal, P.O. Box 25454, Salt Lake City, Utah 84125

WHY THE END ?

Internet:

Art Bell (www.artbell.com)

Richard Hoagland (www.enterprisemission.com)

Contact Newspaper (www.contactnews.com)

Earthchanges TV (www.earthchangestv.com)

Gordon-Michael Scallion, Earth Changes Report
(www.earthchanges.com)

=====================*===========*==========*

WHY THE END ?

Information Pioneers Publisher